CAMP CONCORDIA

German POWs in the Midwest

CAMP CONCORDIA

German POWs in the Midwest

by
Lowell A. May

Rae,
Enjoy this bit
of history
Lowell A. May

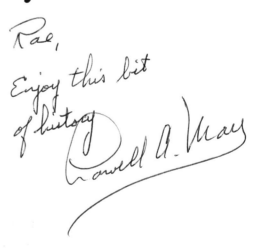

Sunflower University Press®

Box 1009 • 1531 Yuma • Manhattan, Kansas 66505-1009 USA

ISBN 0-89745-192-9

Edited by Sonie Liebler

Layout by Lori L. Daniel

This book is dedicated
to all who have served
in the
Armed Forces
of the
United States,
past and present.

Contents

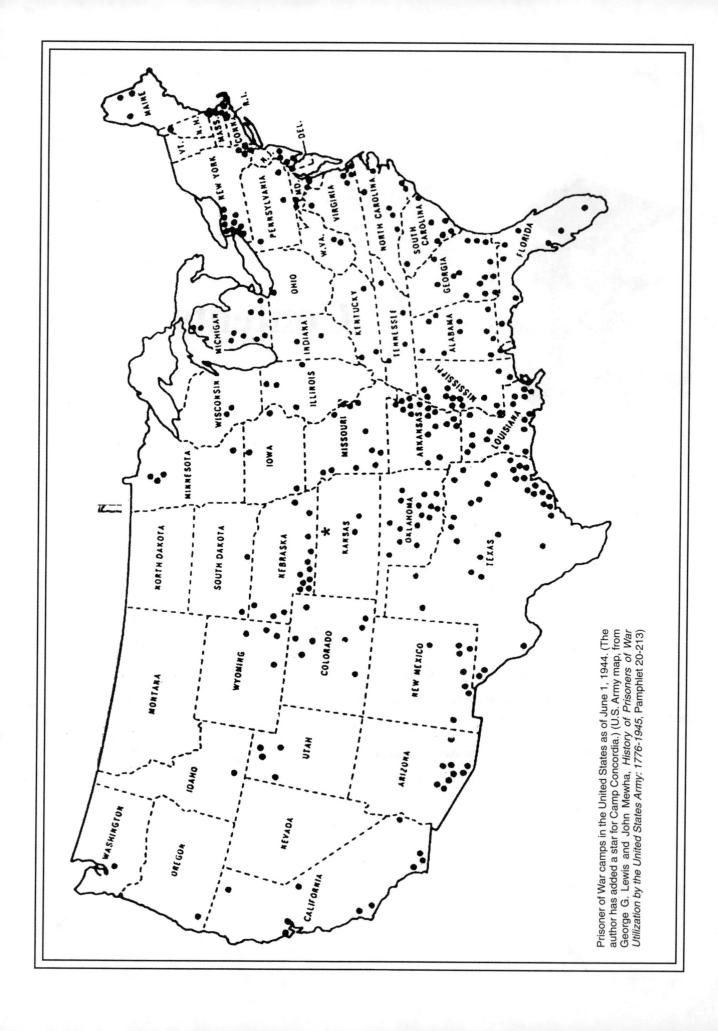

Prisoner of War camps in the United States as of June 1, 1944. (The author has added a star for Camp Concordia.) (U.S. Army map, from George G. Lewis and John Mewha, *History of Prisoners of War Utilization by the United States Army: 1776-1945*, Pamphlet 20-213)

Foreword

$\mathcal{D}$uring World War II, there were eight German POW camps in the state of Kansas, one of the largest at Concordia. Designed to hold over 4,000 prisoners, the camp operated from 1943 through 1945.

In the beginning, camp discipline was rather lax, often giving the impression that the prisoners were in charge. But with the change of Commanding Officers, discipline was enforced and work details as well as educational classes were established, thus making Concordia a model camp.

Due to a shortage of civilian agriculture labor, prisoners were allowed to work on nearby farms. Originally the pay was $1.60 per day for enlisted POWs. Noncommissioned officers were paid the same amount, but they were used in a supervisory role only. Officers were not required to work, but were paid $20 to $40 per month when they did. Individuals were allowed to keep only half of the money and the government retained the rest. Most of the money was used to make purchases at the camp's canteen.

Education classes were originally set up by the prisoners, and by the end of the war these courses were recognized by both the University of Kansas and several German universities. Among the courses were subjects dealing with democracy and democratic forms of government. The strength of these programs is that they provided a positive influence on German prisoners who would return to their homeland, as evidenced from the written comments Lowell May has received from former prisoners.

The strength of May's work is that he has used not only official reports and newspaper accounts, but also personal memories. These reflections — both military and civilian — provide us with an insightful picture of life in a Midwest POW camp. As you read this work, you can be proud of the way the prisoners were treated by the civilian population and the military staff.

Terry Van Meter
Chief, Museum Division, Fort Riley, Kansas

Acknowledgments

$\mathcal{M}$any institutions and individuals have assisted me in research and in preparation of this manuscript. The National Archives in Washington, D.C., and in Kansas City, Missouri, provided much helpful information. The Kansas State Historical Society Library in Topeka provided photos, newspaper clippings, and other material. The staff at the Ablah Library, Wichita State University, Wichita, Kansas, headed me in the right direction with access to magazines and books. The Cloud County Historical Society at Concordia, Kansas, provided a wealth of information through newspaper articles, microfilm, photos, and interviews. The staff at the Frank Carlson Library in Concordia not only provided access to an extensive collection of newspaper microfilm, but also gave me use of the "life-saving" interlibrary loan.

Terry Van Meter, Chief of the Museum Division at Fort Riley, Kansas, provided information that saved considerable time while searching at the National Archives, and also offered suggestions concerning research that made my task easier.

My good friend Richard Wahl, fluent in the German language, served as correspondent with former German prisoners of war. Without his letter-writing and his able translations, much valuable information would have been lost. A special thanks to all of the Germans who answered with information and photos — *Danke!*

Thanks also go to the many people I interviewed and to those who responded to my letters seeking information — soldiers assigned to and civilian employees of the camp, and citizens of Concordia and the surrounding area. All have played a vital role in helping this manuscript come to life.

The task has proven to be monumental. I realize it never would have come to completion had it not been for the computer skills of Mary Mendenhall and Margo Gilster Hosie. Not only did they do the word processing, but they also proofread as they worked. An added thanks goes to Margo for her editing and for encouragement when obstacles arose.

I cannot close without a special thanks to my wife Janice. She not only assisted me in the research and conducted interviews, but mostly, she put up with me through the time-consuming project. A note of appreciation also goes to my daughters Elizabeth and Laura for their encouragement and support.

Introduction

*W*hen I was attending Military Police School in 1959, I learned that there had been enemy Prisoners of War (POWs) in the United States during World War II. The more I read and learned about the subject, the more intriguing it became. I had lived in Concordia for almost two years before learning that a German POW camp had been located there.

In the spring of 1993, after finishing reading Arnold Krammer's *Nazi Prisoners of War in America*, I became a member of a committee to plan a celebration commemorating the closing of the POW camp at Concordia. A year later, committee chairman Everett Miller, of Concordia, was searching for someone to write a book. The timeline was short, as the project needed to be completed by October 1995, the 50th anniversary of the camp's closing. Because of my interest in learning more about the camp, I volunteered to take on the task. The manuscript that follows is the fruit of many hours of travel, research, and interviews.

Once I began my research, I learned what a difficult task I had undertaken. The number of POW camps in the United States differed according to the source that was read. For instance, in his book, Krammer states there were 155 main and 500 branch camps; but Robert DeVore, in his October 1944 article in *Colliers*, "Our Pampered War Prisoners," claims there were 362 camps. In *History of Prisoners of War Utilization by the United States Army: 1776-1945* (Pamphlet 20-213), published by the U.S. Department of the Army, the main and branch camps numbered 150 and 340, respectively. A map, showing the location of the camps, appears in both Krammer and the Army pamphlet, but it does not show Concordia, unless it is in the wrong location.

I was disappointed when I found out that in the 1950s the National Archives had thrown away many of the POW camps' records, but I went to Washington, D.C., anyway, to see what they had. I found information, though not as much as I had hoped for — there were no complete rosters of POWs, information on the work of POWs at Concordia was nonexistent, and there was nothing on the daily operation of the camp.

I went to the Still Photo Archives in College Park, Maryland, and found they did not have a single picture of the camp. I went back to the Archives in Washington where I had noticed photos in a series of reports put together by Captain Karl C. Teufel, before the camp closed. This work, *The History of Camp Concordia from Site Survey to Deactivation* (1945), was the cornerstone of my research. The only official copy is in the National Archives. However, the Cloud County and Kansas State Historical Societies have copies. A few, without pictures, are in private hands.

In Kansas, I found a great deal of information in the Concordia newspapers and other publications of the time. I started interviewing anyone who might have any knowledge of the camp. Some, due to their age, could not remember much. I traveled to other states to interview former guards, and I wrote numerous letters. I did discover that both former guards and even the former POWs had numerous pictures of the camp, and many were quite good. Also, former civilian workers at the camp have been able to provide valuable documents such as prisoner rosters, engineer reports, and maps.

In doing research, I found that there are very few books on German POWs in the United States currently in print. At the present time, only five have been published, and of these, only one covers all aspects of the German POWs in the United States. Of the remaining sources, one is composed mostly of pictures, two are about specific geographical areas, and one is about the reeducation of POWs.

I also was surprised to learn that many people, including some students of history, do not know that enemy POWs were held in the continental United States. In all, there were 371,683 Germans, 51,156 Italians, and 5,413 Japanese prisoners held in camps scattered all across the country, according to Department of the Army Pamphlet 20-213.

The more I researched and interviewed, the more my fascination for the subject grew. I am now convinced that the POW camp at Concordia has had an effect on the future of Europe and, for that matter, the world. A large number of the POWs became professors, diplomats, and business leaders in Germany. I firmly believe that what they saw and learned while POWs in the United States influenced their thought, and thus helped keep Germany in the Western cause during the Cold War. More importantly, how these POWs were treated here has helped bring the two countries closer together.

Even though the POW camp at Concordia was officially named the Alien Internment Camp, Concordia, Kansas, the camp's official stationery read Prisoner of War Camp, Concordia, Kansas. Locally it is referred to as Camp Concordia, the name many of the people stationed there called it. The reader will find that I have used each at different times in the text.

Events of Camp Concordia are treated chronologically in the text. It is my hope that this book will give the reader more of a feeling of what took place here during World War II.

Lowell A. May
Command Sergeant Major, Retired, U.S. Army
Concordia, Kansas

Chapter 1

Building the Camp

$\mathcal{E}$ven before the United States entered World War II, it was realized that there was a need for internment camps within the continental U.S. Enemy aliens and captured crews of enemy ships and U-boat crews were expected to be the first prisoners of war. Three permanent camps with a total capacity of 9,000 were estimated to be sufficient, and if there were a need for more, temporary camps could be used for three to five months. Due to a lack of funds, however, no camps were built before the United States entered the war on December 8, 1941.[1]

The urgency of providing internment camps for enemy aliens and POWs then quickly became apparent. Camps were necessary not only for civilian aliens, who came mostly from the West Coast, but also for the captured Japanese, Germans, and Italians. In addition, the British wanted the U.S. to take some Germans they had captured, as their camps were filling to capacity.[2]

The success of OPERATION TORCH, the American and British invasion of North Africa in November 1942, brought the Allies large numbers of Italian and German prisoners. The question was: Where could they be safely kept? It was soon realized that American ships were carrying supplies and troops to North Africa, and they had to return empty to the U.S., so why not have them carry POWs.

Transporting these POWs stateside accomplished two things: 1) food did not have to be shipped to them; and 2) they were removed from the combat zone. Also, according to the Geneva Convention, they could perform some types of work for the detaining country. It was, therefore, more efficient as well as in keeping with the Geneva Convention of July 27, 1929, to bring the prisoners to the U.S.

But, if camps were to be built, where could they be located? Policy and security reasons at the time kept them from being set up on either coast. Some believed the camps should be built in the South, where the weather was mild and construction and maintenance cheaper. However, due to the increase in the number of prisoners expected, policy was changed, and the decision was made to construct camps farther north, which would allow the prisoners to be employed in agriculture.[3]

In March 1942, the U.S. Army Corps of Engineers considered four sites in Kansas and Missouri for internment camps. Three of these sites (Nevada, Missouri; Concordia, Kansas; and Newton, Kansas) were evaluated as to availability of land, roads, railroads, water, sewage, electrical power, heating fuel, and climate.

The evaluation team visited Concordia and made its recommendation. The town fathers wanted the camp, which would provide jobs, put money from the garrison into the economy, and be a visible means of supporting the war effort. Letters and telegrams flowed into Washington, D.C., from Concordians. On April 27, 1942, Concordia Judge E. W. Thompson wrote Senator Arthur Capper, who then wrote Major General Allen W. Gullion, the Provost Marshal General (PMG), requesting that the camp be built at Concordia. Milton Eisenhower, Director of the War Relocation Authority and brother of Kansas's General Dwight D. Eisenhower, wrote Colonel Ralph H. Tate, Executive Officer to the Secretary of War, inquiring about such a facility at Concordia. On May 7, 1942, Congressman Frank Carlson wrote General Gullion, stating he had received a large number of letters and wires from townspeople about the project.

On May 15, 1942, Beldon Bowen, Concordia Chamber of Commerce secretary, wrote Colonel B. M. Bryan, in the Provost Marshal General's office in Washington, D.C., stating:

> I assure you the people of Concordia want this camp and are ready to extend any assistance possible to bring it here.[4]

According to Captain Karl C. Teufel's *The History of Camp Concordia*, the town of 5,647 could provide for the camp

15 or 20 apartments and 137 hotel rooms

needed to house an additional 1,000 persons. Recreation facilities included two theaters, two swimming pools, one bowling alley, three dance halls, one 18-hole golf course, and a 20-acre fairground. . . . Semi-skilled labor . . . available at .35-.50 per hour, and skilled labor from .75 to $1.00 per hour. . . . Four grade schools, a junior-senior high school, then accommodating about 1,250 students, . . . capable of absorbing an additional 500 students.[5]

However, not everyone in Concordia was anxious for a prison camp to be built near their town. According to Concordian Beryl Ward, some citizens were apprehensive, because they had heard it was going to house Japanese. Others had husbands, brothers, or sons off fighting the war and did not want the enemy near. Many were not vocal in their thoughts, perhaps believing it would never happen.

Rosella Harris, wife of Concordia's mayor at that time and owner of *The Concordia Press*, a weekly newspaper, noted:

> The camp didn't bother me. I was not for or against it. I was [occupied] with our business and my family. I never went to the camp until after it closed.

During World War II, Charles Everett and his father operated a hardware store in Concordia. He explained:

> There was a mixed attitude [about the camp being built]. Some people welcomed it, and other people didn't like it. Some . . . were afraid the German soldiers would get out and harm people. Others thought it was great to have something here that would bring people into town — soldiers and so forth. It was the end of the Depression and it made a difference that way.

Mrs. Rachel Forsberg and her husband had moved to Concordia during World War II; she shared her feelings:

> All of my children were in the service. I never felt comfortable having the Germans

Looking east down Sixth Street, Concordia's main street, in 1942 or 1943. (Courtesy, Richard Palmquist)

near. I was glad they were that far out of town.

In 1943, Jane Wilson was 22, living at home, and working in an abstract office in Concordia. She commented:

[The people in Concordia] didn't really want the prisoner of war camp. They thought the prisoners would escape, and they would be killed in their beds. They were just a little leery of bringing Germans to the United States.

Even with the letters, telegrams, and political pressure in support of the camp, it did not look as if the town would get the internment facility. In fact, on July 16, 1942, *The Concordia Kansan*, another weekly newspaper, reported:

According to present indications Concordia has no chance of getting a prison camp in this vicinity. . . .[6]

Unknown to the citizens of Concordia, the funds for a 3,000-man camp were authorized on Septem-

ber 9, 1942, and the site was approved on December 15, 1942.[7] The first that the local people knew about it was when officials started arriving to make arrangements for workers, and to purchase the land. On January 21, 1943, *The Concordia Press* headlines read: "U.S. To Build Camp Here." News stories explained that the camp would cost over two million dollars and would take up to 1,500 men between four and six months to build.[8] By the end of January 1943, officials and guards had arrived and set up offices in the old Civilian Conservation Corps (CCC) camp on the northeast edge of Concordia.

The camp was to be built two and one-half miles northeast of Concordia, on the north side of U.S. Highway 81, the east side of present U.S. Highway 81. The Chicago Burlington & Quincy, the Union Pacific, and the Missouri Pacific railroads would easily provide the facility's transportation needs. The camp would encompass 640 acres of Section 15, with room for expansion to the north. Captain Teufel explained:

The terrain [was] relatively high and rolling, giving adequate natural drainage as well as freedom from flood hazard from

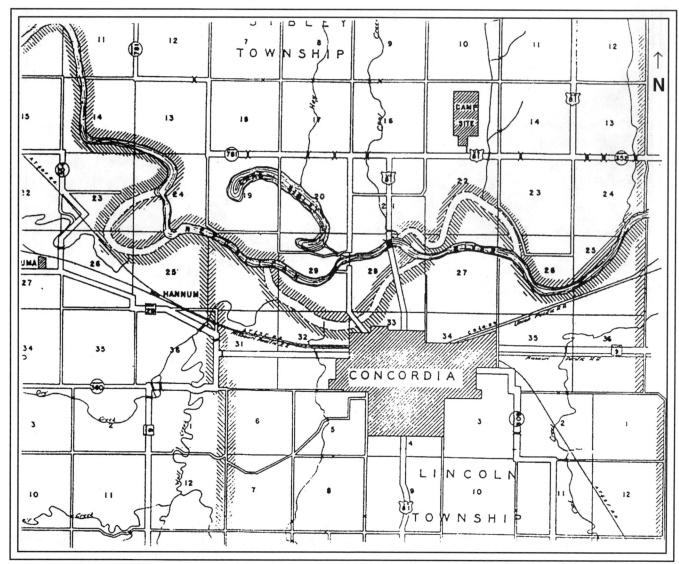

The camp in relation to Concordia. Today, U.S. Highway 81 goes straight north and is a mile west of the camp site. (Courtesy, U.S. Army Corps of Engineers)

the adjacent Republican River [south of the site].

The area was being used at the time for agricultural purposes and contained few improvements, these being valued at only $2,200.00. No churches, schools, cemeteries, power lines, pipe lines or other utilities were present to complicate construction. . . . Four ownerships were involved, but no difficulty was foreseen in acquiring the land, although it was hinted that condemnation proceedings might expedite the acquisition. Assessed

value for the land and improvements was $27,800.00, representing about two-thirds the actual value of the land. Owners were expected to ask from fifty to seventy-five dollars per acre, and some crop loss was anticipated. . . .[9]

The government bought the land from Ella McBride, Harry Vanek, Albert Palmquist, and Anna Larson.[10] According to Richard Palmquist of Concordia, Albert's grandson, one of the conditions of the sale was that when the government no longer needed the land, the previous owners would have first chance at repurchasing it. Even so, the land-owners were not happy. They were upset that the government did not give them what they thought was a fair price, and, according to Dale Cool, who had farmed with his father near the POW camp, they were displeased that they would not be allowed to harvest the wheat crop. Even today, some of the farmers resent the way they were treated. Dale notes:

[Farmers in the area] didn't care too much for having [the camp] around.

Richard Palmquist recalls what his grandfather and father have told him:

My grandfather only had the land two or three years before the government got it. There were some hard feelings. My dad was only on the land twice while the government had it. We farmed the land after we got it back.

Nevertheless, construction began in February 1943. The contract for 289 buildings and water and sewer lines went to Olsen, Assenbacher, and Rokaka, of Lincoln, Nebraska, for $1,270,176.02.[11] The road construction contract had earlier gone to the Roush Construction Company, McCook, Ne-braska.[12] Workers were draft-deferred, which was an incentive. Because all workers were supposed to belong to the union, a union headquarters was established in Concordia. Men came from near and far to work on the camp, and soon numbered near-ly 500, causing a housing shortage in the commu-nity. To alleviate the problem, over 100 house trail-ers were brought in.

Delmer Harris, son of Concordia's mayor, Delmer, Sr., was a 14-year old when the camp was built.

My dad bought some of the farm buildings [on the site]. I remember cleaning bricks from a shed that was torn down. The silo was torn down, and some of it was used for sidewalks at our shop south of town. The town was crowded during the building. A lot of houses

were subdivided into apartments. I never went out to the camp, but would see the trucks with prisoners.

Charles Everett noted:

Coming home one time [on a train from Kansas City] . . . were a bunch of men [on the way] to Concordia to work on the camp. Later on a lot of these guys were in [our hardware] store. Some of them I don't think ever had a hammer in their hands before, but they were looking for used tools. That way [with used tools] they could show they could carpenter.

Dale Cool added:

There was a lot going on in Concordia when they were building it. Concordia was really a country town up until that time. Dad and I would go to town on Saturday night and [would] have to sit in the barber shop until midnight to get a haircut. Anybody who had a hammer and saw could go over there and get a job as a carpenter and draw big wages.

Concordian Donald Kerr worked at several jobs during the building of the camp, and then at the Post Exchange (PX) warehouse. He now owns building T-9, the camp's quartermaster and engi-neer warehouse, which is located on its original site.

I started when they began making the roads. I worked with [Walter] Johnson. We were constructing culverts and stuff. Then I got a chance to drive a truck hauling shale . . . from south of town. I saw that job was playing out so I got on as a carpenter — bought myself a hammer and a saw. I saw that was playing out, too, and I had a chance to get on at the post exchange. So, I worked in the warehouse and delivered to the compounds and to the PX.

Problems arose during the camp's construction because not all of the men hired were union mem-bers. Donald Kerr recalled:

You could work a couple of weeks until

they found out you didn't belong to the union. Then they gave you a choice. I never did join the union. I just changed jobs.

On February 27th and 28th, after demanding a closed-shop agreement with contractors, about 100 union workers of the Building and Trades Council of the American Federation of Labor walked off the job because nonunion workers were being hired. The nonunion men remained on the job, but negotiations with the union were held quickly in Lincoln, Nebraska. By Monday, the 28th, there was a settlement which stated that all workers must be members of the union, and the men who were returned to work.[13]

Even with this settlement, all did not go smoothly. Absenteeism was a major concern. One day in mid-March, 100 carpenters were absent from work. In an attempt to solve the problem, fake dollar bills were given to absent men that read: "This is a present from the Emperor of Japan for your time off."[14] However, even this attempt to shame the workers did not help, and on March 25th, the Concordia papers printed this "Notice":

The following notice was sent to all Contractors, Concordia Internment Camp, Concordia, Kansas:

Gentlemen:
The problem of absenteeism on this project is of a very serious nature. Labor has been habitually absent from work due to allegedly inclement weather and other fancied causes. A conference was held with the draft board in this regard this date, and the chairman of the draft board has requested that any cases of unauthorized absences should be referred to that board for necessary action. This procedure was concurred in by the State Selective Services Headquarters, with the further request that names of flagrant absentees be referred to that office for action.

Labor affected by this action will include all men under 45 years of age and in classes 1A, 2A, and 3A.

You are requested to give this notice such publicity as required to inform all your

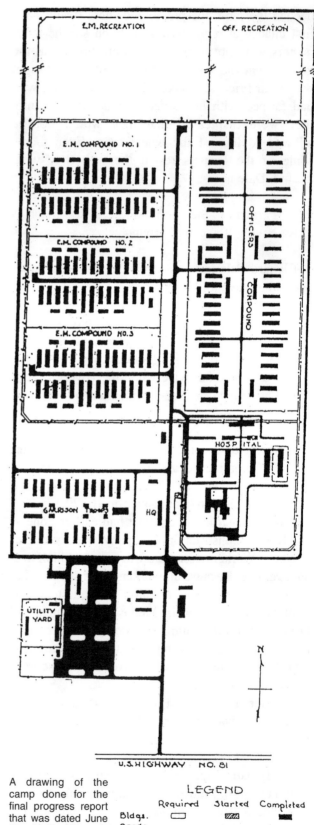

A drawing of the camp done for the final progress report that was dated June 26, 1943. When it became an officers camp, the Enlisted Mens (EM) Compounds 1, 2, and part of 3 were changed to accommodate the officers. (Courtesy, U.S. Army Corps of Engineers)

Donald Kerr and the truck he used to haul shale when the camp was being built. (Courtesy, Donald Kerr)

employees of its contents. For further details as to action required, you are requested to contact this office.

Very truly yours,
/s/ Alfred B. Plaenert
Alfred B. Plaenert
Major, Corps of Engineers

March 19, 1943   Area Engineer[15]

Once the labor problems were solved, work moved rapidly. According to Kerr, the three farm-

houses remaining on the land were moved to other locations, and the barns and silos were torn down. The size of the camp was increased so that it could hold 4,000 prisoners, and a water tower was built, which had a 100,000-gallon redwood tank.

Even before the camp was finished, the press and other citizens of Concordia were invited for a tour and were impressed with the camp's size. *The Concordia Kansan* reported:

The main gate at Camp Concordia. (Courtesy, Cloud County Historical Society, Concordia, KS)

The gate to the POW compound. (Courtesy, Wayne E. Rosen)

one more major problem. The wells were discovered to have a high saline content. Thus, new wells had to be drilled west of the camp, and a mile of eight-inch water main was laid.[18]

Mrs. Helen Blochlinger started working at Camp Concordia as the chief payroll clerk in May 1943, and she remained in that job until her husband returned from overseas in February 1944:

I worked in the headquarters building. A lot of the buildings were not completed when I started. In fact, the big building where I worked was finished while I was there. The roads were mud and water. The civilian workers had to wear boots to get to the buildings.

I was there when the first prisoners came. It was really kind of exciting. Nobody was afraid of them, never thought about being afraid of them. The ones I knew, who came in to clean, were quite young. They were rather small, but were very polite.

Mrs. Beryl Ward worked in the Fiscal Department during the camp's construction:

I missed a day's work. I was really sick. I received a fake check signed with fake signatures of Hitler and Tojo [the Japanese general and premier]!

The whole town turned out to watch the first trainload of prisoners unload. It was very quiet. [You] could only hear military noises. The prisoners looked very young.

Every modern convenience is provided for the officers who will be permanent residents, as well as for the enlisted men and prisoners.[16]

There was even a stable for 30 horses, as all vehicles within the camp except for fire trucks were to be horse-drawn.

On May 1, 1943, after less than three months of construction, the camp was officially turned over to the Army.[17] However, work continued and would do so throughout the camp's duration. But there was

Looking down Reybold Road on the west side of the camp in the fall of 1943. The water tower is to the left and the POW barracks are to the right of the guard tower. (Courtesy, Cleon Snodgress)

Below: View of camp looking east from the water tower. (Courtesy, Kansas State Historical Society, Topeka)

There were about 400 prisoners on the first train, mostly enlisted men; their average age was 22.[19]

Camp Concordia's first commander, Colonel John A. Sterling, named its streets for past and present military men and politicians (note that the spelling was incorrect for the names of General MacArthur, Provost Marshal Gullion, and General George Goethal, but that spelling appeared on street signs and maps of the camp): McArthur [*sic*]— commander in the Pacific; Lee — Southern commander, Civil War; Grant — Northern commander, Civil War; Houston (Sam) — soldier, Texas governor; Crockett (Davy) — frontiersman, politician, Alamo hero; Guillion [*sic*] — Provost Marshal General; Gotthals [*sic*] — builder of the Panama Canal; O'Riley — former Surgeon General; Gregory — Quartermaster General; Osborne — Chief of Special Services; and Carlson — Congressman Frank Carlson from Concordia.[20]

Concordia's Enemy Alien Internment Camp was ready to receive its garrison and prisoners, after the Army officially took possession of the camp on May 1st. There were enough barracks and mess halls for 815 U.S. troops and 4,000 prisoners, a complete hospital, a Headquarters building, an Officers Club, and warehouses, as well as other support buildings.[21]

Captain Teufel sums up the completion:

As a whole, the enterprise was well performed, and laid the foundation from which the Camp developed, through later efforts, into one of the most physically attractive prisoner-of-war camps in the United States.[22]

The following supplemental material, also from the Teufel report, offers detailed description of Camp Concordia:[23]

Climatological Data: Rainfall, temperature

The fire department of Camp Concordia, located outside the compound and just north of the Officers Club. Notice the firemen are both military and civilian. (Courtesy, Cloud County Historical Society, Concordia, KS)

and wind data were furnished by the United States Weather Bureau station at Concordia.

The highest temperature ever recorded . . . was 116 in August 1936, and the lowest -25 in January 1888 and February 1899. Prevailing winds are from the south in Summer and north in Winter, and have an average velocity of from six (6) to nine (9) miles per hour. Wind velocities occasionally exceed fifty (50) miles per hour. There are no swamps or malarial conditions, and both the climate and environment are considered healthful. (The record takes in a continuous service of 57 years, and the details are available at the above-mentioned station.)

Water: The Camp was expected to require approximately 350,000 gallons of water per day. The early investigation determined that two (2) wells, drilled to the depth of seventy feet (70') near the southern boundary of the site, and from the same location from which Concordia obtained its supply should produce 864,000 gallons of good quality water per day. The cost of the wells, pumping equipment, storage tanks of an elevated design and the distribution system was estimated at $114,000. . . .

Sewerage: The Republican River was considered to furnish sufficient dilution to receive

sewerage without treatment, especially since Concordia itself dumped raw sewage into this river, and since the State Board of Health had no objections. Site contours permitted an economical collection system, and the sub-soil was not expected to furnish difficulties. It was estimated that 6,000 feet of ten-inch (10") outfall main would be required to carry the sewerage to the river. Estimated cost of the entire collection and disposal system was $83,000.00.

Roads: In addition to the highway [U.S. 81], the camp site was bounded by sand-surfaced roads on west, north, and east sides. Roads within the project required a minimum of grading, and were recommended to consist of a mile and a half with a crushed-rock base and bituminous surface, and two and one half miles of compacted gravel. Estimated cost of these roads was placed at $30,000.00.

Electric Power: Representatives of the Kansas Power Company at Great Bend, Kansas, assured the Board of its ability to furnish 350 kilowatts for Camp consumption, to be secured from the steam-generating station at Concordia, which had a capacity of 3,000 kilowatts, and if necessary from neighboring stations. Standby emergency equipment with a capacity of an additional 600 kilowatts was also available at Concordia and other local stations. The Power Company agreed to increase the size of its transformer bank and estimated the total cost of the feeder line and the internal distribution system at $29,500.00. Energy was offered at a cost of one and half [*sic*] cents ($0.015) per kilowatt hour. An emergency fence-lighting system was also recommended, motivated by a high-speed gasoline engine, driving a 37.5 KVA generator with automatic control, and estimated to cost $5,000.00.

Fuel: Coal was recommended as the most suitable fuel, and was obtainable three hundred (300) miles southeast of Concordia at prices ranging from $5.80 to $6.10 per ton, f.o.b. Concordia.

Summary Estimate: The Board recommended the construction of the Camp, and estimated the total cost to be $1,525,000.00. . . .

Final cost of the camp was actually $1,808,869.00, which demonstrates that the estimate was $283,869.00 short. However, changes in plans later on resulted in a new estimate which was only $44,964.00 over estimate. . . .

The original layout plan was submitted on 29 December 1942 to the Missouri River Division Engineer, with the request that it be sent through channels to the Provost Marshal General for approval, and that such approval be given by wire. . . . On 3 January 1943, the District Engineer advised Howard, Needles, Tammen, and Bergendoff, the architect-engineer selected, that authority had been received by teletype for an estimated expenditure of $2,900,000.00, and stating that an AA-3 priority had been received. . . . On 5 January 1943, a new layout plan was submitted in place of the plan of 29 December 1942. . . .

The quarters designed for the Commanding Officer had to be moved to the west in order to get them out of the present north-south drainage area. The original cannon stoves designed for installation in the guard towers had to be rejected in favor of kerosene stoves because of the cramped interiors of the towers, and these, in turn, were later replaced by electrical units.

. . . In June, Mr. Jake Vanek, a farmer residing south of the Camp, and adjacent to the Republican River, alleged that the Camp's sewer system had, through reaction with the River, inundated his property, and caused him crop losses, and that he was entitled to damages. This claim was denied by the Investigating Officer on 15 June 1943. . . . Probably the worst problem was in connection with the Camp's water supply. Tests made in the Summer of 1942 had demonstrated a plentitude of water to the south of the Camp. Early specimens had apparently been skimmed from the top of the supply, and proved potable; but in the Spring of 1943, it was discovered that the chloride content was so high as to render the water unusable. A geological survey was made and a report submitted in April by the United States Department of the Interior's Geological Survey and State Geological Survey of Kansas, to the District Engineer, which evidences [*sic*] some little chagrin and the hope that drawing the water off the top of the subterranean stream, and drilling the wells to different levels might remedy the situation. This recommendation apparently proved helpful for water was finally secured in which the chlorides constituted less than one hundred parts per million. . . .

In the meantime, the work went forward rather rapidly. The first sub-surface water exploration was arranged by the contractors on 6 January. On 11 January, joint telephone facilities were arranged for the Engineer and the Signal Officer. Plans for grading, clearing roads, and drainage were submitted by the Area Engineer on 22 January 1943, and the same date, a report was made on available water supply. On 2 March 1943, the sewerage collection and disposal plan was approved by the Kansas State Board of Health, and on 5 March the fire prevention system design was submitted. In April, layouts for service drives, sidewalks and the fire-reporting telephone system were completed. On 17 April, a coal-storage area was selected and approved. . . .

The Architect-Engineer assigned Mr. Bergendoff and Mr. Carl Erb, their Resident Engineer to the work, and these men were mainly responsible for efficient supervision and the commendable cooperation generally existing with the sub-contractors. The latter are listed below:

Crawford Electric Co., North Platte, Neb. (Interior wiring).

Frankamp-Parker, Omaha, Neb. (Water supply and distribution).

Layne-Western Co., Kansas City, Mo. (Well drilling).

L. S. Fisher, Woodward, Okla. (Water tower and tank).

Healy Plumbing and Heating Co., St. Paul, Minn. (Plumbing and heating).

Midwest Roofing Co., Lincoln, Neb. (Roofing).

Fox and Co., Denver, Col. (Sheet metal and warm air heating).

Iowa and Nebraska Painting & Decorating Co., Omaha, Neb. (Painting and decorating).

Baker Ice Machine Co., Omaha, Neb. (Refrigeration).

Bunting Hardware Co., Kansas City, Kansas (Hardware).

Roush Construction Co., McCook, Neb. (Clearing, grading, roads, and drainage).

Crawford Electric Co., North Platte, Neb. (Electrical distribution and fence lighting).

Eby Construction Co., Wichita, Kansas (Construction of RBC-A-T Building).

American District Telegraph Co., Kansas City, Kansas (Automatic fire alarm system).

Fire Protection Co., Chicago, Ill. (Automatic sprinkler system).

M. W. Watson, Topeka, Kansas (Service roads, sidewalks, coal storage area, and drainage).

Frankamp-Parker, Omaha, Neb. (Extension of water supply and distribution system).

Ratings of these contractors show that the majority rendered prompt and satisfactory service, with only a few being criticized with the remarks, "weak administration," "poor cooperation," "constantly behind schedule," and "failure to prosecute the work diligently. . . ."

Captain Charles W. Holderbaum was appointed Area Engineer on 27 January 1943, and was responsible for starting actual construction on 3 February 1943. He was replaced on 5 March 1943 by Major Alfred B. Plaenert, who was, in turn, replaced on 1 May 1943 by Major Paul M. Long. . . .

The Concordia Camp, as finally finished on 26 June 1943, fulfilled its original purpose of providing housing, mess facilities, recreation, and hospitalization for one thousand (1,000) officer internees, three thousand (3,000) enlisted men internees, and the required American garrison of 815 officers and men. Within the 640-acre reservation, the Camp proper contains 157.5 acres, being approximately 4,600 by 1,700 feet. 30.85 acres were devoted originally to officer internees, 36.65 acres to enlisted men internees, 14.69 acres to the hospital, 13.52 as a garrison area, and 12.87 acres to the general service area. The hospital was designed with a capacity of 177 beds, and housing was provided for sixty-five (65) Officers and 750 Enlisted Men of the garrison. In addition to internee quarters, garrison quarters, and essential administration buildings, there are five (5) warehouses, one (1) cold storage building, and quarters for fourteen (14) nurses among the major installations contemplated in the original plans. . . .

Water Supply and Distribution System: Two 350-gallon-per-minute wells, operated by electrically-driven turbine pumps, and supplemented by standby emergency gasoline engines, as well as one standby well of 100-gallon-per-minute capacity (of rather high chloride content), furnish the Camp's water. Main wells have semi-automatic chlorinators, and the supplementary well a manually-operated system. 41,930 feet of main, ranging from 1¼ to 8-inch, cast-iron throughout, serves for distribution. There are thirty-seven (37) fire hydrants. Storage is afforded by a 100,000-gallon elevated wood-stove water-storage tank. The system easily provides the required actual consumption of approximately 330,000 gallons per day, and is capable of furnishing 750 gallons per minute for two hours in event of fire demand.

Electrical Distribution System: The system is composed of a 7200 volt, 3-phase, 60-cycle, 3-wire primary, and a 120-240 volt, single and 3-phase, 60-cycle secondary system. Street and protective fence-lighting systems are both 6.6 ampere, constant-current-series systems. Guard towers are equipped with two (2) eighteen-inch search lights and a siren, and will operate from storage batteries in case of power failure.

Heating: Steam heat is provided for the hospital, Nurses' Quarters, and Officers' Club. Recreation Building RBC-A-T is steam-heated by means of cast-iron radiation, forced draft, and ventilating units. Infirmaries and the Paint and Carpentry Shop are heated with forced warm air. All other buildings are heated with cannon stoves, and all heating units burn coal.

Sanitary Sewage Collection and Disposal System: The collection system and the outfall sewer are gravity-operated, and no storm sewers are provided. No sewage-treatment facilities were constructed, and raw sewage is discharged directly into the Republican River, one mile south. A 12-inch outfall sewer travels south one-quarter of a mile to a water-flushing system, and from thence by an 8-inch line to the River. Twenty-three (23) feet of water head can be developed in the outfall sewer during time of high flow, since it operates as a pressure conduit.

Steam Distribution System: A central heating plant furnishes all steam for the hospital area, and involves 4,700 feet of steam line. Three cast-iron boilers, rated at 61.6 horsepower each, and operating on a gauge-pressure of five pounds per square inch, and composing a vacuum-return system, furnish the steam. A two-boiler utility system is also available. All are hand-fired. Nurses' Quarters and Officers' Club are individually heated by means of low-pressure systems.

Automatic Sprinkler and Fire Alarm Systems: All buildings in the hospital area, except the central heating plant, are served by one or the other of these two systems. Operation of the Sprinkler system automatically actuates the fire system. There are three fire department pumper connections. The system is a closed-circuit, supervised, noncoded, automatic system, and has storage batteries in event of power failure.

The final Field Progress Report, included in the Completion Report . . . , is a highly interesting statistical study. Together with the final accounting report, completed some nine months later on 31 March 1944, it comprises a wealth of important facts. . . . It is impossible to deal with all the details, but a consolidated summary of the basic statistics is certain [*sic*] indicated, and is given hereafter:

EMPLOYMENT, MAN-HOURS, AND PAYROLLS AT THE SITES . . .

PROJECT EMPLOYEES	TOTAL MAN HOURS	TOTAL PAYROLL
Architect-Engr.	16,523	$20,548.99
Area Engr. Office	58,687	52,572.69
Contract Labor	438,167	479,595.64
All Employees	513,377	552,717.32

A total of $1,786,379.00 was estimated to have been spent by 26 June 1943 on Projects T-1 and T-2 (but this was corrected by 31 March 1944, at the conclusion of accounting procedure, to $1,808,860.00 [*sic*]). This had been allocated as follows:

Architect-Engineer Plans and Specifications	$20,500.00
Supervision and Inspection of Project T-2	33,250.00
Clearing, grading, roads and drainage	79,938.00
Electrical distribution and lighting	17,803.00
Building construction	1,128,562.00
Water supply and distribution	80,132.00
Sewerage System	52,453.00
RBC-A-T Recreation Building	21,877.00

Automatic fire alarm system	3,920.00
Automatic sprinkler system	7,410.00
Service roads, walks and coal-storage area	23,453.00
Added wells and service	27,000.00
Government-furnished materials	63,114.00
Central Procurement (Office Chief Engineer)	53,331.00
Area Engineer Overhead (Office Chief Engineer)	73,636.00

TOTAL ESTIMATED COSTS
   AS OF 26 JUNE 1943   1,786,379.00
            [*actual* = $1,757,421.00 — *Ed.*]

Project T-2, involving the construction of additional facilities for 208 Officer internees in the Compounds, a Guard House, and an Ordnance Storage Magazine, not originally included in the initial layout planning, added a total of $71,042 [*sic*] to the total estimated cost. . . .

By 31 March 1944, the resulting figures showed an actual increase of $44,964.00 over the estimated costs of 26 June 1943, as shown in the Final Detail Cost Statement. . . . In times of rapid economic change, this is excellent proof of engineering efficiency.

As a subject of some curiosity, the costs of some of the installations are given below to supplement the information on the foregoing pages:

Enlisted Men Internees' Barracks (75 built)	$2,832.00
Officer Internees' Barracks (50 built)	3,948.00
Internees' Messhalls	6,331.00
Guard Towers	1,625.00
Nurses' Quarters	22,115.00
Officers' Club	23,946.00
Guard House	9,275.00
Fire Station	3,793.00
Cold Storage Warehouse	23,665.00
Flag-pole	306.00
Thirty-horse stable	4,782.00
Hospital Wards (average)	18,226.67
Heating Plant, with boilers	57,024.00
Fencing	23,000.00

Chapter 2

Trouble in the Compounds

*L*ieutenant Colonel John A. Sterling, who had retired from the Army in 1935, was called to active duty at the outbreak of World War II and became the first commander of Camp Concordia.[1] His wife joined him shortly after his arrival, and they lived in a small house south of the Officers Club, near the main gate.

American troops for the garrison had started arriving at the camp even before it was turned over to the Army on May 1st. On May 18, 1943, a few Military Police, some medical personnel, and 24 Quartermaster personnel arrived.[2] The camp was fairly well staffed by the end of May, except for the Military Police Escort Guard (MPEG) Companies.

According to Captain Teufel's report, the 456th and 457th Military Police Escort Guard Companies, two of the six that would be assigned to the camp, arrived by train on July 3, 1943, after having finished training at Camp Custer, Michigan, the Army base where all MPs received their training at

that time.[3] However, according to Privates Joe Pickering and Cleon Snodgress, who had come with the 456th MPEG in July, the 456th had *not* completed training and, thus, in February 1944 the unit was sent back to Camp Custer, to finish these exercises before shipping out to Europe. Pickering, now of New Castle, Indiana, recalls that when he arrived at Camp Concordia, he thought they were "out in the middle of the boondocks."

Newspaper reporters might have thought the camp had every modern convenience, but the soldiers knew better. The latrines were in separate buildings from the barracks; the only heat in winter was provided by three pot-bellied stoves in each barracks; and there were no recreation facilities on post. Private Casey Stangel, who had also arrived with the 456th MPEG in July, described their quarters, without any insulation, as "tar paper shacks just like what the prisoners had."

Bernadine (Blochlinger) Cummings started

First Sergeant Mullenforth of the 456th MPEG in 1943 at Camp Concordia. (Courtesy, Cleon Snodgress)

Inspection of the Guard prior to being posted. Notice the different uniforms. The guards for the gates have sidearms, and those on horse patrol are wearing riding boots; the remaining guards would probably work the towers. In the summer of 1944 the guards started wearing sun helmets. (Courtesy, Wayne E. Rossen)

Cleon Snodgress, right front, and three other members of the 456th MPEG, Camp Concordia, 1943. (Courtesy, Cleon Snodgress)

Second Lieutenants Herbert Ellis and Joseph Siegel, 456th MPEG, 1943. (Courtesy, Cleon Snodgress)

Seven members of the 642nd MPEG in front of their barracks, after their arrival at Camp Concordia in February 1944. Back row (left to right) — Manthey, Keller, Dixon; Second row — Bloch, Scena, Gueecci; and in front, Kerrigan. (Courtesy, Joe Bloch)

working at the camp in June 1943, and continued until it closed. She worked in the Quartermaster and Transportation offices:

I wasn't even aware of the camp until it was built. I was only 19, and my thoughts were on other things. I don't know what people thought about it. I was thrilled to get a job there making more money than I was at the AAA [American Automobile Association] office. Being around prisoners never bothered me at all. I never thought about it. My folks

Six members of the 642nd MPEG in the summer of 1944. The top two are Barnett and Konkolowski, at the side of the steps is Boxwell, and the three in uniform are Manthey, Thomas, and Frishey. (Courtesy, Joe Bloch)

Joe Bloch, 642nd MPEG, 1944. (Courtesy, Joe Bloch)

The Camp Concordia baseball team in the fall of 1943. Back row (left to right): Dorman Stecker, Cleon Snodgress, and George Yunt. Front row center is Lawrence Stemle; the other two are unidentified. (Courtesy, Cleon Snodgress)

Below: The baseball team of the 456th MPEG in the summer of 1943. Games were played between the companies, other military posts, and local teams. (Courtesy, Cleon Snodgress)

and the people I was around didn't object.

Cleon Snodgress, now of Mooreland, Indiana, remembered his time at Camp Concordia:

Bob [Stanford] was a civilian, had something wrong, and couldn't go into the service. Anyway, I met him and he liked baseball — was a good pitcher. He helped us get a ball team started. I liked the camp better after that. They had a nice baseball park [in town] that had covered bleachers. I used to go in to Bob's house and eat dinner with them. His folks were real nice.

Private Al King was assigned to Camp Concordia in October 1943, as a member of the 592nd MPEG Company. He met his wife, Jean, while on pass in Concordia:

The guys didn't appreciate going to Kansas, but when I got out here I liked it. I was here three weeks before I met my wife. After

I got married I was only at the camp when I was on duty. We [soldiers] got along pretty good, never had any trouble. Quite a few married girls from Concordia.

In the winter of '43 the snow was about waist deep, and there were rabbits galore. We took sticks and knocked them in the head. The Army wouldn't let us cook them in the mess hall, so my wife cooked them.

Jean, who had been raised near Concordia, was living in town when she met Al:

. . . We only knew each other three days, and we got married. My folks just about had a fit. I was 18.

Concordia readily made adjustments to accommodate the soldiers from the camp, according to Delmer Harris and Vicki Roberts, who was a 19-year-old girl living in Concordia when the camp was built. In addition to the many houses that were divided into apartments for married soldiers, the community opened a USO (United Service Organization) downtown where GIs could relax, have some homemade cookies, or attend dances, which were well attended by both local girls and soldiers. The USO also had contests and drawings for phone calls home and for bus tickets.[4] The bowling alley on Washington Street and the two movie houses were also popular spots. So were the bars. And to help keep the soldiers in line, the Army had Military Police (MP) patrols working out of the local police station.

Jane Wilson described activities at the USO:

People were curious about the soldiers. They came to town when they got a pass. We had the USO. There were the older ladies, one of them was my mother, who always went down there at night [as hostesses]. Junior Hostesses — I suppose that would have been me — went to the dances. We caught the USO on fire once. We were in charge of cleaning up and emptying the ash trays. There was a butt left in there, and we had a little fire. It didn't hurt very much, just filled it with smoke. The night watchman found it and called the fire department.

They had dances [for the American soldiers] out at the Prisoner of War Camp. The hostesses, the older ladies including my mother, went out. We rode in the back of the Army trucks. The older ladies [chaperones] sat on the sidelines and watched things. One time the German orchestra played, and they were used to going down in the crowd. They started walking through the crowd, and my mother became most alarmed. Somehow they got the message conveyed and got the band back up on the stage. [The Germans] played beautiful

music. [The camp] had a nicer dance floor than the USO [downtown], and they had a live band. The soldiers played, too. They had their own instruments.

The Fahlstroms farmed on the section of ground west of the camp. Their son was in the U.S. Army during World War II. Harriet shared their memories:

My son was in New Guinea, and the camp didn't seem such a big thing to us. We had work to do and relatives in bad places. We heard the prisoners were coming to town, so we went to the depot that night. There were several hundred people there to see them. You felt kind of sorry for them. Here it was night, and they were in a place they had never seen before.

We heard that we could hire prisoners. We would feed them dinner. I was used to cooking. We had hired help. When they came in, I pointed to the dining room. They each gave me a [little bow] German greeting. The guard followed them. He had to have his hat on and his gun beside him at the table because he was on duty. We didn't visit with the prisoners [we couldn't speak German], but we did visit with the guard. He wasn't very big and was from Kentucky. Someone passed the butter to one of the prisoners. He looked at it, and then looked at his friend next to him and said something. I wondered what was going on. Then I saw I hadn't put a butter knife on. So, I reached in the buffet and got the butter knife and put it on. Then, they passed it around. They saw my son's picture, in uniform, on the buffet. They discussed that. Then one of them looked at me and said, "Mother." I thought that was nice of them.

Bessie Payton was a young lady living in Concordia during the time that the POW camp was in operation:

We would go down to see the prisoners when they came in. There was always a crowd when the prisoner trains [arrived], but the guard would not let us get too close. The prisoners looked frightened and were very quiet as they got off the train.

The American soldiers were received in town real well. We thought some of the guards were 4Fs [those not qualified for military service]. I used to go to the USO with my mother to take cookies and cakes.

The camp helped the economy of the town. Most of the time people were not worried about the camp, but the escapes didn't go by unnoticed. They scared people.

Chester Erickson, who lived in Belleville, and worked at Camp Concordia from mid-July 1943 until October 1943, observed:

One of my first jobs was driving a truck to haul prisoners when the first load came in. The train stopped by the old creamery. The prisoners were in regular passenger cars [actually obsolete coaches from Eastern rail lines], but the windows had bars. Their heavy uniforms were sweat clear-through. You could smell them a half block away.

I hauled prisoners out to work, and I hauled food to the mess halls. When I went in [the compound] a guard would check the cab and the trip ticket. One of the [German] cooks would have a sandwich for me at 11:30 a.m. every day — German bread and mutton — a big sandwich. The Germans would sing and sway in the truck, and would almost wreck it. I liked to hear them sing when they marched — good marchers.

Vicki Roberts added:

People didn't want the Germans around. My mother was against the camp, but my dad didn't say much. I had mixed emotions about it. When prisoners were coming in, the train whistle sounded different than usual. It was long and low. Sometimes we would get up at 3:30 or 4:00 a.m. to go watch the Germans unload. They looked dirty and frightened. I used to go to dances at the USO. A lot of girls went, and there were big crowds. One kid

could really boogie-woogie on the piano. I only went to one dance at the camp. It was at the NCO [Noncommissioned Officer] Club.

When the camp was built, Wilma Johnson was 37. Her husband worked at the ice plant. She remembered:

I got up real early one morning and went down to the railroad to watch the prisoners come in. I think all of Concordia was there. I felt bad for [the prisoners]. They were away from home and looked so depressed. They didn't look up. They looked down.

I belonged to the Justamere Club, and we had to do so many things for the community. The USO was one of them. We would make cookies and sandwiches for the USO. We would answer questions and see that they had reading material, cookies, and coffee. They had a juke box, and they played the music loud.

Ellen Dixon was 13 when the camp was built:

I was out at the camp several times as a guest of the Renfros. I was completely in awe of the Officers Club because I had no experience with the military. In fact, I had always thought of the military as pretty far down the ladder. It was such an entirely different atmosphere than I had ever been subjected to that I just sat and watched the world go by. There was a band but I don't remember if it was a German band.

I was instructed not to have anything to do with the soldiers. I was pretty well sheltered. I used to play the violin in the school orchestra, and as I walked home I had it in my mind that it was my protection. I remember them being on the street a lot. People in the church would invite them to Sunday dinner. I don't recall any fear of the prisoners. I was more afraid of the GIs walking down the street.

I went with my mother to the USO several times. One of the clubs she belonged to would furnish cookies and act as hostesses. It was in the building where Sherwin Williams is now

[114 East 6th Street]. I remember setting up cookies and having drinks at the back of the building. As I recall, there were tables set around the outside [of the room] where they would play cards. They could dance if they wanted.

When Ellen married Seth Dixon, he became a career Army officer.

❧❧❧

The first 400 prisoners, who were mostly enlisted men in the *Deutsche Afrika Korps*, had arrived on July 15, 12 days after the first two MPEG companies. The Afrika Korps, commanded by Field Marshal Erwin Rommel, had operated in the Western Desert of Africa in 1941-1943, to assist the Italians. A large number of the townspeople were on hand to watch as the POWs were unloaded from the Missouri Pacific train, placed on trucks, and taken to the camp. *The Concordia Kansan* reported:

The advent of these prisoners of war into Concordia gives this community its first close-up realization of the actualities existing in the prosecution of this great world-wide undertaking to make the world free for all time to come.[5]

❧❧❧

In *The History of Camp Concordia*, Captain Teufel listed the requirements for treatment of POWs as set forth in Articles 2-5 of the July 27, 1929, Geneva Convention (Treaty Series 846), noting that "the U.S. has consistently adhered to the letter and spirit of the [Geneva Convention] which bears its signature and . . . has become one of the commitments of its national honor . . .":

. . . 2. Prisoners of War . . . must at all times be humanely treated and protected, particularly against acts of violence, insults, and public curiosity. Measures of reprisal against them are prohibited.

3. Prisoners of War have the right to have their person and their honor respected.

4. The Power detaining Prisoners of War is bound to provide for their maintenance.

5. No coercion may be used on prisoners to secure information relative to the condition of their army or country. Prisoners who refuse to answer questions may not be threatened, insulted, or exposed to unpleasant or disadvantageous treatment of any kind whatsoever.

❧❧❧

Once at Camp Concordia, the POWs were showered, fed, and assigned temporary quarters. The next day, after more processing, they were assigned permanent quarters, depending on their rank. Enlisted prisoners were assigned 50 to each barracks. Officer barracks were divided into apartments with four men per apartment and a total of 40 per barracks.

According to the Geneva Convention, all prisoners could choose to wear their German uniforms, with their insignia of rank, while in the compound. Enlisted prisoners were also provided blue uniforms that were either denim or old Army uniforms dyed blue with PW stenciled on the legs, seat, sleeves, and back, to wear when they went out to work. There was a German leader for each 250 prisoners. The leader wore four white stripes.[6] Prisoners, depending on rank, were allowed to write two letters and one postcard each week, and could send one 15-word message (telegram) per year. They could receive packages, but no books, and all mail was censored.[7]

Less than a week after the first POWs arrived, they were in the employment of local farmers, who had been told to work alongside the prisoners. Farmhands, however, were to dress in something other than the prisoner blue.[8]

According to the Articles of the Geneva Convention, the prisoners were not to operate machinery, but this rule was not always followed. Because of a shortage of guards, the number working on farms was small — only 15.[9] Charles Blosser had prisoners working on his farm; they loaded trucks and drove tractors. He reported that they were "good workers . . . nice and polite. . . ."[10] They worked in groups of three prisoners with one guard.

German POW work detail at the Concordia Depot. (Courtesy, Beryl Ward)

Charles was one of the leading citizens of Concordia. His wife, Isabell, noted:

We had about ten prisoners working for us. They picked up bales and did farm work. One time Charlie caught one carving a swastika on a tree. He reported him, and he never came back on a detail. Charlie took the prisoners to a cafe to eat at noon. They ate in the back room. We couldn't put them on display. The prisoners got a kick out of going to a restaurant to eat. Some people resented the POWs and soldiers. We were criticized for having POWs work for us. I felt sorry for them.

. . .One time, while the prisoners were waiting to be picked up, they asked to see the house. As they walked through, one of them [dragged] his hand across the piano keys. I asked if he could play and he said yes. I told

him to play something, and he played beautifully.

Mrs. Vida Tucker, whose husband worked at the camp as a mechanic, also noted the POWs' musical talents:

My husband had a harmonica that he played and enjoyed. He found a prisoner who also liked to play. He could really play it. He enjoyed it so much my husband gave the harmonica to him.

Casey Stangel continued about the POWs as laborers:

Generally [the POWs] went out in the country for farm labor. [But] there was an ice company here in town where they made cake

A group of POWs standing beside their barracks. Notice that the legs and arms of the shirts are stenciled with PW. (Courtesy, Kurt Waechtler)

Below: A group of enlisted POWs in March 1945. Notice the PW markings on their trouser legs. (Courtesy, Adolf Weber)

ice that was used in refrigerated railroad cars. They had prisoners loading the cars with ice. The prisoners worked on the railroad, but they were under pretty strict guard to prevent sabotage.

Cleon Snodgress added:

The thing I like about the duty was we would go out on the farms with the prisoners. They would cut the kafir corn. The farmers would always have a big dinner. I always liked that.

Dale Cool commented:

I helped bale hay with [the POWs]. I helped down on Charlie Blosser's. He worked a bunch of them. They were good workers. They were a big help because you couldn't get any other help. All of our guys were off in the Army. They helped a lot putting up silage, and in the hay fields.

[On one occasion,] Harriet Fahlstrom said a nice collie dog came to her place, and she wanted to know if I wanted it. She knew we were getting married and didn't have a dog. I said we would take it, so she brought it down.

A group of enlisted POWs. Notice that there is no PW marking on their clothing. (Courtesy, Gunter Klein)

It was the most beautiful collie and it was from an officer [POW] over there at the camp. We kept him 15 years.

Dale's wife, Mary Jane, who was a lifetime resident of Concordia and had married Dale shortly after the camp closed, added:

A lot of girls got jobs out there and got a lot better wages than in town.

June (Avery) Gilkison, who went to work at the POW camp after she graduated from high school, noted:

I went to work in the Adjutant's Office and worked for Captain [Karl C.] Teufel. The camp was well-kept and well laid out. As a civilian, I had to eat lunch at the PX. The food was excellent.

The prisoners were very intelligent and well mannered. Sometimes they wore their German uniforms, and they were impeccable. One of the prisoners did a beautiful oil painting for me and

Above: A group of German POWs at Camp Concordia. Notice the variety of uniforms, mixed uniforms, and even a striped shirt (front row, second from the right). (Courtesy, Al Purdy)

A group of enlisted POWs wearing their German army uniforms. (Courtesy, Gunter Klein)

another made an octagon inlaid box for me. It doesn't have a nail in it. I still have the painting and the box.

I remember they announced Germany's surrender over the camp's loudspeakers. The Germans' faces were downcast when they heard the news.

Lorene Baxa's parents, Henry and Blanche, operated a farm near Agenda, Kansas, about 13 miles from the camp. Lorene's memories come from the stories her parents told her about the German prisoners working on their farm:

A tornado hit the barn in the fall of 1943. Prisoners were asked to pour a new foundation. There were four prisoners and one guard. Since they were only helping with the foundation, they were only there three or four days. Mom prepared lunch for them each day. The camp had given her a list of foods so

The enlisted POW compound at Concordia. Notice the board sidewalks and the benches by the steps. (Courtesy, Adolf Weber)

Five of the local women that worked at the camp. Left to right: Celine McCall, Helen Balthazor, Barbara Stevenson (Walters), and unidentified. (Courtesy, Cloud County Historical Society, Concordia, KS)

Miss Lorene Baxa, Master Sergeant Hobson, and Mrs. Richey in the Post Headquarters. (Courtesy, Wayne E. Rosen)

there would be a large enough portion of meat and a balanced diet. When they came in for lunch, the guard would take notes as to what foods were prepared. The [POWs] were polite and hard workers. One day when they came in for lunch, one of the prisoners asked about the baby's age. He said he had a daughter about the same age. He asked if he could hold the baby and Mom let him. He thought that holding the baby was great.

The POWs were pouring the floor in the barn, putting limestone rocks into the cement, and picking up rocks and putting them in a wagon. Dad said they could use his horses to pull the wagon. One of the prisoners commented that they had similar horses in Germany, and he enjoyed using them. They were using a small cement-mixer with a gasoline engine. They had to count the shovels of sand, gravel, and cement. The prisoners would count the shovels in German.

We did not have running water, and the well was located between the house and where the prisoners were working. Mom went out to get water and was carrying the baby girl and had the two-year-old boy with her. One of the prisoners came up and pumped the water for her.

Mom was always apprehensive when the prisoners were coming, but they were always

polite and kind. What made her nervous was that at lunch the guard would put his rifle in the corner. She was afraid her two-year-old would get it without being seen.

The Garlows lived with their two children on a farm about three miles northwest of Camp Concordia. Fern explained the value of the POW help:

We hired the prisoners one day to shock wheat. My mother-in-law and I fixed dinner, and they laughed and talked while they were eating. Of course, it was in German and we couldn't understand them. At the time I was a little leery of them. They were our enemies.

Most of them were farm boys. [Our] farmers were hard hit because most of the young men were gone, and they depended on [the POWs]. It helped our country by having them here. Otherwise, how would we have gotten the harvest in?

In late July, the wage of the prisoners had been set at $1.60 per eight-hour day, plus one-half cent per mile round trip, for a maximum payment of $2.40.[11] Of this amount, only 80 cents went to the prisoner; the remainder went to the government. Enlisted prisoners who did not work received $3 per month, while those who did had up to $13 per month to spend in the canteen. NCOs could only be used in a supervisory role and were paid at the same rate as other enlisted prisoners. According to the Geneva Convention, officers were not required to work, though they could volunteer. Depending on their rank, officer-prisoners received from $20 to $40 per month. The money could be spent in the canteen, or it could be saved.[12]

If a prisoner had a relative in another POW camp in the United States, he could pay the transportation costs to be taken to the same camp. As a result, there were several brothers, uncles, and cousins at Camp Concordia.

Fritz Vogt had been serving with the 10th Panzer Division in North Africa when he was captured. He was sent to the United States and on to the POW camp at Concordia. In *Prisoners on*

POWs building a fence at the camp under the supervision of a civilian (second from the left). (Courtesy, Wayne E. Rosen)

The three POWs that worked as projectionists at the theater. Left to right: Hans Fungeling, Gunter Lehmann, and Gunter Klein. (Courtesy, Gunter Klein)

the Plains: German POWs in America, Glenn Thompson recorded Vogt's impressions:

The first POW camp we were sent to was at Concordia, Kansas. We were registered there on August 29, 1943. Each of us was given a number which we kept during the entire time of our imprisonment. They gave us new clothing which was marked with a large PW. Then they took our old uniforms, and we never did see them again. The camp was furnished adequately, and the meals were good and plentiful. I worked on street repair, always under strict guard.

After about five months at Concordia, we were sent to Camp Atlanta, Nebraska, arriving January 26, 1944. We were the first prisoners there.[13]

Concordian Richard Wahl, who is fluent in German, has corresponded with Gunter Klein of Dusseldorf, Germany, a former Camp Concordia POW. The following is a portion of what Klein has written about his experiences there:

After training as a rifleman in the armored corps, I was sent to Africa. I was captured in

May 1943, and taken to an American prison camp. I was then taken to Algiers, Scotland, and finally landed in New York. On August 12, 1943, I arrived at Concordia, Kansas. After a short period of working in the PX warehouse, I, along with two of my comrades, became projector operators in the post theater. After October 5th, films were also shown to POWs there. I did the office work, sold tickets (admission was 15 cents), stood at the ticket box during admission, filed invoices, and was responsible for keeping the theater clean (including the toilets). I worked daily at the projectors, usually five days a week, with three showings for officers and men. On October 20, 1945, I was transferred to the release camp at Atlanta, Nebraska, and then through Boston to Europe.

• • •

I have no knowledge of a Munich city band [being at the camp]. It is possible that this [band] was in the officers' camp. I know of a large symphony orchestra from the officers' camp which gave beautiful concerts for everyone in the post theater. In the enlisted camp, we had a large brass orchestra. If I remember correctly, it was supposed to have originally been a Hamburg police orchestra. The men in the orchestra were taken prisoner in Tunisia and finally came to Concordia. The band concerts brought us much happiness.[14]

Erik Kosin was a native of Yugoslavia, but was drafted into the German army after the fall of his country. He was only 19 when he was captured in North Africa. He was sent to Camp Concordia, and worked as an interpreter. After the war, he returned to Yugoslavia and became a pharmacist. In 1976, he returned to Concordia for a visit and was interviewed by KNCK radio and *The Concordia Blade-Empire*. Kosin told KNCK:

I felt relief [when captured], to get rid of the German army, and I was safe. I arrived at Concordia in the summer of 1943. When we came into the camp and compounds, we were surprised everything was so nice.

An excerpt from an article in *The Concordia Blade-Empire*, quoted Kosin:

In general, all of the prisoners were treated as they deserved. We had all of the reading material we wanted, records, and we could get food, beverages, and cigarettes from the canteen. We had plenty of exercise. I even played some tennis in the recreation area. I took some university courses in Spanish, American history, civics, and geography. I was glad to get off [from the war] — glad to get out of that mess.[15]

❦

The arrival of the 480th MPEG in August 1943 and the 592nd MPEG in November solved the shortage of guards at the camp and soon prisoners were assisting farmers in Cloud, Mitchell, and Republic counties. The farmers were glad to have them. There were times when the farmers could barely keep up with the prisoners' pace.

Concordian Keith Buss was 13 years old when his father had POWs working on their farm. His parents were from Germany. He remembered:

We started getting POWs in the fall of 1943. There were four prisoners and one guard. They built a cement-block tool shed without using a level. They just used a nail and a string. We still use the building. One time the guard laid down his rifle and helped.

In 1944, they helped cut up alfalfa. Dad could speak German, and he would tell them what to do. They were glad to work for someone who could speak their language. Dad had to tell them how to use the pitch fork to put the hay on the stack. Once they got the hang of it, they could bury the guy on the top of the stack. There was one who would not cooperate. Dad told the guard, and the next day, there was a different prisoner on the detail. I was not afraid of them. They were good workers.

My mom fed them at noon. They liked the food and ate a lot. They thanked her every day. One said it was the first time he had eaten with a family in four years.

Joe Pickering remembered:

The wind always blew — hotter than heck in the summer, and colder than heck in the winter. One time the commander had us out for close-order drill in front of the barracks. It was ten below. Finally, we went back inside. Didn't finish whatever it was we were doing.

I took a detail of four or five to shuck corn. It was colder than the dickens so I rode in the cab of the truck; [the POWs] weren't going any place.

We went out on a hike and killed rabbits with sticks. I forget how many. We brought them back and were going to have the mess sergeant cook them. The commander wouldn't let him.

They used to catch guys asleep in the towers, leaning against the tower. We couldn't have chairs and couldn't sit down. It was a long four hours.

Private Mike Yaksich arrived at Camp Concordia

POW work detail at the Buss farm. (Courtesy, Keith Buss)

on November 1, 1943, with the 592nd MPEG, and he remained there until it closed, by which time he had been promoted to Staff Sergeant. He met his wife while stationed at the camp. Yaksich noted:

When we boarded the troop train at Fort Custer, we didn't know where we were going. Thought it would be overseas. When we got to Davenport, Iowa, we learned we were going to Concordia, Kansas. Most of the men were from the East, and we were surprised. . . .

. . . One time I helped take two prisoners to Douglas, Wyoming. The guards were MPs in uniform, and the prisoners were in their German uniforms. We went through Union Station in Kansas City [Missouri], without any trouble. Then, on the train, a drunk started trying to agitate the prisoners. We had to ask the conductor to have him put off the train.

Casey Stangel, originally from Nebraska, notes:

They sent me to Fort Custer, Michigan, where I went through basic [training] and [then we] were split up for orders. When units were shipped out, we were lined up on the dock. The 456th was one of them. They were five people short and had to be at full strength before they could ship out. They said, "You, you, and you are volunteers," so I volunteered.

I thought Kansas is close to Nebraska, and I might get to go home. About an hour out of town, they told us we were going to Concordia.

When his 456th Company left Camp Concordia to return to Fort Custer for additional training, Stangel remained at Camp Concordia and worked in the Provost Marshal's Office (PMO) until the camp closed.

It appears that Camp Concordia's commander, Lieutenant Colonel John A. Sterling, was a very relaxed officer. Perhaps he didn't want to command a POW camp, or maybe he had never been strict. Officers did not have to report for duty at any set time, and they started drinking at the Officers Club at 11:30 a.m. There were no guard regulations.[16] It also appears that Sterling let the officer-prisoners run the compound.[17] Perhaps, because the officer-prisoners had maintained discipline before they were captured, he was able to justify their being in charge.

However, with this type of atmosphere in the camp, unfavorable incidents soon began to happen. On August 9, 1943, the first POW death occurred when Captain Gustav Dormann hanged himself only one week after his arrival.[18] Then on October

Gerhard Gruenzig, upon his arrival at Camp Concordia in 1943. (Courtesy, Gerhard Gruenzig)

16, 1943, one of the guards shot and killed a prisoner, Corporal Adolf Huebner, who was going after a soccer ball, but went too near the fence.[19]

Gerhard Gruenzig was in one of the first groups of POWs that arrived at Camp Concordia. He recalled the shooting of Huebner:

Our boys played in an area where there was some open space. The guards in the tower observed this pick-up ballgame. Several times the ball went into the security zone, and the guards permitted us to get the ball. Then they would not permit it anymore, and the guard shot our comrade through the head as he stood. A forced murder from the death tower. Now came our anger. We answered with stone-throwing and a two-hour demonstration. The guard was relieved [of his duty]. This young comrade was the first death in Camp Concordia and, I believe the first death of a German Prisoner of War in the USA.

Casey Stangel also remembered the incident:

When the prisoner [Adolf Huebner] was shot, I was in the latrine getting cleaned up to go to town. I was halfway through when the alarm went off, sirens, and we knew something was happening. I had heard a noise prior to that, but didn't know it was a shot. Anyway, we were all sent to the supply area to get ammunition and weapons. We were all confined to the post and had to be ready. It was a kind of hurry-up-and-wait thing. The prisoners got in their formations and started marching up and down the road in the compound singing German songs. They kept it up for 48 hours or longer. We were kind of outnumbered, four to one, and didn't know what was going to happen.

Harriet Fahlstrom also described that night:

The area in which Corporal Adolf Huebner (7WG 14363) was shot on October 16, 1943. The guard was in the tower on the left. (Courtesy, Gerhard Gruenzig)

Colonel Eduard Waltenberger (front center) became the senior German spokesman after the Tropschuh incident. He is seen here with some other German officers, probably his staff. Colonel Waltenberger was respected by the Americans as well as his own men. (Courtesy, Bernadine Cummings)

One Saturday night we went to town to make our purchases. When I went in the store, soldiers were on the street with the local people. I made my purchases and came out. There wasn't a soldier in sight. My husband came down the street, and I told him that something was going on and [that] I wanted to go home. So we got our groceries and [left]. When we drove up to the garage, I opened the door to get out, and I heard the [noise]. It was screaming and yelling like you never heard. It was a mile and a half away, yet I could hear it that plainly.

The Germans protested by shouting and singing patriotic songs, but there was not a riot.

Donald Kerr added:

Well, I remember when the guard shot the prisoner. Why, it was about four days before I

was even allowed to go back up into the compound with supplies. When Fairmont Dairy used to bring milk out, if the driver was a woman, I would take their truck up into the compounds and deliver for them.

The Germans marched from one place to another. Boy, they were high-steppers, and they would sing everywhere they went.

As a result of the shooting, all soldiers who were on pass were recalled to the camp.[20] The POWs called it a murder, and, according to Donald Kerr and Chester Erickson, tension within the camp was high. POWs were kept in the compound, while civilian workers were kept out of the compound. According to Mike Yaksich, the guard was in the 456th MPEG. He was court-martialed, but it was determined he had fired in the line of duty.

Then, on October 19, 1943, POW Captain Felix Tropschuh, who had arrived on August 9th, was

Lieutenant Franz Kramer (7WG 16327) in Officer Compound 4 in 1945. (Courtesy, Bernadine Cummings)

found dead in his quarters.[21] On the surface it appeared there had been another suicide, but an investigation would reveal that Tropschuh had expressed anti-Nazi sentiments in his diary and had been slow to obey orders of the compound spokesman. A meeting of the entire camp had condemned him.[22] He was convinced that if he did not take the "proper" action, his family would suffer after the war. He was given a rope, put in a room, and few hours later, he was dead.[23]

The German senior spokesman at the time demanded that Tropschuh not be buried with Dormann and Huebner, because he was not a good German. Lieutenant Colonel Sterling agreed to the demand, and Tropschuh was buried by the Ameri-

cans on the opposite side of the cemetery. The Germans refused to attend the funeral.

Franz Kramer, of Gundelfingen, Germany, has also written to Richard Wahl about his time at Camp Concordia as a POW. A portion of his letter follows:

I wouldn't say that the Nazi officers . . . were putting pressure against the other officers in the camp. But, let me describe a few other measures taken by the Nazis. I am sure notes were taken concerning officers who openly dared say that Germany would be defeated. Surely those notes would have been dangerous had Germany been victorious. But could it be a real threat? Almost every prisoner felt or knew that Germany would lose the war.

In the beginning, the camp was controlled by a very small group of German officers. The American officers were at first very reserved, and these Nazi officers were bold enough to do things which perhaps went beyond what was right and lawful. There was a deplorable mysterious death. An officer was found dead. Apparently, he had made notes that were not friendly to these officers. I don't know the exact circumstances, but he committed suicide, or so the German leaders said. Nevertheless, rumors persisted that there happened to be some help by Nazi officers.[24]

The German leaders owned a short-wave radio. They would listen to German news, especially the army report. In the evening, we would meet at a named place in the camp. There the German news concerning the war in Europe would be read and commented on by a high-ranking officer. The officer commented on the events as success for the German armies and signs of winning the war. Presence at this meeting was, so to speak, a national obligation and demonstrated a belief in a final victory. Absence was taken note of.

There existed in the camp a so-called university where we could take courses of all kinds. These courses were not influenced [by the Nazis]. The subject had priority. I was a customs official as were others. There was

Captain Giles H. Strong, the stockade commander in 1945. The POWS referred to him as "Papa Strong." Many of the POWS corresponded with him after their return to Germany. (Courtesy, Bernadine Cummings)

meet our expectations. We didn't know why it was necessary to shorten the rations. Since the shortening coincided with the end of the war many believed it was done without fear of retaliation against American prisoners of war in Germany. Others were of the opinion it was a kind of punishment for crimes committed by Germans. Be that as it may, time passed and all was forgotten.

There was no reason to criticize American authorities. The prisoners felt that they were well treated. We learned a little of the American way of life and saw part of the vast country.

Captain Giles H. Strong, referred to by Kramer, was the commander of the officers compound and, later, the stockade. He was respected and well liked by the POWs, who referred to him as "Papa Strong."

ಌಯ

By this time, Camp Concordia was getting a bad reputation in the local press and throughout the Army as the worst POW camp in the country.[25] Then, on October 23, 1943, an incident occurred at the Officers Club that was a direct result of the "country club" atmosphere. Captain David Roberts, the Commander of the 456th MPEG, was the Duty Officer and was at the club, where he had been drinking. He got into an argument with Captain Joseph R. King's wife and her daughter, Betty. Mrs. Sterling, the Colonel's wife, saw that Captain Roberts was about to pull out his service pistol so she stepped between them. She was shot in the back.[26] Mrs. King and her daughter scuffled with Captain Roberts until others that were in the club came to their aid. He was disarmed by Lieutenant John N. Hummel and placed under arrest by Captain King. Captain Roberts was immediately relieved and taken to the guardhouse and placed under guard. Mrs. Sterling recovered from her wound.

Isabell Blosser noted:

We went to the Officers Club to parties and dances. A German band would play. Quite a few civilians would be invited to the parties.

also an officer who had been a customs teacher before the war. He liked to teach in the camp and wanted all officers to join his lessons, but some did not. He expressed the opinion that those who did not take part in his classes would have disadvantages after repatriation. I have no doubt that this teach[er] would have welcomed a German victory.

After the end of the war, the food rations were drastically shortened. It is not that we suffered from starvation in the real sense of the word. However, our stomachs grumbled heavily. We tried planting melons to improve our nutrition. [The stockade commander] Captain [Giles H.] Strong tried to increase the rations. The result was moderate and did not

We were at the club the night Colonel Sterling's wife was shot, but had left before it happened.

Mike Yaksich, of the 592nd MPEG, remembered the incident:

When Captain Roberts shot the Colonel's wife, they had to have NCOs guard him, so I was promoted to Corporal. I guarded him while he was at the camp.

Casey Stangel, on guard duty that night, commented:

When I went on my tour early that morning, I went past the guardhouse and there [Captain Roberts] was behind bars. I could hardly believe it. He was my Company Commander at the time. So I did some inquiring around, and the Sergeant of the Guard told me what had happened. It was quite a deal. Seeing your own Company Commander behind bars was quite a thing. He was a really good man, had been in the British army and was well liked.

Cleon Snodgress mentioned the shooting, as well:

I was on the main gate when I heard the shot at the Officers Club. It was early morning, and they were having a party. [The Officers Club] was pretty close to the main gate and you could hear the music. I know some of the guys on guard duty had to take [Captain Roberts] to the guard house. He was the Officer of the Guard. He was real strict.

❧

Martin H. Lutzke was commissioned a Second Lieutenant in the Signal Corps and assigned to the Prisoner of War Camp at Concordia on August 9, 1943. He was the Commanding Officer (CO) of Compound Number 1 and later the stockade commander. He was promoted to Captain and remained at the camp until it closed. He spoke fluent German,

which helped in his dealings with the prisoners. Lutzke explained:

More than anything, I would like people to know that the prisoners more than earned their keep.

We [the soldiers] felt we were not wanted. [Concordia] wanted an Air Corps base, but they got us. We didn't get along with the newspaper. We wouldn't give them information, so they got it from the people who worked at the camp. That information was not always right.

One time, two prisoners hollowed out a lumber pile, and one of them hid inside. That night, there was a good Kansas thunderstorm, and he got soaked. In the middle of the night, he came up to the gate and wanted back in.

Bernadine Cummings added:

The editor of the *Blade* [*The Concordia Blade-Empire*] Nosey Green and the camp were in a constant battle. When prisoners came in, the only ones who knew about it was the commandant, the post adjutant, executive officer, Captain McShane, and myself. We were the only ones aware of the exact time of the POW movements. But, Nosey Green would have it out in the newspaper. The only thing we could figure out was the AP [Associated Press] might see the prisoners debarking at the port and getting on trains. He never found out when they were shipping out.

The prisoner who worked with me was Ernest Rudolf. He was a nice kid. He was a file clerk in Quartermaster and also translated the reports of the garbage men. They drove the horse-drawn wagons in the compounds and made their reports in German. Rudolf translated these reports for our office. He was very reserved and quiet. He was also very concerned about his family. He had not heard from them for a long time.

The janitor was an enlisted POW. You didn't dare say anything to him about Jews or he would go into a rage. Something was mentioned one time, and he took his broom and pushed my chair clear across the room. When they had the raid to separate the Nazis from the anti-Nazis, he was picked up and shipped out.

Marvin Stortz, who was a Sergeant, had spent 22 months in the Pacific Theater and then was assigned to the POW Camp at Concordia, his home town. He remained there until it closed:

Four of us came in, the first ones to [arrive] who had been overseas. The German prisoners would meet us on the sidewalk. Of course, we had "Hershey bars" [overseas combat-zone duty stripes] and ribbons, and they would get off the sidewalk. They thought we might have a bone to pick.

A little POW sergeant, name was Blum, was from Potsdam, Germany. He was an interpreter and spoke three languages. He had been in the movie business and knew Eva Braun [Hitler's mistress]. When anybody came on post in a two-button suit, like the FBI, it was like the Gestapo to him, and he was very frightened. When we were shipping [the POWs], he wanted to stay here. His parents were in Potsdam, and he hadn't heard from them. He assumed they were all dead. We used to sneak him into the theater. He had this little book, and he would rate the movies with one star, two stars, propaganda, etc. He kept track of the Colonel for us. We knew where he was all the time.

❧❧❧

In November 1943, Camp Concordia was at its highest strength, consisting of 793 American military, 171 civilians, plus 3,012 German enlisted men, and 1,015 officers.[27] In addition, a branch camp at Hays, Kansas, from mid-September until October 8th had employed 100 POWs, and a second branch camp at Peabody, Kansas, employed 112 POWs.[28]

In December 1943, Captain Robert B. Heinkel of the Provost Marshal General's Office inspected Camp Concordia. His report, of the 23rd, noted that the treatment of prisoners was on the lenient side

and that the prisoners were running their own companies.

. . . Prisoners are allowed to attend the movies shown in the War Department theatre outside of the compound.

. . . There appeared to be sufficient games and sport equipment to satisfy the demands of the prisoners. The eleven sets of athletic equipment furnished through this office were in use.

He described the "complaints" of the POWs:

. . . The ranking spokesman complained that the buildings were not insulated properly for winter weather. However, it appeared that these buildings were built according to specification, that they were in good repair and that they were similar to the quarters assigned to the American personnel.

He also suggested that Lieutenant Colonel Sterling had lost interest in the camp.[29]

The following duty roster is from Captain Heinkel's Inspection Report:

Colonel John A. Sterling, Commander, Post
Lt. Col. Lester Vocke, _____, Post
Major Roy M. Inbody, Executive O, Post
Major Carl L. Mangiameli, Post Surgeon, Hospital
Captain John J. Austin, Stockade O, Stockade
Captain Ralph T. Coverdale, Labor O, POW
Captain Curtiss S. McCallister, Post Dentist, Hospital
Captain Harold C. Rininger, Dispensary O, Hospital
Captain Donald M. Renfro, CO, Compound #3, POW
Captain Marvin C. Johnson, Exchange O, Post
Captain Samuel P. Davalos, Chief Engr Br, Post
Captain Earl S. Charles, CO, Compound #2, POW
Captain Max Simons, Chief EENT Clinic, Hospital

Captain William C. Biehle, Personnel O, Post

Captain Carl I. Dietz, Claims O, Post

Captain Russell H. Mulder, Asst Executive O, Post

Captain Richard D. Harding, CO, Officer Compd, POW

Captain Giles H. Strong, CO, Compound #1 POW

Captain Robert R. Bates, Chief Surgical Hospital

Captain Frederick E. Rawdon, Asst Chief Engr Br, Post

Captain Josiah R. King, Transportation O, Post

Captain David Roberts, _____, 456th MPEG Co

Captain Marty Ball, Commanding O, 480th MPEG Co

1st Lt. Harry G. Bracken, Commanding O, 592nd MPEG Co

1st Lt. Frank D. Gomez, Post Veterinarian, Post

1st Lt. Wilburn E. Wright, Dental O, Hospital

1st Lt. James W. Chambers, Chief Medical Br, Hospital

1st Lt. Russell L. Compton, Canteen O, POW

1st Lt. Charles E. F. Gentes, Chief Q.M. Br, Post

1st Lt. Kenneth J. McShane, Sales O, Post

1st Lt. Bernice A. Pollock, Chief Nurse, Hospital

1st Lt. Carl J. Bergman, Post Chaplain, Post

1st Lt. Herbert C. Ellis, Commanding O, 456th MPEG Co

1st Lt. Neal A. Broyles, Company O, 480th MPEG Co

1st Lt. George J. Rohn, Adjutant, Hospital

1st Lt. Clarence P. Hanse[n], Medical Supply O, Hospital

1st Lt. Martin H. Lutzke, Asst CO, O. Compd, POW

2nd Lt. Peter L. Doyle, Asst Exchange O, Post

2nd Lt. John N. Hummel, Adjutant, Post

2nd Lt. Joseph A. Siegel, Company O, 456th MPEG Co

2nd Lt. Philip E. Sitzman, Commanding O, 457th MPEG Co

2nd Lt. Hubbard W. Wells, Finance O, Post

2nd Lt. Sol Zaretzki, Company O, 457th MPEG Co

2nd Lt. Oke E. Carlson, Company O, 457th MPEG Co

2nd Lt. Wilkie B. Dye, Asst. CO, Compd #1, POW

2nd Lt. Ewald S. Schoeller, Company O, 480th MPEG Co

2nd Lt. Vincent B. Hughes, Commanding O, Hdqrs Det

2nd Lt. Jacob A. Yockey, Asst. CO, Compd #2, POW

2nd Lt. Angus M. Shipley, Laboratory O, Hospital

2nd Lt. Clem J. Denicke, Company O, 592nd MPEG Co

2nd Lt. Roy C. Fanning, Salvage O, Post

2nd Lt. Paul V. Folkenson, Asst. T Officer, Post

WOJG Bill M. Strange, Asst. Personnel O, Post

· · ·

Permanent Details:
  Station Hospital:
    Kitchen:
      Cooks, KPs 66
    Labor:
      Painters 12
      Clean-up detail 42   120
  Medical Assts:
    Interpreters 12
    Dental Aides 12
    Medical Aides 144   168
          288 weekly — 48 daily
Officers Compound:
  Kitchen:
    Cooks, firemen
    Latrine detail 462
  Orderlies:
    Mail 18
    Barracks 780
    Personal 48
    Barbers 24
    Tailors 24
    PX 72   1374
             [*actual = 1428 — Ed.*]

Labor:
    Carpenters 234
    Sign painters 18
    Stone Masons 588   840
Clerks:
    Office 48
    Educ. Supvr. 6   54
        2268 weekly — 378 daily
Engineer:
    Architect 12   2
               weekly — daily
    Labor 1273   212
Miscellaneous:
    Officers Mess 48   8
    Transportation 54   9
Subsistence:
    Cold storage 30   5
    Commissary 30   5
Quartermaster:
    Warehouse T-10 12   2
    Warehouse T-11 30   5
    PX Warehouse 12   2
    Stockade Hdqtrs. 30   5
    KP's Garrison Kitchens . . .186   31

Total No. Men Daily on Permanent Details
                              — 710

The paint and carpenter shop, T-20, in 1944. (Courtesy, Wayne E. Rosen)

The fire station, 1943. (Courtesy, National Archives)

Agricultural:	Men	Details
Monday	42	6
Tuesday	63	9
Wednesday	44	7
Thursday	0	0
Friday	28	4
Saturday	28	4

Total No. of Men working on Agricultural
    Projects: 205
Daily Average No. Men working   34
        [actual = 29.3 — Ed.]

Camp Projects:	Skilled	Unskilled	Total
Monday	82	398	480
Tuesday	56	413	469
Wednesday	64	426	490
Thursday	52	398	450
Friday	68	401	469
Saturday	61	335	396

  Skilled Labor:
      Week: 383
    Daily Average: 64

  Unskilled Labor:
      Week: 2371
    Daily Average: 395

    Total Labor:
        Week: 2766 *[actual = 2754 — Ed.]*
    Daily Average: 461 *[actual = 459 — Ed.]*

Summary: Daily Average
    Permanent Details 710
    Camp Projects 159
    Compound Overhead (Class I) 220
    Agricultural:
        Concordia .34
        Peabody .112
        Total Daily Average 1235

❧❧❧

The prisoners had planted trees and flowers to improve the look of the camp. Drainage ditches were lined with stone, and bridges were built across them. With scrap lumber, the prisoners built tables

Certificate given by the POW University, for a course in American History. (Courtesy, Kurt Waechtler)

beer, which was "all right," but the men bought more soft drinks than beer. The prisoners' food was plentiful, and one prisoner said he "didn't know anyone in the world was rich enough to have so much meat to eat."[30] There had been some adjustment of rations to suit the German taste.

Like the POWs, the garrison soldiers were also making improvements to their way of life. Baseball teams had been organized, and games were arranged with teams from Fort Riley and nearby towns. Later, according to Cleon Snodgress, basketball and even golf teams were formed. A liberal policy was adopted which allowed for passes for off-duty soldiers, many of whom were dating local girls. Several of these soldiers married the girls and remained in the area after the war. Leave was given whenever possible. The theater showed movies, and, occasionally, USO theater troupes would perform. The soldiers also organized local talent shows.

In early December 1943, Lieutenant Colonel Lester Vocke, a Regular Army officer, replaced Lieutenant Colonel Sterling as the Commander of Camp Concordia. The "country club" atmosphere that the American staff had enjoyed, as well as the lenient treatment of the POWs, came to an abrupt end. The slot machines were removed from the Officers Club, and the bar was closed, except for beer after duty. Within 24 hours, guard regulations had been written. Vocke was constantly out of his office checking mess halls, labor details, and POW compounds.[31]

Everyone knew Vocke meant business when a large number of the officers and senior NCOs who had been on Lieutenant Colonel Sterling's staff were transferred. The Germans who had been controlling the compounds and some of the educational instructors who were determined to be Nazis were sent to other camps.[32] Meanwhile, the POWs

and chairs and made improvements to the interior of the barracks and casinos (clubs). Libraries were started in the enlisted mens and officers compounds, and educational classes were started. The prisoners also had their own newspaper, *Neue Stacheldraht Nachrichten* [*The New Barbed Wire Nightly News*]. The prisoner canteens served 3.2

Above: The north end of the Headquarters building with the hospital compound in the background. Besides the headquarters offices it contained the PX, post office, and restaurant. All of the landscaping was completed by POWs. (Courtesy, Gunter Klein)

Left: The guard tower at the corner of the hospital compound. The hospital is in the background. (Courtesy, Wayne E. Rosen)

key, and carols at night.[33] For the Americans, Christmas was a holiday when only the guard reliefs worked, and there was a big meal in each mess hall.

By the end of 1943, the prisoners had harvested 20,000 bushels of corn, 15,000 bushels of kafir corn, 15,000 bushels of soybeans, 5,000 bushels of wheat, 1,000 bushels of oats, 3,500 sacks of potatoes, 2,200 tons of alfalfa, and had dressed for market 4,000 chickens and turkeys.[34] The prisoners were proving to be a valuable asset to the local farmers and to the country as a whole.

continued with their labor details and the beautification of the camp.

For Christmas 1943, the German government sent $9,000 to be spent on the prisoners. There was a Christmas tree in each compound, a dinner of tur-

HEADQUARTERS
Prisoner of War Camp
Concordia, Kansas

EDUCATIONAL COURSES IN OFFICERS COMPOUND
MASTER SCHEDULE
College Instruction
25 Aug 1943 - 25 Dec 1943

LEGEND

Instructor Group

A - Theology	G - History	N - Biology	T - Agronomy
B - English	H - Geography	O - Technical Courses	U - Forestry
C - French	I - German	P - Architecture & Applied Arts	V - Medicine
D - Italian	K - Physics	Q - Jurisprudence	W - Veterinary Medicine
E - Spanish	L - Chemistry	R - Economics	
F - Latin	M - Mathematics	S - Stenography	

SUBJECT	INSTR GROUP	TOTAL HOURS	HOURS PER WK.	NUMBER OF CLASSES	NUMBER OF STUDENTS
Historical Theology	A	13	1	1	15
Systematic Theology	A	13	1	1	12
Practical Theology	A	17	1	1	12
English, Beginners	B	34	2	6	250
English, Advanced Course	B	34	2	9	340
English, Conversation	B	34	2	3	80
American Civilization (Lecture in English)	B	17	1	1	100
French, Beginners	C	34	2	3	83
French, Advanced Course	C	34	2	3	80
French, Conversation	C	34	2	1	40
Italian, Beginners	D	34	2	3	49
Italian, Advanced	D	34	2	1	20
Spanish, Beginners	E	34	2	3	140
Spanish, Advanced	E	51	3	1	10
Latin, Beginners	F	34	2	1	14
Latin, Seminary	F	34	2	1	15
History	G	17	1	1	300
Geography, Seminary	H	14	1	1	80
Geography, General Survey	H	17	1	1	300
German Literature, Seminary	I	34	2	2	70
Educational Science, Survey	I	34	2	1	80
Physics, Beginners	K	30	2	1	50
Physics, Advanced	K	30	2	1	90
Chemistry, General Survey	L	30	2	2	80
Organic Chemistry	L	15	1	1	90

SUBJECT	INSTR GROUP	TOTAL HOURS	HOURS PER WK.	NUMBER OF CLASSES	NUMBER OF STUDENTS
Physiological Chemistry	L	15	1	1	90
Mathematics, Beginners	M	51	3	2	75
Mathematics, Advanced	M	51	3	1	100
Geometry	M	12	1	1	50
Mathematics, Seminary	M	34	2	2	100
Biology, General Survey	N	14	1	1	250
Technical Mechanics	O	34	2	1	90
Electrotechnics	O	34	2	1	60
Building Materials	T [sic]	15	1	1	20
Planning	P	102	6	1	20
Drawing	P	51	3	1	80
Act [sic] and Anatomy	P	51	3	1	80
Sculpture	P	51	3	1	20
Book Binding	P	34	2	1	30
Civil Law, General	Q	68	4	1	150
Civil Law, Creditor-Debtor	Q	34	2	1	120
Penal Justice	Q	51	3	1	120
Introd. Into the Jurisprud.	Q	17	1	1	130
History of German Law	Q	17	1	1	110
Military Penal Law	Q	17	1	1	80
Civil Law, Seminary	Q	34	2	1	20
Penal Law, Seminary	Q	34	2	1	20
Civil Law, Suit	Q	34	2	1	15
Management, General Survey	R	34	2	1	200
Money and Banking	R	17	1	2	240
Hist. & Prob. of Ec. Areas	R	17	1	2	240
Bookkeeping	R	17	1	1	150
Bookkeeping, Advanced	R	34	2	1	30
Management and Balances	R	17	1	2	80
Shorthand, Beginners	S	34	2	5	127
Shorthand, Advanced	S	34	2	1	20
General Agronomy	T	17	1	1	60
Farm Management	T	17	1	1	50
Gardening	T	14	1	1	50
Zoology for Farmers	T	15	1	1	50
Physiology of Domes. Animals	T	15	1	1	50
Diseases of Domes. Animals	T	16	1	1	50
Forestry, Introduction	U	13	1	1	40
Anatomy	V	15	1	1	15
Embryology	V	15	1	1	15
Physiology	V	15	1	1	25
Hygiene	V	15	1	1	25
Bree. & Sterility of D. Anms.	W	30	2	1	12
Parasitology & Protozoology	W	15	1	1	17
Bacteriology & Immunology	W	15	1	1	17

High School and College Entrance Preparation
25 Aug 1943 - 25 Dec 1943

SUBJECT	INSTR GROUP	TOTAL HOURS	HOURS PER WK.	NUMBER OF CLASSES	NUMBER OF STUDENTS
English, Beginners	B	2	34	1	50
English, Advanced	B	2	34	1	25
English, Conversation	B	2	34	1	10
French, Beginners	C	2	34	1	60
French, Advanced	C	2	34	1	40
Latin, Beginners	D	2	34	2	65
Latin, Advanced	D	2	34	1	15
History	G	2	34	2	65
Geography	H	1	17	2	85
German Grammar	I	2	34	1	30
German Literature	I	2	34	2	75
Physics	K	2	34	1	90
Chemistry	L	2	34	1	90
Mathematics	M	3	51	2	80
Biology	N	2	34	1	70

(From Captain Robert B. Heinkel, Inspection Report, December 23, 1943.)

Left and right: The interior of the prisoners' libraries. Altogether there were over 7,282 books in three libraries, the largest selection in all of the POW camps in the U.S. (Courtesy, Kansas State Historical Society, Topeka)

Chapter 3

An Officers Camp

*I*t appeared that 1944 was going to be a better year for Camp Concordia. The country club atmosphere was gone, and other positive changes were taking place. The camp population had dropped to 3,926 prisoners, 740 American soldiers, and 122 civilian employees. The Nazi influence among prisoners was being weeded out, and the Americans were firmly in charge of the compounds. Branch camps were in operation in Peabody, Kansas, and Hebron, Nebraska.

On January 4, 1944, the court-martial of Captain David Roberts convened at Camp Phillips, near Salina, Kansas, the Army training camp that also had POWs. On January 5th, Roberts was found guilty of shooting Mrs. John A. Sterling, and of shooting at Mrs. Joseph R. King. Mrs. Sterling had recovered and testified in Roberts' behalf. However, the court-martial recommended dismissal from the service and forfeiture of pay.[1]

The prisoners had a belated second Christmas when in early January a freight car of 433 food packages, containing sardines, canned meats, candy, and coffee cake arrived from Germany via the Red Cross. These welcome gifts were distributed by the German officers.[2]

On January 11, 1944, there was another apparent suicide. Private Franz Kettner was found in his cell in the guardhouse with his wrists slashed. Two weeks earlier, Kettner, an anti-Nazi, had stated that he feared for his life, having been threatened by other prisoners. It is not known exactly, but the threats were probably against his family in Germany. He had been placed in the guardhouse outside the compound, while awaiting transfer orders.[3] He may have thought that by killing himself he was protecting his family. As with Captain Tropschuh, the Germans wanted Kettner buried in a separate part of the cemetery. This time, however,

Sergeant Al Purdy, of the 480th MPEG, and Corporal Charlie Fisher on Sunday, April 2, 1944, in Concordia. (Courtesy, Al Purdy)

Hasert was found dead in his hospital ward; he had used his pajamas to hang himself.[6] He had made two previous attempts and had been kept in a locked ward. This time, however, the German officers took part in the funeral.

During February, side or branch camps were opened at Remer and Bena, Minnesota, to which were sent 386 prisoners and 73 men from the 480th MPEG.[7] The POWs in these camps worked in the forest cutting trees for pulp and fuel. The branch camps had a smaller number of prisoners, who had been sent there for short periods until the work for the local farmers was finished. At that point, the branch camp would be closed and the POWs would be returned to the main camp.

❧❧❧

Corporal Alfred W. Purdy came to Camp Concordia with the 480th MPEG Company in August 1943. He departed as a Sergeant in June 1944 and was sent to the Pacific Theater. He met his wife while stationed at the camp. Working mainly on town patrol, Purdy provided an incident report on December 18, 1943, which is summarized as follows, indicating that at the time tensions still existed between civilians and the camp garrison:

A civilian was trying to instigate a fight at the Brown Derby bar. The MPs and civilian police went to the Brown Derby, but the police left without taking any action. Corporal Purdy told all of the soldiers to leave except one who was with his wife and one who was with his girl friend. Purdy then started to walk back to the police station. On the way, he met the MP and civilian police cars and returned with them to the Brown Derby. It seemed the proprietress had asked the two GIs to remove the civilian from the premises. As the two soldiers were leaving, the civilian challenged one of them, and a fight followed. The police took the civilian to jail. No action was taken against either soldier.

Purdy added:

I spent some time at the branch camp #403

Lieutenant Colonel Vocke denied the request. Although no Germans attended the funeral, Kettner was given full military honors by the Americans.[4]

On January 20, 1944, the Camp Concordia Fire Department made its initial run to the Officers Club. The boiler that supplied heat was not working and the fireplace was being used to heat the entire building. The wall became too hot and a fire started.[5]

Another suicide occurred. Lieutenant Karl

Members of the 480th MPEG on the steps of one of the barracks. Standing in the rear, left to right: Privates First Class Walter A. Bailey, Howard E. Lee, Edward B. Megginson, Corporals George M. Pruett, Alfred W. Purdy, and Private First Class Charles H. Roenish. The three in the middle are Private Charles L. Carney, Technician 5 Edmund E. Pizzinski, and Private First Class Stanley R. Pierson. Standing to the left is Sergeant Ernest L. Mattord and seated are Private Harold P. Greenberg, Private First Class Thomas S. Ursetti, Private Louis J. Engles, and Private First Class William F. Holmes. (Courtesy, Alfred W. Purdy)

Below: Two of the guards, Staff Sergeant John E. Walser and Sergeant Foster, and their carryall. Notice the guards have their protective gas masks. (Courtesy, Wayne E. Rosen)

at Owatonna, Minnesota, and was the acting First Sergeant there. The prisoners worked in the nurseries and liked the work. The thing I remember most about the branch camp is the good conduct and good discipline of the prisoners and soldiers.

While at Concordia, I helped escort two prisoners to the camp at Alva, Oklahoma [where the most radical Nazis were imprisoned]. One was a very arrogant Colonel who was accused of conducting a kangaroo court that killed one of the prisoners [forced suicide]. The other was a large German Sergeant.

In February 1944, Private First Class Joseph L. Bloch arrived at the camp with the 642nd MPEG. Up to his departure in February 1945 he remembered the friendly townspeople and the good home cooking:

The people of Concordia treated us fairly well. One party came out to the camp and picked me up every so often. After an evening of entertaining, they would bring me back. There was a restaurant in town that served delicious fried chicken. We called the woman who ran it Ma.

The best duty was taking [prisoner] details out to the farms. The PWs helped the farmers with the crops and worked in a dairy handling milk cans or egg crates. The best thing about the detail was the food — it was just like home.

The worst thing was the tower duty on the night shift. The duty was long, cold in the winter, and very quiet.

Four of the women who worked in the PX, located in the Headquarters building. (Courtesy, Cloud County Historical Society, Concordia, KS)

Below: The guard tower on the north side of the recreation area. Note the searchlights and the machine-gun. The towers were also equipped with a siren and an electric heater. The awnings were built over the catwalk on some towers to provide shade for the guards, but the Kansas winds would cause the tower to shake. (Courtesy, Gunter Klein)

I was at the branch camp at Peabody, Kansas, as well as others. They were small operations, about 200 PWs and 20 MPs. Each was friendly duty, and we had semiprivate rooms.

Improvements were still being made at Camp Concordia in early 1944. The guardhouse was converted into a club for the enlisted guards, and a restaurant was opened in the Post Exchange. At the PX, a clothes-pressing service was started, offering two-day service. Due to the winter weather and constant movement of men and vehicles, mud had become a problem and was tracked everywhere.[8]

Movement of guards and POWs continued. In January, 250 POWs had been sent to the new camp at Atlanta, Nebraska, and another 250 to Clarinda, Iowa. The 457th MPEG, which originally had been assigned to Camp Concordia, was by then spread over four camps in three states. The 456th MPEG had returned to Fort Custer, Michigan, after spending six months assigned to Camp Concordia.[9] According to Vicki Roberts, a big crowd was at the train station to see the 456th off.

In March 1944, the camp was reviewed again, and the inspector noted on the 26th that it had come out of chaos and was much improved. The 642nd MPEG had arrived from Fort Custer in February,[10] and in March, the 361st MPEG arrived.

In April, branch camps were opened in Deer River and Owatonna, Minnesota, which involved 39 guards and 251 prisoners.[11] Also, in April there

was an administrative change. All MPEG companies were deactivated, and the Service Command Unit (SCU) 4750 Guard Detachment was activated.[12]

The garrison's day room was improved, thanks

CAMP: Prisoner of War Camp, Concordia, Kansas.

LOCATION: Four miles north of Concordia.

TELEPHONE NUMBER: Concordia 467

DATE: 26 March 1944

CAMP COMMANDER: Lt. Colonel Lester Vocke

OTHER KEY OFFICERS: Lt. Colonel George W. Eggers, Executive Officer, Lt. John W. Rogers, Adjutant, Major Roy M. Imbody, Provost Marshal, Major Carl L. Mangiameli, Post Surgeon.

DATE OF ACTIVATION: 30 November 1943.

CAPACITY OF CAMP: 3,000 EM, 1,000 Officer

NATIONALITY: German

HAS PROCESSING BEEN COMPLETED: Yes

CAMP SPOKESMAN: Colonel Eduard Waltenberger, a Regular Army Officer of the old Army, a gentleman and a soldier.

A. PHYSICAL PLANT

1. General Camp Appearance. The camp is composed of Theatre of Operations type barracks mostly covered with a tan, sanded composition board with tar-paper roofs. The area is rather level but barren. To rectify this condition, the Commanding Officer has had planted about 3,000 Chinese elms which have been secured without cost. There is no grass yet and the area is quite muddy after a rain. Soil erosion presents a problem. Plans are made to seed the entire area in grass.

2. Geneva Convention.

a. Description of quarters including adequacy of space and equipment.

No more than fifty enlisted men are assigned to the enlisted men's barracks and no more than two officers per room are assigned to the officers' quarters. Field officers are assigned individual rooms. The appearance of the Officers' barracks has been improved by the addition of front porches on each.

b. Sanitary measures.

Standard latrines and other sanitary facilities are provided. The grounds are well policed and the interior of the buildings is kept in immaculate condition as the result of frequent and most rigid inspections by the Commanding Officer.

- 1 -

3. Security features.

   a. Guard towers. Small type, five sided, towers are used. There
      is one guard in each tower during the day and two at night. In
      order to employ prisoners in the garrison echelon area without
      a large number of guards, the Commanding Officer has inclosed
      this area within a fence and is erecting two stone towers on the
      corners.

   b. Fences. The fences are of non-graduated hog wire with a barbed
      wire overhang. The fence posts are not painted and therefore
      detract from the appearance of the camp.

   c. Line of Fire. The terrain is uniformly flat and a clear field
      of fire is provided except that many defliladed areas occur
      because of erosion or drainage ditches.

   d. Proximity of buildings to fences. All but the stockade office
      are at least 75 feet from the fence.

   e. Dogs. There are ten dogs of which six are used in the side camps
      in Minnesota. All are attack and trial dogs.

   f. Proximity of railroads, defense installations, airports, etc.
      The closest railroads are in Concordia which is four miles distant.
      The municipal airport is five miles away.

B. ADMINISTRATION AND OPERATION

   1. Geneva Convention.

      a. Segregation of officers and enlisted men. Prisoners are separated
         by ranks into one officer compound and three enlisted men's
         compounds.

      b. Treatment of prisoners. All prisoners are treated strictly as
         soldiers. Their administration is kindly and their welfare is
         assured by constant attention. However, commands are firm and
         there is never doubt that American officers are in complete
         command. Because the Commanding Officer treats the officer
         spokesman as one soldier to another and thereby secures complete
         cooperation, it has been possible to assign many administrative
         duties to the prisoners. This procedure has improved the morale
         of the prisoners and has relieved, to some extent, the lack of
         sufficient American personnel.

      c. Labor Detachments.

         (1) Type of class one labor. K.P. by roster. Table waiters.

         (2) Type of class two labor.

- 2 -

(2) <u>Type of class two labor.</u>

Orderlies for Off. Prisoners
Post maintenance
Tree planting
Construction of fences and towers
Clerical administrative assistants
Restaurant .
Officers Mess

Camp Farm
3 Pulpwood side camps
5 Agricultural side camps
(See attached pictures taken at side camps in the North woods).

(3) <u>Availability of class two work projects.</u> Requests have been received from the War Manpower Commission for the establishment of five side camps for agriculture in Kansas. A total of 1700 prisoners of war will be required for these projects. They have not been established because all but a few of the present prisoners are employed.

d. <u>Food.</u>

(1) <u>Kitchen and mess equipment.</u> The equipment is standard and the kitchens are immaculate.

(2) <u>Special rations.</u> The Regular Army mess with the exception of breakfast is served by the prisoners by their own choice. At their request, only a light breakfast is provided. Food saved thereby, as eggs, is used in other meals.

(3) <u>Supplemental rations from vegetable gardens.</u> None at present but a large garden is planned. There will be 190 acres of potatoes and a truck garden of 30 acres will be used to raise onions, carrots, beans, beets and cabbage.

e. <u>Clothing.</u>

(1) <u>Marking of enlisted men's outer garments.</u> All issued outer garments have been re-marked within the last week.

(2) <u>Exemption of officers' garments from marking.</u> No officers' garments are marked.

(3) <u>Sufficiency for work details.</u> Supplies are adequate even for the side camps in the North woods.

f. <u>Medical attention.</u>

(1) <u>Average size of sick call.</u> Forty.

(2) <u>Hospital and infirmary.</u> The hospital is spotless. It is of standard type for a prisoner of war camp.

(3) <u>Number of wounded to be considered for repatriation.</u> 35

(4) <u>Mental and neurotic cases.</u> None

- 3 -

(5) Use of prisoner medical personnel and number of prisoners used.
All prisoner medical personnel is used in the hospital. The
doctors, dentists, and orderlies are well trained and have
rendered valuable assistance.

g. Side camps and agricultural details.
(1) Rations. Quartermaster rations furnished through Prisoner of
War Camps Concordia, Camp Phillips or Fort Snelling.

(2) Transportation. Mostly the camp vehicles are used. They are
used from the base camp and at the logging camps. In the
agricultural works, the farmers furnish much of the transportation.

(3) Sanitation. All carefully inspected prior to arrival of prisoners
of war and tests are made of the water. Contract surgeons are
employed.

2. General.

a. Recreation facilities.

(1) Moving picture entertainment. Provided at base camp by using
the Post Theatre at the rate of 15¢ each.

(2) Games, sports and recreation kits. The camp has been provided
completely with PMG recreational kits, but little has been
received from welfare organizations. However, the prisoners
have ample funds as canteen profits to purchase anything needed.

(3) Prisoner orchestras and theatricals. There is an officers'
orchestra of 40 pieces and an enlisted men's orchestra of 30
pieces. They present occasional shows and concerts.

(4) Recreation rooms. There is a standard recreation building in
each enlisted men's compound. There are four recreation buildings,
"Casino's" in the Officers' Compound. All interior decorations
and furniture have been made by the officers from scrap material,
paper and tin cans. It is impossible to describe the beauty of
the rooms and their fixtures or the ingenuity of the prisoners
but the finished product would put to shame all but a few night
clubs.

(5) Garden tools. Sufficient tools are available. The Seventh
Service Command also is furnishing two tractors for the camp
farm.

(6) Work Shop. With the exception of the shop in the Officers
Compound, the work shops have been converted to other uses.
However, a large work building is provided outside the stockade
for the prisoners. This building is well supplied and the prisoners have made beautiful furniture.

- 4 -

(7)   Library. Large libraries have been donated through the University of Kansas, the YMCA and others, and many books have been purchased by the prisoners.

    b.   Records maintained at camp. See attached

C.   PERSONNEL

    1.   Headquarters Detachment.

        a.   Strength. 34 officers
                    120 Enlisted men
                    106 Civilians.

        b.   Familiarity with Geneva Convention. All military personnel has been schooled thoroughly and the school is repeated frequently.

    2.   Military Police Escort Guard Companies.

        a.   Strength. Four Companies nearly up to strength.

        b.   Efficiency. Excellent.

        c.   Equipment. Complete.

        d.   Attitude toward prisoners. Nothing adverse.

D.   SPOKESMAN.

    1.   Complaints. Mail is the only complaint.

E.   RECOMMENDATIONS OF THE CAMP COMMANDER.

    1.   All prisoner of war camps be classified as exempted stations, under the command of the Provost Marshal General's Office. The Service Command, as an intermediary, serves no useful purpose and merely delays action. (This opinion is shared with many other commanding officers in the Seventh Service Command).

    2.   Principal officers in the Prisoner of War Division, PMG, should visit camps more often in order to study the practical application of the theories expounded in the Prisoner of War Circulars.

F.   REMARKS.

    Several months ago, Concordia was probably the poorest prisoner of war camp in the United States. The administration was weak and inefficient. The prisoners of war ran the camp as they pleased and there was no one concerned enough or who was man enough to interfere. After talking to all officers who were there at the time, it was learned that the previous commanding officer, Colonel Sterling, was a kindly old gentleman who did not have the qualifications

for a commanding officer. No addendance was taken for the officers on the
Post and, if they appeared at their assignment at all, they did so only
at a convenient time. The SOP was for all officers to gather at the Officers
Club Bar at 11:30 a.m. and procede to get drunk. There was no further work
done during the day. As an example of the inefficiency, no guard regulations
whatsoever were prepared by that administration. It was during this regime
that prisoner of war suicides occurred and that the Commanding Officer's
wife was shot in a brawl at the Officers Club. Lt. Colonel Vocke, who had
distinguished himself as the commanding officer of other prisoner of war
camps, was ordered to Concordia to relieve Colonel Sterling and bring
order out of chaos.

Upon arrival, Colonel Vocke transferred some of the officers and
reassigned the others. The slot machines were removed from the post and
the bar was closed except for beer after hours. By four o'clock in the
morning, Colonel Vocke had completed the guard regulations. From the time
of his arrival, there has been no doubt in the minds of U. S. personnel or
of prisoners of who is in command. Colonel Vocke has ruled with an iron
hand but at the same time has been most considerate and fair and has
provided his command with all possible comforts. He is a prodigious worker
and his indomitable spirit has been contageous with all officers and men
on the Post. Seldom is he at his desk and then only when necessary or on
passing. Rather, glimpses may be had of him as he rides his horse on an
early inspection before breakfast has been served, as he drives to the
more distant labor details, or as he walks among the prisoners. Indeed,
he seems to be everywhere.

Colonel Vocke is ably assisted by Lt. Colonel Eggers, his Executive
Officer, who incidentally, speaks German fluently. With two outstanding
men at the helm, the success of the camp has been assured.

At present, the camp not only has been brought out of chaos, it has
become a model that is superior to all but a few prisoner of war camps in
the country. The resurrection and transition within the short time of
three months are monuments to the Commanding Officer.

Earl L. Edwards,
Lt. Colonel, C.M.P.,
Assistant Director,
Prisoner of War Division.

One of the trucks hauling a detail of prisoners in Concordia. Notice there are seven prisoners and two guards. One of the guards has his rifle on his hip, and both are at the rear of the truck as prescribed in their orders. (Courtesy, Beryl Ward)

to the women of Belleville, who furnished drapes and furniture. Dances were held at the new NCO Club, where a GI band provided the entertainment. Girls from Belleville and Concordia, who came for the dances, were provided free transportation and given a flower as well as refreshments.[13]

Charles Everett and others recalled events in that first year of the camp's existence:

A lot of our [hardware] business [after the camp was built] was with the German soldiers. They were allowed some money and most of them had a craft. They were never in the store themselves. Several of them bought small hand tools, sandpaper, and tools for carving.

One day, a truck drove up to the back of the store. Charlie [Blosser] came in, and eight prisoners and a couple of guards were with him. He outfitted these boys with shovels, rakes, and hoes, and signed the ticket. They got ready to go, and one of the German boys barked a command of some sort. Those fellows all snapped to attention and goose-stepped out the back door of the store. I always claimed that I was the only store in town that had the German Army goose-step [in it].

My cousin, who was a farmer north of town, had prisoners out there. Lots of times, they would send meals with the work crews, and sometimes the farmers would furnish their meals. They had a great big screened-in porch and invited the men and the guard in to eat on the porch. The prisoners really enjoyed that. . . . She had homemade bread for them. It was nice and warm and they thought it was cake.

[When] the first group [of prisoners arrived] . . . there was such a crowd that we couldn't get close. So we went north of town and parked at the school west of the camp and watched them come by. People were amazed. Here were young men who were singing and laughing. It wasn't what we thought about at all. I think they were glad to be here.

Others remember the POWs as being quiet, though on July 15, 1943, *The Concordia Press* had reported that they seemed happy and glad to arrive.

Charles Everett continued:

[I recall an incident when] an American soldier who was driving [a truck hauling POWs] came off the viaduct too fast and turned west. The prisoners were all on one side, and it threw them and the guard to the other side. The truck slid over on its side and into the curb in front of our store. The guard was knocked out cold. One of the Germans grabbed the rifle [the guard] was carrying and was saying something. Pretty soon he came over to me and said, "You take, you take." So, I took the rifle, and they sat down on the curb. They weren't trying to get away. Fairly soon, the guard came out of it, and I gave him his rifle back.

The November 10, 1943, edition of *The Concordia Blade-Empire* reported that the wreck had been caused by the swaying motion of the POWs; one had a broken collarbone.

Elmo St. Pierre and his wife, Ruby, along with their two young daughters, lived on a farm east of Concordia during World War II. He used POWs to put up alfalfa.

Ruby would fix dinner for them. We fed them on the back porch for a few times, but as we got more used to them . . . they ate in the kitchen with our family. They loved potatoes and gravy and beef. They seemed to enjoy everything we had.

We had combined five or six acres of wheat right south of the house. Some sparks from the train set that field of stubble on fire. I was cutting wheat by Ames [southeast of Concordia] and wasn't home. Ruby was home with the girls so she gave the line ring [on the crank telephone]. Some of the neighbors came over. Charlie Blosser had the farm right east of us down on the river. He had about ten or twelve of [the POWs] working down there cutting weeds. So he brought them over to help fight the fire. By the time I got there, they were there with some of the other neighbors trying to put the fire out. There was a pump on the back porch, [and] one of [the POWs] was pumping water and the others were wetting sacks trying to keep the fire away from the house. Our little girls were there and [the POWs] kept passing the word between them, "Save the mama and the babies." You could hear them, . . . [they] had to save the babies. They had a real desire to get that fire put out, and they got it put out.

During the war, Opal (Chaput) Roy lived near Camp Concordia with her husband Jim Roy. Jim worked on the camp fire department and worked on a truck garden that used POW labor.

They were good artists. They showed my husband [a] picture; it was just exactly like our house. . . . The next day [the prisoner] brought it back framed and gave it to us. [*The watercolor of the house is signed "Merlet Juli 44."*]

They were good workers, but they didn't like to pick strawberries. They said it was a job for women and kids.

Jack Krager was a 13-year-old boy when the camp was built. His father drove a Fairmont Dairy truck and sometimes would take Jack with him to make deliveries to the camp. He remembered:

The enlisted prisoners were friendly and would wave at the truck. But, when we went into the officers compound, they would not get out of the way, even when Dad blew the horn. They would move only when they were ready. If people knew prisoners were coming in, they would flock down to the Missouri Pacific. We used to go watch the prisoners work on the railroad. The guard would not let us get too close. The prisoners seemed to get a kick out of us trying to talk to them.

❧

The camp hospital was truly a joint American-German operation. The Post Surgeon was an American while the pharmacy, laboratory, and the eye, ear, nose, and throat (EENT) and dental clinics were staffed by both Americans and Germans. In other words, an American soldier might have his eyes examined by a German optometrist, and a German may be operated on by a American doctor assisted by Germans. The nurses were American civilians, except for the Chief Nurse who was a member of the Army Nurse Corps. Even though both countries were at war, the medical professionals were working together.

According to Teufel's *History of Camp Concordia*, on July 10, 1945, the civilian nurses were released and replaced by an Army nurse. Teufel notes:

The hospital . . . had 2,261 admissions, 1,966 for disease and 360 for injury. It performed 80 major and 1,761 minor surgical operations, gave 47,603 routine physical examinations, 12,143 Physiotherapy treatments, 28,241 laboratory experiments and tests, 7,313 Xray and Fluorescent examinations, 810 eye examinations, 973 ear examinations, 619 nose examinations, 429 throat examinations, and 185 general (EENT) examinations. 1,008 eye treatments were given, 941 pairs of glasses were ordered, and 1,530 other optometrical services performed. 41,686 dental operations were rendered, ranging from simple extractions to the making of full dentures. . . . Six Post Surgeons and thirty

Adolf Weber (7WG 12865), an enlisted POW, from *Lager* (Compound) #1, had been seriously wounded in the abdomen shortly before his capture. He spent time in a hospital on the East Coast before being sent to Concordia and then had another operation on his wounds while there. He also had an appendectomy. (Courtesy, Adolf Weber)

medical Officers served at the Station Hospital.

Bernadette (Blochlinger) Oeser worked at the station hospital as a civilian nurse from May 1, 1944, to August 13, 1945. She had daily contact with the POWs:

The Germans were very courteous and acted as gentlemen. I don't remember the officers as acting much differently than the enlisted POWs, not in the hospital anyway. Most were well educated and could speak English. They were from diverse backgrounds.

I worked with German doctors and medical corpsmen. The doctors made rounds with the Army doctors. The POW corpsmen took care of the German patients. The corpsmen also worked in most all of the departments of the hospital, x-ray, laboratory, and on the wards.

I thoroughly enjoyed working at the Station Hospital. It was a very good experience for me. I especially remember the great number of malaria patients we had. They had been with Rommel in the African campaigns where they contracted the disease. I also remember the two hangings at the hospital — one German officer and one enlisted POW.

Dorothy L. Swenson, who was only 19 when she started working in the medical supply section of the hospital, noted:

It was one of the better jobs on the post. I think I started about the first of August [1943]. I started out at $60 a month, and when I quit, I was making $160 a month. It was good money at that time.

I had contact with many prisoners. Of course, the hospital was in the compound, and I had to go through it every day. We had two working in our office. One of them was there every day, just like I was. His name was Gerhardt Hauschird. After he got back to Germany, I got a couple of letters from him. He was extremely fluent and had no problem with English. Some people would ask me if I was scared going into the compound. I never had any fear at all.

One prisoner was always telling me he was going to escape at night and come to my house. Of course, I didn't tell him where I lived. I was a little bit leery because I didn't know if he meant it or not.

Older people were a little leery about [the camp]. The [American] soldiers were received in town pretty well. I did hear that some of them complained about some of the service clubs that they were not welcomed in. That is probably because Concordia is such a small town.

A 1943 Christmas dinner menu, courtesy of Dorothy Swenson, lists the following as employees of the hospital:

Major Carl L. Mangiameli, M.C.
1st Lt. George J. Rohn, M.A.C.
Capt. Robert R. Bates, M.C.
Capt. Curtiss S. McCallister, D.C.
Capt. Max Simons, M.C.
1st Lt. James W. Chambers, M.C.
1st Lt. Clarence P. Hansen, M.A.C.
1st Lt. Wilburn E. Wright, D.C.
2nd Lt. Angus M. Shipley, M.A.C.
1st Lt. Bernice A. Pollock, A.N.C.
Bunker, Alice, Nurse
Hobson, Myrtle, Nurse
Stafford, Ruby, Nurse
Hay, Velma, Nurse
Stensaas, Dorothy, Nurse
Balding, Margaret, Nurse
Molz, John G., M-Sgt.
Martinson, Brady, T-Sgt.
Pando, Joseph P., S-Sgt.
Miyata, Itsusuo, Sgt.
Nichols, Oscar E., Sgt.
Geohring, Walter, Tec. 5
Lefferts, Howard, Tec. 5
Slifer, Hugh B., Tec. 5
Thiel, Harold P., Tec. 5
Ehreth, Michael G., Pfc.
Hanson, Jack D., Pfc.
Mayer, Edwin, Pfc.
Musser, Joseph V., Pfc.
Pipkins, James P., Pfc.
Seal, Royal C., Pfc.
Toreson, Kenneth A., Pfc.
Stein, Bernard, Pfc.
Weiss, Francis J., Pfc.
Wenk, Guenther W., Pfc.
Wood, Glen D., Pfc.
Dahlin, Clifford L., Pvt.
Diethert, Fredrich V., Pvt.
Eisinger, Donald C., Pvt.
MacDonald, Malcolm S., Pvt.
Nelson, Russell J., Pvt.
Solberg, Alfred M., Pvt.
Willhite, James W., Pvt.
Zemba, Stephen J., Pvt.

CIVILIAN WORKERS:
Mangiameli, Josephine, Clerk
Shepherd, Dorothy, Clerk
McQueen, Gladys, Stenographer
Bearman, Betty, Lab. Tech.
Lowman, Dorothy, Clerk
Ehreth, Sylvia, Clerk

∽⌒∽

In late May 1944, it was announced that Camp Concordia was to become an officers camp. The only enlisted prisoners kept at the camp would be those necessary to do some of the work for the officers, who were not required to work.[14] Therefore, at the end of May, it was announced that all contracts with farmers would be cancelled,[15] even though there were almost 2,900 prisoners (1,900 enlisted and 1,000 officers) remaining at the camp. By the first week of June, however, this number had dropped by almost 1,000 POWs.[16] The Geneva Convention specified that officer POWs were allowed more square feet per man than enlisted prisoners, and thus the number of prisoners the camp was able to hold was reduced.

The subsequent lack of prisoner farm labor was a disaster for the farmers. They had planted crops, counting on POW help for the harvest. Without that help, and with their own young men still away at war, much would go unharvested. Farmers and farm groups contacted their Congressmen and the War Department. In turn, the Congressmen and Senators Frank Carlson and Arthur Capper pleaded the farmers' case to the War Department. As a result, by June 13th, 60 POWs were made available to help area agriculture.[17]

∽⌒∽

On June 3, 1944, Camp Concordia had its first and largest escape. About 5:00 p.m., a tornado struck the camp, damaging several buildings and knocking out the electric power. The lights did not come back on until after midnight. Three POWs, First Sergeant Herbert Kayser, Corporal Karl-Heinz Ockelmann, and Private Herbert Doerner had escaped. Their absence was not detected until the morning of the 4th.[18] For four days, there was an intense manhunt in the surrounding counties. Finally on the evening of the 7th, the men were caught near Courtland, Kansas, about 23 miles northwest. They had tried to hitchhike, and a soldier on leave saw them. He reported the three to the town marshal who caught them hiding behind trees. The prisoners were wearing their German uniforms and had four duffle bags of clothing and food.[19] The three Germans refused to tell American authorities when or how they escaped, and, in accordance with the Geneva Convention, a POW could not be punished for the act of escaping or attempting escape.

Gunter Klein, a POW at the time, commented:

The escape by Kayser, Doerner, and Ockelmann had nothing to do with the tornado of June 3, 1944. The escape was carefully planned and arranged in advance, and [they] were ready in the afternoon of May 29th. Naturally, in the distant North America, they had to have some plan of action. That was done through a clever manipulation of the formation for the head count. The absence of these three men was first noticed on June 4. . . . Their escape was then associated with the tornado.

Fern Garlow described their hiding place:

At that time it was the job of the women to check the cattle in the pasture. Our pasture was about a mile and a half from the camp, and there was a creek there. The prisoners who escaped [June 3, 1944,] hid in the daytime down in this creek. When we went to check the cattle, we saw the tall weeds mashed down where they had lain. There was also an empty snuff can and some papers, so we knew it was prisoners who had been there.

∽⌒∽

The night of June 6, 1944, D-Day, the Allied invasion at Normandy, was exciting for Germans and Americans alike. For weeks the officer-prisoners had been saying that there would not be an invasion of Europe by the Allies. The prisoners listened to radios the nights of the 5th and 6th to learn the

One of the POW bands, maybe the 47th Grenadier Band, which performed for the other POWs on weekends. It also played at concerts for the public until one of the German officers complained that they were being put on display. Another ensemble, the POW brass band, played for other prisoners and for dances at the Officers Club and the Enlisted Club. (Courtesy, Cloud County Historical Society, Concordia, KS)

latest news; they were unusually quiet on the morning of the 6th. As soon as breakfast was over, all of them, including the cooks and the guards, hurried back to the barracks to listen to the radio reports. One officer-prisoner was heard to comment, "Well, that means the end of war."[20]

In June, the German 47th Grenadier Regimental Band was moved to Camp Concordia from Fort Robinson, Nebraska. The band had been captured in North Africa with instruments, arrangements, and conductor intact. The band members had not been appreciated at Fort Robinson, so they had asked to be moved to a larger camp.[21] Previously, there had been bands or orchestras in both the enlisted and officer compounds at Camp Concordia.

⌒⌒⌒

When the prisoners were not working, they could take part in various activities, in keeping with the Geneva Convention. During good weather, sports were popular, especially soccer. The prison-

ers also liked tennis, and reading was always a favorite pastime. *Gone with the Wind* was a popular novel. The prisoners also could take one of the many courses offered at the camp and accredited by the University of Kansas at Lawrence. Crafts were enjoyed by some, and they made everything from toys to furniture and lamps. The officers who were artists were taken on walks to the Republican River, so that they could sketch the countryside. When the camp closed in 1945, the POWs gave many of these craft items and paintings to soldiers, civilian employees, and farmers.

POWs also could view approved movies each week or spend time in the casinos, which were decorated in a Germanic style. In the canteens, they could use their coupons to buy cigarettes, candy, books, soap, and other toilet articles.

Karl Gassmann came to Camp Concordia as a 21-year-old German Second Lieutenant. While there, he started his studies that led to his career as an architect. He has written to Richard Wahl about his experiences as a POW, and the following are portions of those letters:

In a newly erected POW camp near a small desert town named Chancy [Algeria], I saw my first American soldiers. From then on, I was in U.S. custody. At the end of July 1943, we were shipped from the port of Oran [Algeria] to the USA. We debarked in Norfolk, Virginia, on August 5, 1943. There, after screening and registering, we received, for the first time in months, a hot shower with plenty of hot water, good smelling soap, and snow-white towels — what a relief! We felt like humans again. There were still other surprises awaiting us. We traveled not in freight cars as we had in Europe, but in Pullman cars. What impressed us most was that life in the USA seemed like peacetime, no blackout at night, streets and parking lots at factories filled with cars, everything full of energy and efficiency. We began to understand that this powerful and resourceful land could not be overcome.

We arrived at Concordia on August 8, 1943. Except for a little railway station and many American soldiers and trucks, we didn't see anything of the town. The camp was new, clean, orderly, well planned and constructed, the barracks simple, but adequate. After awhile, we recognized that the U.S. made every effort to fulfill the conditions of the Geneva Convention. We were well cared for, had plenty to eat, and were treated correctly. We officers could not go out to work and thus could not learn anything about the land and people. The environment of the camp was not very inspiring, flat and barren.

After getting acquainted with the new conditions, we began working to make the rooms, the barracks, more comfortable, and to beautify the area. We set up courses, started an orchestra, gave plays, and played sports in the recreation area. Later on, the courses became more professional and were overseen by the University of Kansas and some German universities (via the Red Cross and YMCA). I found additional work that I loved. I became the printer on the camp newspaper. My roommate, a paratroop lieutenant, in civilian life a journalist, founded the *Neue Stacheldraht Nachrichten* and invited me to be the printer.

Karl Gassmann, of Schweinfurt, Germany, in 1994 at age 72. As a 22-year-old prisoner, Lieutenant Gassmann had started his studies to become an architect while at Camp Concordia. (Courtesy, Karl Gassmann)

Take note of the initials: NS! We knew this abbreviation as *National-Sozialistisch*.[22] But the journalist was all-in-all an honest man respected even by the American censor, an emigrated Jew from Frankfurt. For me it didn't matter, I had a job I loved. So, time went by, and nothing very spectacular happened except the "Tropschuh Case." This brutality, forcing a suicide and, worse yet, watching it by [a] few [officer-POWs] from the outside window, shocked the majority of us and made us feel ashamed.

It is untrue, or at least frivolously generalized, that [Camp] Concordia was ruled by Nazis who oppressed the others. I was not a Nazi and never felt oppressed or pushed to do anything against my will. Of course I was only 21, but the majority of the camp was like me. In fact, we lived a mostly untroubled and peaceful life. We didn't see the American

KNOW ALL MEN BY THESE PRESENTS, THAT

LEUTNANT KURT WÄCHTLER 7-WG 16998

while a student in this institution, has completed satisfactorily the following approved courses, in consideration of which he is granted this certificate as an evidence thereof

DATE	COURSE NUMBER	TITLE	TOTAL HOURS	INSTRUCTOR NAME, RANK, POW NO
1945	6 S 1080	THEORY OF TOOLS AND SPORTING MATTERS	10	2nd LT. PRENZEL HORST 31-G-11626
1945	6 S 1081	THEORY OF INSTRUCTION AND EDUCATION	10	2nd LT PRENZEL HORST 31-G-11626
1945	6 S 1083	SELECTED PARTS OF GYMNASTIC EXERCISES	21	2ND LT. PRENZEL HORST 31-G-11626
1945	6 S 1093	PRACTICE OF SPORTS	11	2ND LT. PRENZEL HORST 31-G-11626
1945	6 S 123	ROMANCE, SEMINAR	24	2ND LT. (SOF) VOTH LUDWIG 7-WG-16447

IN WITNESS WHEREOF, WE AFFIX HEREUNTO OUR HANDS & SEALS THIS 1st DAY OF Sept. IN THE YEAR OF OUR LORD 1945

CHANCELLOR, U. KANSAS

POW SPONSOR, U. KANSAS

US - EDUCATION OFFICER

GEORGE W. EGGERSS LT. COLONEL C.M.P.
COMMANDING OFFICER

SENIOR GERMAN SPOKESMAN

GERMAN DIRECTOR OF STUDIES

One of the certificates given for studies at the POW University. Note that it has the seal of the University of Kansas, at Lawrence, and that one of the signatures is that of the University's chancellor. (Courtesy, Kurt Waechtler)

guards very much except for the daily counting.

After the landing on the Normandy coast, we heard about a speech, from the German *Reichspropagandaminister*, Joseph Goebbels, that was intended to give what is an old Roman saying that means the situation is bad, but not hopeless because there are the *triaril*, the experienced veteran soldiers of the third row of the Roman battle formation. Shortly after this speech, the first German officers, who had been captured in Normandy, arrived. They were located in the compound opposite our officers' compound. It had been an enlisted compound before. In comparison to us well-fed and well-clothed "old" POWs, they were exhausted and their clothes were torn. We jokingly called their compound the *Triarier-Lager*. They had not lost their wit and called our compound the *Joseph's-Lager*. This is from the Bible. Joseph, son of Jacob, was sold by his brothers to Egypt and became wealthy and influential. He "wore better clothes and thought to be better than his brothers." We had to look into the mirror and did not find out that the *triaril* were right. Fortunately, all this was only kidding.

Our lives as POWs changed dramatically after Germany surrendered. Now, we were showed that we had lost the war. The treatment became harsher, and the food rations were cut to a minimum. We rapidly lost weight and felt hungry. . . . We regarded this all as childish revenge for something we didn't feel guilty for.

In September 1945, we officers had the opportunity to work outside the camp. Most of us were happy to have the opportunity to finally learn something of the land and people. I was sent to Indiana and later, December 1945, back to Europe.

❧

The steady loss of enlisted prisoners was felt in the branch camps as well. In July 1944, the camp at Owatonna, Minnesota, was closed, and in August, the Peabody, Kansas, camp was turned over to Fort Riley. In September, the branch camp at Hebron, Nebraska, was turned over to Camp Atlanta, Nebraska; in October, Camps Bena and Deer River in Minnesota were closed; and in December, the closing of Camp Remer followed.[23]

At the end of August 1944, the command of Camp Concordia passed from Lieutenant Colonel Vocke to Lieutenant Colonel George W. Eggerss. Eggerss had been the Provost Marshal at Camp Concordia since February 1944. Like Colonel Vocke, he was of German descent and spoke the language fluently. Eggerss dealt directly with the

An awards ceremony in front of the Post Headquarters. (Courtesy, Wayne E. Rosen)

Neue Stacheldraht Nachrichten
Lager Concordia

2.Jhg.No.4   4.Februar 1945

Auf den Deichen

"Kurlands eiserner Mann"

Die grosse sowjetische Offensive hat die Aufmerksamkeit der Weltöffentlichkeit auch wieder auf Kurland gelenkt. Hier halten dreissig geschwächte deutsche Divisionen seit Monaten dem sowjetischen Ansturm stand. Die belagerten, von Feind und Meer eingeschlossenen deutschen Truppen stehen unter dem Befehl eines Generals, den man seit Rommels Tod als einen der markantesten der Deutschen Wehrmacht bezeichnen kann. Generaloberst Ferdinand Schörner ist ein fanatischer Nationalsozialist, Weltkriegsteilnehmer und Inhaber der höchsten Auszeichnung des kaiserlichen Deutschland, des Pour le Merite. Vor diesem Kriege gab er an Kriegsschulen des Reiches weltanschaulichen Unterricht.

Generaloberst Schörner schwor, den Kampf in der abgeschnittenen Festung Kurland nicht aufzugeben. Er hat alle Soldaten zu Spezialisten der Panzernahbekämpfung ausgebildet, auch die Fahrer, Bäcker, Köche und Schreiber. Soldaten, die um Urlaub baten, soll er erklärt haben: "Erbeutet einen Sowjetpanzer und fahrt los!"

An allen Mauern und Strassenschildern, auf allen Kraftfahrzeugen sind Schlagzeilen angebracht: "Wir kämpfen in Kurland, um Ostpreussen zu retten!"

Schon an der Eismeerfront hat Generaloberst Schörner sich besonders Verdienste erworben. Hier lernte er die Kunst der Improvisation, die es ihm nun möglich macht, die Angriffe der Roten Armee immer wieder abzuweisen.

In Berlin erachtet man das Standhalten von Generaloberst Schörner und seinen Soldaten in Kurland als ebenso wichtig wie die Erfolge der Westoffensive. "NEWSWEEK"

Jubel um die Sowjets
(TOPEKA DAILY CAPITAL)

"Die amerikanischen Soldaten an der Westfront interessieren sich mehr für den Fortschritt der sowjetischen Offensive als um den Ausgang ihres eigenen Kampfes. Sie hoffen, dass die Rote Armee bis in das Herz des Reiches vorstossen wird, und der Krieg damit ein schnelles Ende findet. Irgendwelche Eifersucht auf die militärischen Erfolge der Sowjets ist nirgends festzustellen. Alles was unsere Soldaten wünschen ist eine baldige Beendigung des Krieges und schnelle Heimkehr. Es ist ihnen gleichgültig, wer den Endsieg erkämpft.

Allerdings sind auch die Sowjetsiege nur auf Amerika zurückzuführen. Die Sowjets kämpfen mit Waffen, die fast ausschliesslich in den USA gefertigt wurden und auch der grösste Teil ihres Nachschubs geht auf amerikanische Quellen zurück.

Unsere Soldaten kümmern sich nicht um diplomatische Intrigen, sie wollen nach Hause und jubeln deshalb über die Sowjetsiege."

Dieter Wolff.

Das Tal zwischen den Bergen

"Siege sollten nicht verkündet werden, bevor man sie nicht in der Tasche hat", eine Feststellung, die jeder Beteiligte dieses Krieges schon einmal treffen musste und die vorsichtige Betrachter auf alliierter Seite im Augenblick besonders unterstreichen. Da zur Zeit unsere Gegner allein damit beschäftigt sind, die siegreiche Beendigung dieses Krieges zu beschleunigen, bleibt für uns nur die nüchterne Umkehrung dieser Erkenntnis. -- "man sollte keine Niederlage an die Wand malen, wenn die Schlacht noch im vollen Gange ist".

Das Ausmass der modernen Schlachten hat Formen angenommen, die es jedem Aussenstehenden unmöglich machen, vorzeitig ein Urteil über den Ausgang eines Feldzuges abzugeben, von dem Offensiven über hunderte von Kilometern, Verteidigungskämpfe und Gegenangriffe auf einer auseinandergerissenen Front, ebenso wie Einbrüche von durchschnittlich Landestiefe im gegenwärtigen Augenblick der entscheidenden Kriegführung eben nur Teilausschnitte sind.

Der am 12.Januar 1945 -- ein Tag, den wir in den kommenden Jahren niemals vergessen wollen -- einsetzende Generalansturm aus dem Osten hat trotz der überwältigenden Erfolge der Roten Armee seinen Hoehepunkt noch nicht überschritten. Die Folgerung aus dieser Feststellung mag dem einen oder anderen unangenehm, vielen sogar unglaubwürdig erscheinen angesichts der von den Sowjets in diesen drei Wochen eroberten Gebiete und Landschaften. Die Namen der Ortschaften, die im Zusammenhang mit den Moskauer Salutschüssen als erobert genannt werden, sagen uns mehr als strategische Phantasien beim Kartenstudium. Es ist notwendig, das Gefühl und den Verstand fest in die Hand zu

The front page of the POW newspaper, February 4, 1945. (Courtesy, Bernadine Cummings)

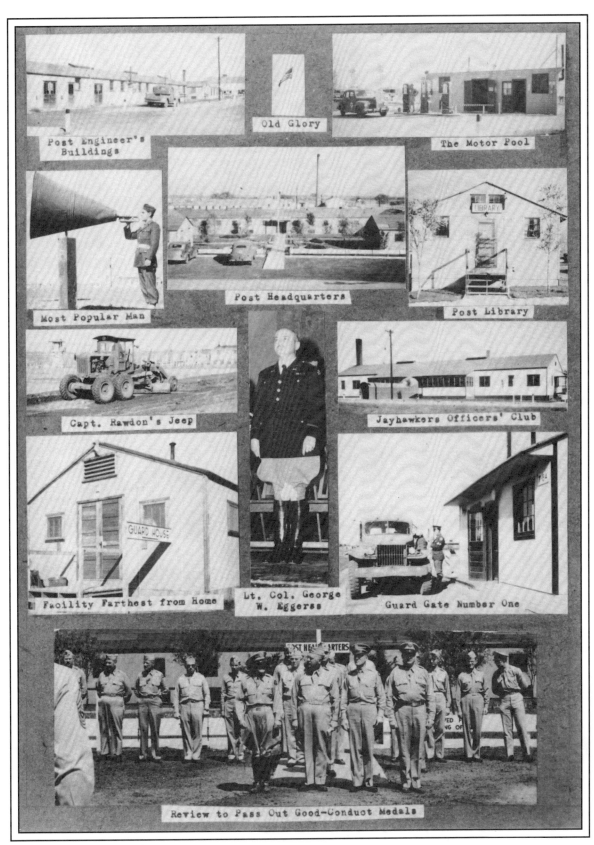

Post Engineer's Buildings

Old Glory

The Motor Pool

Most Popular Man

Post Headquarters

Post Library

Capt. Rawdon's Jeep

Jayhawkers Officers' Club

Facility Farthest from Home

Lt. Col. George W. Eggerss

Guard Gate Number One

Review to Pass Out Good-Conduct Medals

(Courtesy, National Archives)

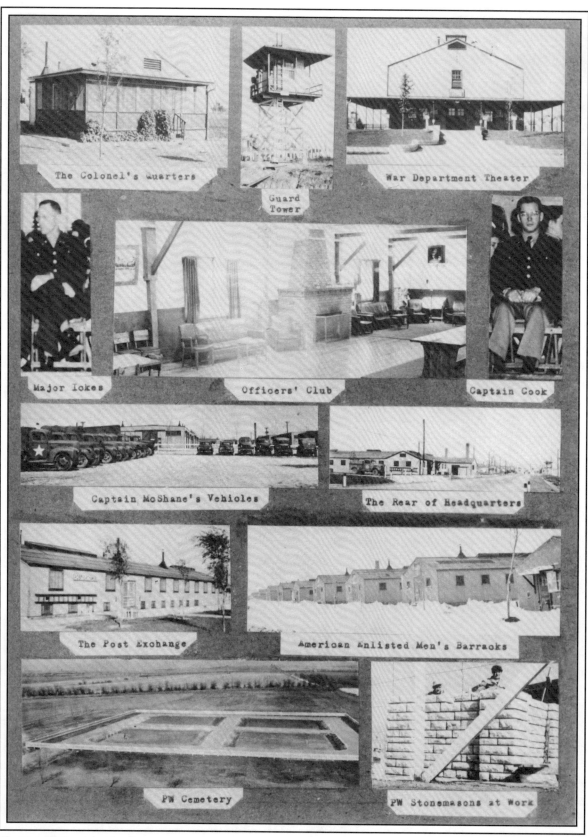

The Colonel's Quarters

Guard Tower

War Department Theater

Major Ickes

Officers' Club

Captain Cook

Captain McShane's Vehicles

The Rear of Headquarters

The Post Exchange

American Enlisted Men's Barracks

PW Cemetery

PW Stonemasons at Work

then senior spokesman, Colonel Eduard Waltenberger, in matters pertaining to the POWs.[24] He was always out checking on the operations of the camp.

On October 5, 1944, there was a second escape from the camp. Lieutenant Wolf Sthamer concealed himself in a depression in the athletic field and escaped when the guards left the area. He made his way 18 miles north, to Belleville, where he purchased a railroad ticket and breakfast. Although he was wearing his German uniform, the reason he was caught was because he was not familiar with American money. By the afternoon of the 6th, he was back at the camp.[25]

❧❧❧

Karl Gassmann, in his letter to Richard Wahl, noted how the lack of food after Germany had surrendered "didn't help much in the 'reeducation' which we were willing and ready to undertake."

This reeducation had been going on for some time, and involved reading material, movies, music, and anything else that would show the positive side of American life, but it was not public knowledge until shortly before the war in Europe ended.

In November 1944, the Adjutant General of the U.S. wrote the following "secret letter" to the camp:

The detention in the United States of ever increasing numbers of German prisoners of war creates an unprecedented opportunity. These men will some day be repatriated and, as a group, will have a powerful voice in future German affairs. Their opinions and feelings concerning America may determine, in a large measure, future relations between Germany and the United States. . . . Accordingly, the Secretary of War directed the Commanding General, Army Services Forces, to establish a program of reorientation for prisoners of war. . . . The purpose of the program is to create and foster spontaneous responses on the part of German prisoners of war towards activities and contacts which will encourage an attitude of respect on their part for American institutions, traditions, and ways of life and thought. Thereby they may be brought

to realize the industrial might and indomitable spirit of the American people. . . . The program is, therefore, designed to encourage self-indoctrination on the part of the prisoner. . . . It does not contemplate any attempt to Americanize them. . . .[The program] also provides for a company grade officer at each base camp who is to be known as the Assistant Executive Officer of the camp. His sole duties are to foster the program. . . .

Teufel's *History of Camp Concordia* called this new program, described by the Adjutant General, "The Re-Educational Program:"

During the Summer of 1944, and even before, there had been a great deal written in our newspapers and periodicals regarding the necessity of re-educating the German people, but apparently, at least as far as John Q. Public knew, nothing concrete was being done about it. Secretly, however, . . . the Camp was informed, in a letter from the Adjutant General [in Washington, D.C.], dated 9 November 1944, of the intention of higher authority to set up a re-orientation program for prisoners-of-war. . . .

On 2 December 1944, Captain Karl C. Teufel arrived at Camp Concordia and was duly assigned to this task. (In May 1945, he was joined by M/Sgt. John Molz). On the following day, he reported to the Commanding Officer the details of his mission. These included the direction of a prisoner-of-war school, a motion-picture program, encouragement of the use of radios, musical activities, hobbies, physical recreation, dramatics, libraries, the establishment of a prisoner-of-war camp newspaper, the orientation of American personnel, and other functions of a more minor character.

A few days later, the Assistant Executive Officer reported to the Commanding Officer on the Camp's situation as it reflected on his assignment. Probably no other camp in the country was so well organized for such a work. Colonel [George W.] Eggerss had long favored keeping the minds and bodies of his wards occupied, not only for reasons of security, but also in order to develop their capabilities for later civil life. This attitude had resulted in a prisoner-of-war university, already in existence for many months. . . .

The curriculum dealt with approximately three hundred (300) subjects, ranging from Beginners' English to Electrotechnics, including twelve (12) languages, Theology, History, Geography, Government, Engineering, Medicine, all the Arts and Sciences, vocational subjects, and so forth, of which it was estimated that about thirty percent (30%) already had re-educational value. Approximately 175 instructors were employed in the University, including some fifty (50) with Doctor's academic degrees and many others with comparable educational attainments. Prisoners had long been accustomed to seeing worthwhile War Department Theater pictures. Approximately 157 radios were in use in the Compounds at this time, affording excellent natural indoctrination. A number of excellent orchestras had been organized, and included among them the 47th Grenadier Band, all the personnel of which were Sergeants, which had been captured intact with its instruments in Tunisia, and had been brought here at the special request of Colonel Eggerss. Recorded music was plentiful, and included many American selections. While hobby programs were not systematically organized, there was a very great deal of individual activity in this direction. A prisoner-of-war theater had been in existence for a considerable period, specializing in dramatic and entertainment presentations. In February, when first counted, the libraries contained 7,282 volumes, of which better than ninety percent (90%) were regarded either as valuable for re-education, or politically neutral in content. 430 subscriptions to 153 different newspapers and magazines were in force. A prisoner-of-war newspaper of excellent workmanship was being printed, but did not always contain perfectly desirable material from the American point of view. This was being supplemented by a daily news bulletin, which while cautious in its

methods, yet managed to lean noticeably toward the Nazi version of the news. Above all, Post Regulations at Concordia were of such character, and so well enforced, and morale was so generally high among enlisted personnel, that there was no need of orientation to create soldiers who were models of dress and deportment to serve as examples of American manhood before the Germans. In ten words, the foundation for re-education had been long and suitably laid.

Not all factors at Concordia, however, were helpful to the Assistant Executive Officer's work. Prisoners had died at the Camp under mysterious circumstances, euphoniously called "suicides," and some of these had been known Anti-Nazis who were buried without benefit of German chaplains or German mourners. In fact, one had been buried in a segregated grave where he would not be able to contaminate his purer Hitlerian ex-comrades, and Colonel [Lester] Vocke had firmly denied a second similar request for an unsanctified "Potter's Field" burial. Many a prisoner kept a stout club at the head of his bed, and made interior arrangements to render unnecessary sallying forth to the latrine at night. Fanatical Nazis were doing their best to control a waxing war-weariness and decaying confidence in Herr Hitler, and were sufficiently successful that the open voicing of Anti-Nazi sentiments was a dangerous and unhealthy pastime. The ever-darkening war situation stimulated these die-hard fanatics to such measures of control that tension and mistrust grew ever worse among the Germans, and any unusual measures of cooperation with American authorities were subject to a threat of fearful physical menace. The Assistant Executive Officer divined that his activities would need be undertaken with subtlety, since he was subject of considerable suspicion, and since open efforts to control educational measures in the direction would only result in hardened resistance and possible danger to those from whom cooperation could be expected. . . .

In consequence, the Assistant Executive

Officer followed two basic lines of procedure. First, he attempted, through the furtherance of justifiable activities within the Compounds, to gain the confidence of the prisoners. Secondly, he began to control by surreptitious means the essential media of his program through the careful cooperation of a small, but long-standing, group of Anti-Nazis, with whom a high degree of mutual confidence quickly sprang up. Anti-Nazis in Enlisted Men's Camps were proverbially known to the [Corps of Military Police] CMP as weak characters, but this group of Officer Anti-Nazis was composed of extraordinary men. Two of them had travelled extensively and studied in the United States. Another had married a Long Island heiress and represented Lloyd's of London and an American insurance company in Paris and Berlin. All were highly educated, lawyers, teachers, ministers, and similar types of professions which are the more susceptible to the mental training leading toward objectivity. These men thought for themselves despite Herr Goebbels and his henchmen at Concordia. As true Germans, their aim was to assist in every possible way in the respectable regeneration of their Fatherland through the destruction of National Socialism. A bit fearfully at first, and always secretly, they began to give active assistance to the Assistant Executive Officer.

They divulged the inner thoughts and activities of the Compounds, kept their fingers on the pulses of the Nazis in behalf of the American authorities, and began a long and careful intelligence procedure designed to transfer eventually the "incorrigible" to places where they would find a homogeneous and congenial flock of similarly-feathered birds. Wherever possible, their information was tallied with information of assured veracity, and in all cases were proven trustworthy and truthful. A great deal of confidence in them thereby became possible. Among their activities was a suggestion, sent to the Office of the Provost Marshal General, concerning possible methods for anti-Nazi cooperation with American Occupational Forces in Germany later on,

which suggestion either inspired action on the part of higher authority, or else constituted a remarkable coincidence with procedure later adopted. As a result of their efforts, an impending riot was averted and forty-four (44) "150%" ring-leaders were shipped out to the Prisoner of War Camp at Alva, Oklahoma. . . . On 21 April 1945, as a result of a strictly forbidden, but relatively mild Hitler Birthday celebration, long-planned segregation measures were invoked with their help, and 101 more "bad boys" were placed in separate custody, and some six weeks later likewise shipped to Alva. Because of them, therefore, the backbone of Naziism was broken at this Camp, and when their activities were added to the psychological effects of V.E. Day, they succeeded completely in restraining any overt Nazi activity in those unconvinced unregenerate still remaining at Concordia.

The Assistant Executive Officer was now able to come out frankly into the open to sponsor re-educational activities. Pressure began to be exerted in a forceful manner so as to secure the complete dominance of the Anti-Nazi elements in the Compounds. Things hitherto impossible were now freely undertaken, including the following:

1. Removal of some 440 subversive books from the libraries and personal possession of the prisoners. These were confiscated.
2. Reversal of the editorial policy of the prisoner-of-war camp newspaper, which had formerly been cautiously under Nazi domination, and now became a forthright instrument of democratic indoctrination, crusading for realism and cooperation with the Western Allies.
3. Tremendous increase in demand for *Der Ruf* [*The Call*], national prisoner-of-war newspaper, the first edition of which had suffered an eighty percent (80%) destruction by calculated arson.
4. Increased attendance on [*sic*] church services despite decreasing numbers.
5. The completion of two questionnaires and one declaration, under the auspices of the

Assistant Executive Officer, in which there was a ninety-eight percent (98%) participation, voluntarily undertaken, by the prisoners, who were inspired by the realistic Senior German Spokesman to write the truth, and were amazingly frank on formerly tabooed subjects. These questionnaires furnished excellent bases for intelligence investigation and evaluation, which when accomplished with the help of the Anti-Nazi group, gave this Camp exceptional intelligence records. Whether the declaration of cooperation was the reason or not, at least no further difficulty of a disciplinary character has been experienced here since. The questionnaires also disclosed a very large participation in re-educational media.

6. Establishment of an Anti-Nazi Privy Council, serving as liaison between the Assistant Executive Officer and the Senior German Spokesman, not known to the generality of the prisoners, but effectively controlling the leadership function among the prisoners, to the extent of becoming the real leadership of the Camp itself.

7. The frank request of the Senior German Spokesman for guidance in the re-orientation of the younger and more totalitarian-istically-indoctrinated members of the Camp.

8. Discontinuance of the regular University of 7 July 1945, and its replacement by a school exclusively occupied with English, American History, Geography and Civics, and which enjoyed eighty-eight percent (88%) participation — practically all those mentally capable of attempting such work.

9. Voluntary purchase of from 6,000 to 8,000 books for re-educational purposes, in addition to between 15,000 and 18,000 of this type already in private possession.

10. Initiation of a series of lectures on re-educational subjects by the Assistant Executive Officer, the Provost Marshal, and the Post Exchange Officer, at the request of the Germans.

11. Articles by the Assistant Executive Officer in the camp newspaper at the request of the Germans.

12. Issuance of more than 4,000 certificates of credit to prisoners-of-war for participation in re-educational work at the urgent request of the Germans.

Many other indications of a psychological transformation could be evoked, but space does not permit. It is sufficient to state that as

Three of the officer-POWs on the porch of their barracks. Notice they put a birdhouse at the end of the barracks. (Courtesy, Cloud County Historical Society, Concordia, KS)

a result of "spontaneous responses on the part of German prisoners of war" and through their own "self-indoctrination," Naziism faded out, and a growing confidence in America and the democratic way of life began to replace it. Re-education was accomplished by natural means from within, by and for Germans, and as it is felt it will have to be done in Germany. The Assistant Executive Officer merely attempted to guide and advise a German-inspired mental movement. In evaluating the trend of the new indoctrination, still incomplete on 17 September 1945, when all but a few German Officers had been transferred out, the following statistics are given. It should be borne in mind that these are, in some cases, estimates of intangibles, and represent only the best opinion of the Assistant Executive Officer and his Anti-Nazi colleagues, unless dealing with specifically concrete details:

Month	Average No. of PWs	Books in PW Libraries	Periodical Subscriptions	School Participation	Church Attendances	School Instructors
Jan.	2,475	7,272	430	App. 75%	2,462	193
Feb.	2,376	8,507	524	App. 75%	2,074	189
Mar.	2,332	7,545[1]	730	76%	3,674	190
Apr.	2,330	7,630	663	64%[2]	3,163	170[3]
May	2,192	8,631	767	73%	4,012	183
June	2,035	8,663	810	74%	3,825	178
July	1,869	8,739	2,207	86%[4]	3,482[5]	75
Aug.	1,844	8,786	2,207	87%	2,749	72

1. 900 books sent to International Red Cross.
2. Due to imposition of restrictions after Hitler Birthday celebration.
3. Nazi teachers graduate to Alva.
4. July and August figures 95% re-educational, compared with prior 30%.
5. Due to bustle of departure of 1200 PWs on 4 September, probably.

From January to September 1945, ability to read and understand English increased from approximately 55% for Officers and 1% for Enlisted Men to approximately 75% and 12% respectively.

On December 2, 1944, POW labor from Camp Concordia was terminated for the winter. During the last six weeks that the POWs had worked, they had put in a total of 1,403 days of labor on 106 farms. Of these farms, 40 percent were in Republic County, just north of Cloud County, where Camp Concordia was located.[26]

Around this time, another suicide occurred, when Corporal Richard Michael hanged himself in the linen room at the hospital. It appeared he had become depressed over a letter from home. There were no political overtones to his death.[27]

At the end of 1944, there were almost three times as many officer-prisoners (1,864) as enlisted prisoners (613).[28] The war was nearing its end.

What was in store for Camp Concordia?

Chapter 4

Mission Accomplished

lthough Camp Concordia had been built to hold 3,000 enlisted and 1,000 officer-prisoners, by January 1945 it held only 613 enlisted men, but 1,763 officers-prisoners. Most of the 433 POW Privates worked in the officers section of the camp as cooks, KPs, or maintenance workers. The remaining Privates worked in the enlisted compound or for the Americans. Seventy of the officers worked in administrative positions, for which they were paid.[1]

The officers that had enrolled in some 230 offerings of courses in languages, physics, engineering, economics, medicine, agriculture, and theology numbered 927. There were eight courses for the enlisted prisoners consisting of accounting, English, and preparatory courses for certificates in food products and other commercial branches. There were only 126 Privates attending these courses, because most of them worked all day.[2]

The prisoners kept improving their forms of recreation and leisure activities. The officers had a technical library of 2,593 books and a fictional library of 3,663 books. The enlisted men had a library of 1,026 books. In addition, both had American magazines and newspapers. All prisoners were allowed to see movies five times a week. Sports and handicrafts were available for those so inclined. The officers in each company had casinos that they had decorated and furnished with handmade furniture. In his 1945 Inspection Report, Captain Alexander Lakes stated: "There is no doubt that the comfort of the German officers in Concordia is far superior to that in other prisoner of war camps. . . ."[3] There were at least three orchestras and bands, including the one transferred from Fort Robinson.

Because at this time in 1945 all of the enlisted POWs were employed at the camp, labor remained unavailable to farmers. It was announced that if work details were to be provided for area farms,

100 POWs would have to be transferred to Camp Concordia.[4]

Meanwhile, Colonel Eggerss was continuing to seek out Nazi influence in the compounds and found that some of the officer-prisoners were interfering with the education program, were planning a demonstration for when the defeat of Germany was announced, and were spreading uncensored literature within the compound. On February 22nd, 44 of these officers were sent to Camp Alva, Oklahoma, which was the camp for incorrigible and radical Nazis.[5]

According to Chapter 7 of Captain Teufel's *History of Camp Concordia*:

[The] political complexion of the prisoners changed markedly. In January 1945, 22% were estimated to be potentially dangerous Nazis, 34.2% luke-warm Nazis, 36% middle-of-the-roaders, and 7.8% Non-Nazis or Anti-Nazis. 155 dangerous Nazis were segregated and 55 Anti-Nazis transferred elsewhere. On 18 August 1945, about three months after V.E. Day, dangerous Nazis were calculated at 2.7%, still totalitarian-minded men at 21.3%, and the balance as either realistic men leaning toward democracy and cooperation with the Western Allies, or Non-Nazis and Anti-Nazis.

On March 2, there was another so-called suicide. Lieutenant Wolf Sthamer (who had attempted to escape on October 5, 1944) became sick while drinking 3.2 beer, which was available in the canteen. It seems he then took an enema with a fire extinguisher. Sthamer died ten hours later of a ruptured colon. There was no reason for a suicide, but there was also no proof he had been killed.[6]

☙❧

Much has been made of the cutting of rations to the prisoners in March 1945. Some prisoners have inferred that their rations were cut because the concentration camps in Europe were discovered and because Allied prisoners had not been treated as kindly.[7] However, at the same time rations to American troops were also cut, and civilians were having difficulty finding meat. At Camp Concordia,

substitutes were made for food items that could not be obtained. *The Concordia Kansan* reported:

Salted fish, eggs, spaghetti, macaroni, beans, and cold cuts as replacements for beef, pork, ham, lamb, bacon, chicken, and other meats, virtually unobtainable at markets, will be made. Oleo-margarine has been substituted for butter at the Concordia Camp for quite some time. Other foods will be served in place of canned fruits and vegetables, preserves, jellies, etc.[8]

The article noted that the POWs received food equal to that served American forces.

In April 1945, the prisoners were warned not to attempt to celebrate Hitler's birthday. However, some disregarded the warning. On April 20th, while the Officer of the Day was making his rounds, he found POWs in a mess hall singing and making speeches in celebration. He quickly reported the breach of discipline. Over 100 prisoners were segregated from the rest, and Colonel Eggerss denied the officer-prisoners the privileges they had previously been accorded. They lost their enlisted POW mess attendants, cooks, and KPs, and had to do things for themselves. They were denied use of recreation areas and lost luxuries from their canteens. All enlisted prisoners were kept in the com-

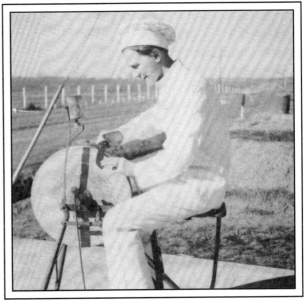

One of the POW cooks sharpening a knife on the west side of the compound. (Courtesy, Wayne E. Rosen)

POW cooks in the 14th Company of the officers compound. Franz Rodel is in the rear with an "X" over his head. (Courtesy, Franz Rodel)

Below: POW cooks at one of the American garrison kitchens in March 1944. (Courtesy, Adolf Weber)

pounds during the time they were not allowed to work for the officers.[9] This hurt the POWs, because they liked earning the extra money.

Once the ringleaders of the celebration were identified and sent to Alva, Oklahoma, the privileges were gradually returned.[10] The cooks and KPs were returned during the first week of May.[11]

Rudolf Wendorff, a First Lieutenant in a panzer (armored tank) regiment in North Africa, had been captured in 1943 and began to write his memoirs for his grandchildren. Wendorff now lives in Gutersloh, Germany, and has graciously allowed the reprinting of portions of the text, concerning his POW time at Camp Concordia. He was eventually sent to the camp at Alva, Oklahoma.

The beautiful place named "Concordia" (harmony) belongs to the most important, positive memories of my life. Close by this small town, in the so-called Midwest of the USA at the point where two diagonal lines across the continent would cross, was our newly built camp which we were the first to occupy. Approximately from September 1943, until May 1945, for some one and one-half years, these were my accommoda-

tions. Barracks were built for us here in tidy, geometric order. As I remember, one living barracks was divided into five or six units for every four officers. Each of these units included an anteroom for all occupants, and two sleeping rooms for two people. In the common room there were two small wardrobes on the left and right. In the sleeping rooms, a bed stood on the left or right in the direction of the

SECRET

HEADQUARTERS ARMY SERVICE FORCES
Office of The Provost Marshal General
Prisoner of War Special Projects Division
50 Broadway, New York 4, New York

CLASSIFICATION CANCELLED OR CHANGED

SPMGX (7) 680.2

TO _____ 18 April 1945 ____
BY _____

MEMORANDUM FOR DIRECTOR, SPECIAL PROJECTS DIVISION
DATE __21 October 1945__

SUBJECT: Field Service Report of a Visit to Prisoner of War Camp, Concordia, Kansas, 17-18 February 1945, by Captain Alexander Lakes.

1. <u>Nature of Camp</u>. There are 1757 officers and 619 enlisted men among the German prisoners of war at this camp.

2. <u>Summary of Progress</u>. Captain Karl C. Teufel, the Assistant Executive Officer, has been accepted by the German officers as a liaison officer for Lt. Colonel George W. Eggers to foster their educational and recreational activities. With diligence and tact he has won their confidence and should continue to have success. An educational program of great magnitude had already been initiated by the German officers in the past year. They undoubtedly have the largest library of any prisoner of war camp. Captain Teufel's objective and influence will succeed only when strong Nazi prisoners of war are removed from the compound, as they predominately influence the thought. German enlisted prisoners of war have not been receiving the same attention in regard to this program as the officers. It was recommended that Captain Teufel pay more attention to their needs.

3. <u>Education</u>. The academic schedule at Concordia includes 230 courses, in which 927 prisoners of war are enrolled. German enlisted prisoners of war have 8 courses and 22 instructors. There has been a lack of supervision and monitoring of these classes and it was recommended that this be corrected in the future.

The Director of Studies, Lt. Colonel Heyse, was Rommell's Plans and Training Officer. He is considered an excellent organizer of moderate Nazi leaning. There are several alleged anti-Nazi officers on the staff of instructors. They have requested transfer to a camp near an American university of high standing where they might be allowed to study, or at least have a scheduled course of lectures by American professors. There are approximately 25 men in this group. They also requested to have the opportunity to visit various phases of American industrial, social, and political life so that they could better appreciate the American way, and be prepared to return to Germany as ambassadors of the democratic way of living. They are men of outstanding talents in teaching, science, business, and law. They offered their services to combat Nazism among the German prisoners of war in this country, and to help weed out Nazi officials who might be accepted inadvertently by the Allied military occupying forces. Active in taking courses from the University of Chicago are six men who received law courses, seven who

SECRET

DECLASSIFIED
Authority NND 770123
NARA, Date 11/4/94

SPMGX (7) 680.2 (Cont'd)

study business methods, and one who receives a course in Egyptology. Mr.
Montgomery of the University of Kansas, the sponsoring school of this
camp, has made a visit to the camp and has surveyed its needs in the
education program. He took back with him a tremendous number of requests
for visual aids, text books, and various educational material. Nothing
has been forwarded as yet from the school to the camp, but Captain Teufel
plans to visit the school to obtain the necessary materials.

4. Library and Reading Rooms. There are two libraries at Concordia,
one a resplendent Wissenschaft or technical library containing 2,593 books
and an incompletely constructed fiction library of 3,663 books. The enlisted
men have 1,026 books in their library. The library building is one of
the finest seen by Captain Lakes. It has an excellent color scheme, fine
paintings on the wall, a superb division of subject matter on various shelves,
and study alcoves with tables and chairs. Everything is conducive to scholarly
activity. The fiction library in a separate building is rather decrepit in
comparison and will need additional work. Both catalogs of reference books
and novels are being submitted to the Education Branch for its study and
censorship. Captain Teufel has not had the opportunity of removing the
disapproved books, but this will be done. Captain Teufel will now act as
custodian of the prisoner of war fund and as censorship officer, two necessary
duties that he has not heretofore performed. A list of the magazines which
are being submitted to the Education Branch, indicates interest in almost
every phase of American life. All that is lacking is the receipt of a good
daily newspaper. The New York Times, Chicago Tribune and others are received
too late to be effective as news. Captain Teufel will investigate the
possibilities of introducing one of the better daily newspapers from some of
the larger cities in Kansas or Missouri.

5. Motion Pictures. All prisoners of war have been seeing the latest
releases at the War Department theater in five programs a week. Pictures
are censored by Captain Teufel before showing. Two 16-mm. projectors in the
compound, which will be necessary for the film circuit, are not in good
condition. For the most part, the latest film releases have been indiffer-
ently received except such pictures as Keys of the Kingdom, and Can't Help
Singing, a story of early California.

Colonel Eggerss has deemed it inadvisable to let them see the newsreel
or any pictures concerning the war. On two occasions they have marched
out of the War Department theater en masse when depictions on the screen
offended their patriotism. Colonel Eggerss has dealt harshly with such
activity by forbidding them to see pictures for several weeks thereafter
and terminating their concerts. The commanding officer has in all cases
shown himself to be the master of the situation and is very well informed
of all activities, clandestine or otherwise, in the compound. This has
resulted in a most orderly and disciplined attitude on the part of the
prisoners of war.

SPMGX (7) 680.2 (Cont'd)

6. <u>Religious Activities</u>. Approximately 225 catholics and 150 protestants attend church on Sundays. The German officers have a lieutenant colonel and a major among their ranks who were divisional chaplains. Colonel Eggerss has faith in their ability and integrity to teach only religion at their services. It has been known in the past that German divisional chaplains have been good propaganda ministers.

7. <u>Camp Publications</u>. The camp newspaper, the <u>Neue Stacheldraht Nachrichten</u>, is one of the cleverest pieces of Nazi propanganda fostered in a German prisoner of war camp in this country. The editor-in-chief of the paper, along with others responsible for its rabble-rousing articles, is due to be transferred out of the camp with the other SS men and leaders. The colonel was advised of the significance of the initials "N.S." (National Socialism) contained in the name of the paper and he will inaugurate a more stringent policy of control on publication once the Nazis are removed. The paper is printed on a press that the Germans bought, and just recently it has been removed from the compound into the stockade area where it can be more closely supervised by American personnel. Captain Lakes had occasion to read several articles and the obvious intent of the paper is to intimidate the Germans into Nazi belief for self-defense against Allied activity in postwar Germany. Captain Teufel was advised to exert more control and supervision over the paper than he has heretofore.

8. <u>Recreational Activities</u>. Picturesque casinos or rathskellers have been set up in every company in the officers' compound. The best productions of art are hung on the walls in these casinos. Need was expressed for tennis courts and gymnastic material. Certain officers are very adept at handicraft, sculptoring and coppersmithing. There is no doubt that the comfort of the German officers in Concordia is far superior to that in other prisoner of war camps, and it is based on the policy of Colonel Eggerss to make concessions to them only if they cause no insubordination.

9. <u>Segregation</u>. The Compound Spokesman, Colonel Waltenberger, appears to be unusually pleasant and lacking in the arrogance of the usual German career officer. His aide, Lieutenant Zander, is the leader of the anti-Nazi group of officers at Concordia. This may explain the former's trend of thought. The Nazis have been attempting to depose Colonel Waltenberger in favor of one of their own men. It was the fortune of Captain Lakes to be present when an incident of greatest significance took place. Captain Teufel was informed by one of the German lieutenants that a plot was being hatched by one of the SS Colonels and other Nazi leaders in the compound for a demonstration and riot on V-E Day, the proportions of which would have dire consequences. This was the first crystallization of actual information at Concordia that concerted revolt and probably mass escape is being contemplated by the Nazis in desperation of their fate on V-E Day. This knowledge at once prompted Colonel Eggerss to compile a list of some 40 to 50 men from his blacklist and have them immediately transferred to Alva.

10. <u>Radio</u>. They have 150 radios at Concordia, which appears to be sufficient for most prisoners of war to hear programs daily.

SPMGX (7) 680.2 (Cont'd)

11. <u>Music</u>. They have several orchestras among the officers and enlisted prisoners of war. The German noncommissioned officers' orchestra at Concordia was captured intact in Tunisia after having been sent there to build up the morale of the German troops in the waning days of the African campaign. At the time of the visit, a Beethoven appreciation program was being conducted in the theater building with recordings and explanations by a German officer.

12. <u>Theater</u>. The theater group was presenting a play during the week of the visit. They prefer comedies or light operettas. The stage facilities, costumes, and make-up are rather limited.

13. <u>Morale of the Guard Personnel</u>. The general appearance, attitude and morale of the guard at Concordia is above average. They have adequate facilities and a very active special service program. Colonel Eggerss is a strict disciplinarian and his attitude is personified in a guard that is better dressed, has better bearing, and executes the proper military courtesies. Captain Teufel, because of his religious background, has induced many more men to go to church on Sundays than have gone heretofore. There is a lively interest in learning the German language at this camp among the officers and enlisted men, and Captain Teufel will serve as instructor. Orientation in the understanding of German psychology and history is being planned in a lecture series by the assistant executive officer.

PAUL A. NEULAND
Major, (QMC) CMP
Chief, Field Service Branch

window. In front of the window stood a small table with two folding chairs. In the common room was also the stove to heat the entire "apartment" with coal and wood to make a fire. Close to the living barracks, each company had a mess hall and a washroom and toilet. In addition, for the camp as a whole, there were buildings for classes, a library, and a community room where we would get together in the evenings. Naturally, there was also a sport field here. Around it all were high, secure fences with watchtowers here and there.

Close to our camp was the compound for the American guards with all that belongs to such a compound. There was also a theater in which we were able to see films often without pay. That was always a nice change. Here we saw the same program the American soldiers saw, and we were able to experience what was new and what amused us: film shorts with requests to sing along with American folk songs. That was very nice. Another enjoyable thing was that the regular words and music were shown so that we too, could sing along. So in a chance and casual manner, we could see something of the American mentality as well as their historic personality which we

found to be very kind. Around the camp stretched the level, wide fields. We were well isolated. Occasionally the camp captain, with permission of the post commander, would take a small group of us for a walk in the near vicinity, especially to a romantic little stream, the Republican River. There we rested a short while, and then we marched back. For this we were very appreciative to the nice captain. At first, there were about 1,000 to 1,500 officers. Later, after the invasion of France by the Allies, about another 1,000 officers came here from that Theater. As is customary, the compounds for the noncommissioned officers and

Above: Rudolf Wendorff in 1943. (Courtesy, Rudolf Wendorff)

Left: A group of officer-POWs in front of their quarters. (Courtesy, Rudolf Wendorff)

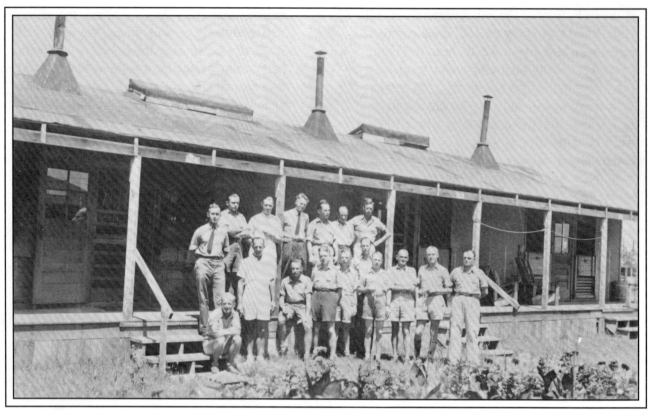

A group of officer-prisoners in front of one of their barracks. Note the homemade chair on the porch and the flowers in the foreground. (Courtesy, Karl Gassmann)

Sergeants James West, Jr., and Wayne E. Rosen in the Finance Department. (Courtesy, Wayne E. Rosen)

enlisted men were located close by the officers' compound. Between them there was some illegal "small border traffic [smuggling]."

Twice a day we had to go to formation on the main camp street to be counted. This was to check whether anyone had escaped. The ceremony was quite mindless. When they wanted to annoy us, they made us wait a long time, . . . useless standing around in formation . . . [but usually] the nice Americans settled the matter quickly. We, ourselves, took care to awaken the officials in the morning, and in the evening, about 2200 hours, gave the tattoo with the call, "Camp quiet! Lights Out!" Of course, sometimes we had the desire to read a little longer or be together. To do that we had to be very careful to black it out. Understandably, the times for meals and for class were fixed. With the rest of the time we could do what we wanted to. In line with this, the outline of the German camp routine was established, and a staff officer, usually a colonel, functioned as spokesman. He looked after our interests with the Americans and wrote about occasional problems to the agent of the International Red Cross in the USA. As for orga-

HONOR AGREEMENT
Prisoner of War Camp
Concordia, Kansas

.....................1944

American:

In return for the courtesy of the walk allowed this date under the supervision of the accompanying American officer, I give my word of honor that I guarantee the return of the .... Officers comprising this group and accept responsibility for their conduct and order on this walk.

Deutsch:

Bei dem heute stattfindenden Ausgang von .... Offizieren unter der Aufsicht XXX eines amerikanischen Offiziers, gebe ich mein Wort, dass ich fuer die Rueckkehr und die Ordnung waehrend des Spazierganges verantwortlich bin.

Genehmigt:

........................., Oberst
Deutscher Lagerfuehrer

....
Verantwortlicher Offizier

German officer-prisoners had to sign this Honor Agreement before leaving the compound for a walk. (Courtesy, Bernadine Cummings)

nized activities, first was the camp school, other cultural activities, and sports. Whoever believed he knew much about a field, had knowledge to lecture at a university level, [or] had practice or work related to a field, was encouraged to pass the knowledge on to others. In the great number of officers, there were many academics who would dedicate them-

selves earnestly to such a job. There were three trimesters which were separated only by a short pause. (What meaning could semester vacations have for us?) For attendance at the courses, one had to properly enroll by application form. Following the course, the camp leadership issued certification under seal and signature, and the certificate was recognized

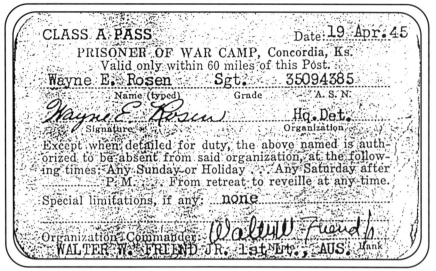

CLASS A PASS   Date: 19 Apr. 45

PRISONER OF WAR CAMP, Concordia, Ks.

Valid only within 60 miles of this Post.

Wayne E. Rosen   Sgt.   35094385

Name (typed)   Grade   A. S. N.

Wayne E. Rosen   Hq. Det.

Signature   Organization

Except when detailed for duty, the above named is authorized to be absent from said organization, at the following times: Any Sunday or Holiday . . . Any Saturday after   P.M. . . . From retreat to reveille at any time.

Special limitations, if any: none

Organization Commander *Walter W. Friend Jr.*

WALTER W. FRIEND JR. 1st Lt., AUS.   Rank

The Class A pass that allowed Sergeant Rosen to go downtown when not on duty. (Courtesy, Wayne E. Rosen)

studies to art history, geography, science of justice, business management, etc. After breakfast, the POWs all left their barracks with a folding chair under their arm to go to the designated room for the lectures. At the breaks, for a change of scenery one would go here and there in the camp with his chair.

From the beginning, I retained a lecture, "Theory of Education," for several trimesters. At first I had no literature for a basis, and I had to search for, sort, and arrange everything myself. I worked out every hour of instruction exactly as when one writes an essay. That had the advantage so I always could fill exactly 45 minutes. I believe that usually I needed 15 pages for this.

in Germany for the studies. The courses of study covered all important fields, from courses in speech, mathematics, and nature

POW Camp Concordia, 1945, a drawing by POW Eugen Grittmann in 1945. He has stated that this is the "West Camp" and that it was not as elegant as the east part with the "old" prisoners from the Afrika Korps. (Courtesy, Beryl Ward)

A scene along the Republican River drawn by one of the prisoners. Officer-prisoners were taken on walks so that they could sketch the countryside. (Courtesy, Gunter Klein)

bauer, a Bavarian from Panzer 8, and my friend Kurt Wolff, very soon a camp newspaper was put out. At first, it was just a copy available on the bulletin board. A large area was filled and arranged with essays, illustrations, poems, etc. The entire text was written by one industrious man on the pull-out table, with a wide artistic pen in easily read script. Later, the newspaper was written on a machine, duplicated, and distributed to everyone in the camp along with its illustrations and mistakes. There are certainly few "newspapers" that were as intensively read as this page.

I want to mention something of the cultural area. Sometimes on Sunday mornings an event with literature and music was undertaken. It was similar to a favorite radio program of that time. In addition, sometimes the camp orchestra gave a concert, or a theater group gave a play on a temporary stage. On Sunday afternoons, we often heard simply magnificent symphony concerts. In good weather, loudspeakers were set up outside so that we could then hear a concert from Carnegie Hall in New York and observe the play of the clouds in the sky, or let our gaze wander indefinitely

From the second trimester on I also initiated a lecture on Nietzsche [the German philosopher, philologist, and poet], but just for one hour a week. I also had this complete text in front of me. With this moderate schedule and the preparation for both lectures, I was quite occupied. To make matters more difficult, there was very little literature available to me, and it was mostly in English.

Under the leadership of Hauptmann Hof-

```
              Abbreviations:
  Mon  = Monday          1.Lesson   8.30 − 9.15  o'clock a.m.
  Tue  = Tuesday         2.   "     9.25 −10.10    "     "
  Wed  = Wednesday       3.   "    10.20 −11.05    "     "
  Thur = Thursday        4.   "    11.15 −12.00    "     "
  Fri  = Friday          5.   "    19.00 −19.45    "   p.m.
  Sat  = Saturday        6.   "    19.55 −20.40    "     "
  I.E. = Infirmary East  7.   "    20.50 −21.35    "     "
  I.W. = Infirmary West  8.   "    21.45 −22.30    "     "
```

I. DEPARTMENT OF PHILOSOPHY AND SCIENCES

English Language.
Department Head: Capt. Penzel.

English, Beginners	Capt. Penzel	Tue & Fri 1.L.	Bar.	319
	1st Lt.Krause	Tue 1.L.	"	363
		Sat 2.L.	"	315
	1st Lt.Willert	Tue & Thur 1.L.	"	456
	2nd Lt.Pechascheck	Wed & Sat 1.L.	"	456
	2nd Lt.Riese (I)	Mon & Thur 1.L.	"	300
	(II)	Wed & Sat 1.L.	"	363
English, Advanced	Capt. Penzel	Mon & Fri 2.L.	"	421
	1st Lt.Darwig	Fri 2.L.	"	472
	1st Lt.Kodytek	Mon & Fri 1.L.	"	469
	2nd Lt.Pechascheck	Tue & Fri 3.L.	"	363
	2nd Lt.Licha	Tue & Thur 1.L.	"	322
	2nd Lt.Meinhardt	Mon & Fri 1.L.	"	363
	1st Lt.Willert	Wed 1.L.	"	421
	1st Lt.Aeberli	Mon & Wed 2.L.	"	300
English, Conversational	Capt. Penzel	Mon & Thur 1.L.	"	462
	Capt. Grossmann	Mon & Thur 1.L.	"	472
	1st Lt.Weber-Andreae	Sat 1.L.	"	411
	2nd Lt.Zander	Tue 1.L.	"	472
	2nd Lt.Lepine	Wed & Sat 1.L.	"	300
Technical English	Capt. Grossmann	Thur 4.L.	"	463
Business English	1st Lt.Gutzeit	Wed 1.L.	"	411
Course on Shakespeare	2nd Lt.Dr.Kurtze	Sat 2.& 3.L.	"	411
Danish	2nd Lt.Kuska	Tue 4.L.	"	469
		Fri 4.L.	"	462
Swedish Seminar	2nd Lt.Wagner	Mon 2.L.	"	469
		Thur 4.L.	"	421

Lectures on America.
Department Head: 2nd Lt. Dr.Blanke.

Survey of American Civilization				
	2nd Lt.Dr.Blanke	Thur 5.L.	"	456
Seminar	" "	Mon 5.& 6.L.	"	469

Romance Languages.
Department Head: 2nd Lt. Voth.

French, Beginners	2nd Lt.Wimmer	Mon & Thur 1.L.	"	353
	2nd Lt.Dr.Treichl	Tue & Fri 2.L.	"	315
French, Advanced	Capt. Heidt	Tue & Thur 2.L.	"	300
	2nd Lt.Waechtler	Wed 1.L & Thur 2.L.	"	472
	2nd Lt.Biber	Wed & Sat 4.L.	"	419
	2nd Lt.Wallraf	Tue & Fri 1.L.	"	300
French, Conversational	2nd Lt.Dr.Treichl	Wed & Sat 2.L.	"	472
	2nd Lt.Albrecht	Wed 7.L.	"	469
Romance Seminar	2nd Lt.Voth	Mon 5.& 6.L.	"	472

The curriculum for the Department of Philosophy and Sciences for the term of April 19 to July 7, 1945, at the Prisoner of War Camp University, Concordia, Kansas. Notice that the courses are taught by qualified POWs. Dr. Blanke gave lectures on America and after the war became a professor at Mainz University, Germany. He has since given lectures at several colleges and universities in the United States. (Courtesy, University of Kansas, Lawrence)

In the officers compound the menu was posted at the door of the mess hall each day. The watercolor artwork was done by one of the POWs. The menu is for 4 May 1945, and translates: Morning: Milk, cornflakes, bread, marmalade, and coffee. Noon: Dr. Samig's special meatballs and pasta, bacon sauce a la Gideon (from ham), and oranges. Evening: Bean stew, bread, and tea. (Courtesy, Rudolf Wendorff)

evening hours with floor exercises and much sweating.

I should still tell something about the general conduct of the camp. I spoke about the canteen and the bookstore. I now must write that we regularly, monthly, received a sort of pay which was somehow divided between officers, noncommissioned officers, and enlisted men. We received $20 a month in the form of little vouchers or script, worth from one, five, ten and more cents. With these we could purchase merchandise in the canteen or, when we were together in the evening in the commons rooms, we could get a beer or a Coca Cola. We could get the important articles in the canteen such as soap, toothpaste, paper, drinks, cigarettes, tobacco, ice cream, and also beautiful briar wood pipes. I purchased many pipes in various sizes and shapes, which I still have all. The availability of American pipe tobacco was tempting. Sometimes, I thought that pipes were a secure investment, perhaps more secure than the trust fund into which we could

over barracks and fences. In Concordia toward the end, we regularly read American newspapers and magazines, such as "Life."

Although I was not a sport type, I did participate in some sport, mainly the distance run, alone or in group competition. Eventually, I ran in a group together with Reinhard Mohn who taught me and others the basics of Judo. Those were wonderfully strenuous

A group of officer-prisoners relaxing in one of the casinos. The prisoners were able to purchase 3.2 beer. (Courtesy, Cloud County Historical Society, Concordia, KS)

Below: The interior of one of the casinos in the officer-prisoner compound. The POWs made the lamps and furniture. (Courtesy, Rudolf Wendorff)

pay. I didn't trust it. (In this instance the thought was not justified.)

Here we were treated the same as replacement troops of our captors, and we received the same good food as the American soldiers (until we lost the war and no "reciprocal treaty" existed anymore). For breakfast, there was always milk and cornflakes, also bread, butter, and marmalade, and often also scrambled eggs, or scrambled eggs and bacon. The noon meal was good and varied. In the course of time, we succeeded, after difficult negotiations, to get through two deviations from the American menu — once a week, on Wednesdays, our cooks could offer simple stew, and in place of the very soft, fine white bread, we could also have dark bread. We Germans could not eat as much as was apparently usual for the American soldiers. The kitchen regularly received more flour and sugar than they could

use. It was not usual to give back or make a gift to the American enemy, [but] occasionally the white paths and boundary lines on the sport field were marked with scattered flour. During meal times the latest daily news was read, including taking into account the illegal news from listening to the short-wave German radio, including the official report of the German army.

As I already said, we could buy beer in the canteen. It was of good quality and even had

German-sounding trade names. One favorite American brand was *Alpenbrau*. It is suspected that brewing knowledge in the USA was entirely established by Germans. Schnaps and whiskey were naturally not available. Occasionally, the resourceful among us secretly made something. Some time in May 1945, I was isolated along with perhaps 40 or 50 comrades within the camp. We were placed in one or two barracks outside the normal area; we had absolutely no room to run about. Instead, we had to remain in one primitive barracks or sit directly in front of it. They wanted the supposed militarists or Nazis, who had known influence in the camp, to be secured before the final collapse of Germany so there would be no emotional attempt to escape under their leadership. Perhaps I came into this group on account of the Nietzsche lectures in that some people held, or hold, Nietzsche as a forerunner of Hitler. I took the matter no further to heart, particularly since I was in a group with many good comrades, above all, with Neuron and Wolff. We were harassed for several weeks in all. For instance, we could not have anything to drink between meals. To ease that, I always had with me, as did some others, a jar with a screw-on lid, when we marched to breakfast or evening meal in a mess hall. The jar was then filled with tea and to camouflage it, after the march back to our sleeping barracks, it was stuck in a sock. So during these warm days I could now and again have a swallow. For the rest of the isolation was not really so bad. Here one laid or sat on the bed in one room for the entire day with perhaps 30 mostly, also quiet comrades and had time for reflection about all the facts of Germany or National Socialism.

Up to this point in Wendorff's memoirs, the publicity the camp had received remained largely negative. The negativism was not always in the open, but was sometimes implied. Newspapers across the country would pick up stories from the area papers

and, as noted, the camp soon gained the reputation of pampering prisoners and allowing Nazis to run the camp.

Perhaps this negative perspective was due in part to the Army releasing very little information about Camp Concordia's operations. But, finally, on June 1, 1945, the camp opened its gates to reporters, who were allowed to circulate throughout the compounds. They went into barracks, the mess halls, and casinos, and they talked to prisoners. The reporters were impressed with the way the POWs had decorated the buildings.

The Concordia Press reported:

> . . . One quickly realizes that although the prisoners are treated fairly, according to rules laid down by the War Department and the Geneva Convention, they most certainly are not pampered. They are, however, slowly becoming acquainted with American ideals and our "way of life," and respect the treatment they are receiving at our hands.[12]

In the spring of 1945, the loss of the prisoner labor continued to be a problem for the farmers, and the Concordia Chamber of Commerce again contacted Senator Carlson who contacted the Army. He was told again that there were not enough enlisted prisoners in the camp to provide labor to the farmers, but that the Army would try to get more.[13] Once again it looked as though the farmers would not be able to get in all of their crops.

There was no farm labor until June 14, 1945, when an arrangement was finally made. But because by that time Germany had surrendered and for the Germans the war was over, the procedures were different from before. *The Concordia Kansan* reported the new rules for using POWs:

> Farmers may use any number of prisoners they need. Prisoners will work without guards, but the farmers must furnish transportation from and back to the camp. Wages will be 40 cents per hour for time actually at work on the farm. A credit for transportation of one cent per mile per prisoner up to fifty

cents per prisoner will be deducted from the labor charge. A credit of 25 cents per meal will also be given. The camp will, at frequent intervals, send a roving guard to check up on the prisoners on the farms. Farmers will agree to inform the camp immediately if an escape attempt is made. All requests for prisoner labor will be handled at the Farm Bureau offices at Concordia and Belleville. Republic County farmers will order through their office at Belleville. Two work days will be provided for: Out at 7:30 a.m. — Back at 5:30 p.m. and out at 9:30 a.m. — Back at 7:30 p.m.[14]

ᗍᗎᗍ

Up until the Germans officially surrendered on 7 May 1945, the prisoners had been allowed to use either the Nazi salute or the American salute. After the surrender, the Nazi salute was outlawed in all POW camps, as well as Nazi emblems, Nazi flags, and swastikas.[15]

Earlier, the POWs had walked out of movies that they felt were unpatriotic.[16] But, on June 15, 1945, they were forced to watch films depicting German and Japanese war atrocities, and they were very sober as they left the theater.[17]

On August 22, 1945, another prisoner died. This time it was not a suicide, but rather a death from natural causes. Captain Ernst Weychardt had suffered from a spontaneous intraventricular hemorrhage brought on by arteriosclerosis (coronary artery disease) and hypertension and had died in the camp hospital.[18]

During late August 1945, a survey was taken to find out how many officer-prisoners would be willing to give up their rights as officers not being expected to work. They were asked if they would be willing to volunteer for labor on the same basis as enlisted men. Every officer in the camp volunteered! On September 5, 1945, 1,200 of the officer-prisoners were sent to Indiana to help with the tomato harvest;[19] only about 300 enlisted and 330 officer-prisoners remained at Camp Concordia. Also, over the months, the size of the garrison had been continually decreasing. By August, there were only 185 military and 80 civilians working at the camp.[20] It was clear that with the small number of prisoners and the small garrison, Camp Concordia's days were numbered.

On September 19, 1945, the prisoners remaining in the hospital were transferred to another hospital. About this same time, the dogs that had been used to help guard the compounds were returned to Fort Robinson, Nebraska.[21]

On September 27th, the editor of *The Concordia Kansan* received a telegram from Senator Frank Carlson, which read, "War Department advises Concordia Prisoner of War Camp declared surplus today. Probably means closing camp within 30 days."[22] Even though the paper had received the telegram with the news, the soldiers at Camp Concordia did not get the official word until October 6th when Colonel George W. Eggerss told his staff.[23]

The camp was scheduled to be closed on November 5, 1945, and turned over to the War Assets Administration. In the meantime, all prisoners had to be shipped out, and surplus supplies, including 15,000 tons of coal, had to be moved.

The last prisoners departed on October 30 and 31, 1945. The 47th Grenadier Regimental Band and 18 officer-prisoners were sent to the POW camp at Trinidad, Colorado, and the remaining 100 were sent by truck to Camp Atlanta, Nebraska. A contract was let to move the coal to Fort Riley and Fort Leavenworth within 30 days. Bodies of the eight German prisoners who had died were moved from the camp cemetery to two rows of Section J of the Fort Riley cemetery, along with other German and Italian POWs who had died in captivity. The trucks and other motor vehicles, except the fire trucks, were taken to Fort Riley. The last day for civilian workers was November 2nd. The last U.S. soldiers departed on November 8, 1945,[24] after the camp was officially turned over to the War Assets Administration as scheduled. The only remaining activity was that of a small maintenance crew, which also acted as a fire department and served as guards.

A summary of personnel strength during the camp's 31 months' existence and its accomplishments is provided in Chapter 7 of Captain Teufel's report:

Precisely, one hundred and two Officers have served tours of duty. . . . Of these, only

The camp cemetery was located outside the fence at the northwest corner of the recreation area. This picture was probably taken in early 1944. (Courtesy, Cloud County Historical Society, Concordia, KS)

eighteen remain as this is written (8 October 1945). The Camp's greatest personnel strength was reached in November 1943 when 4,027 prisoners were being handled by 39 Officers, 754 Enlisted Men and 171 Civilians. Greatest Officers' strength was 50 in May 1944, and greatest Enlisted Man strength was 801 in April of the same year. Approximately 5,300 prisoners were brought here, of which approximately 2,000 were Officers. All but 319 of this 5,300 have been transferred out at some time or other, and no prisoner movement has ever resulted in overt difficulty. . . .

We at Concordia are not unproud of our record. We feel that we have enjoyed, under difficult circumstances, a notable degree of success. We will depart with the sincere assurance to our self-respect that we did our best, and that the best does not require that we be ashamed. As soldiers, engaged in a type of activity strange to this continent, we have conducted ourselves according to the requirements of our basic assignment, and when we leave, we shall experience the meaning of the Army's benediction, the two terse words that express the satisfaction of higher authority for a task well performed, "MISSION ACCOMPLISHED."

Chapter 5

Dismantling the Camp

On November 8, 1945, the War Assets Administration declared the 308 temporary frame buildings of Camp Concordia surplus real property.[1] For the remainder of that year, the camp was unoccupied, and no action was taken to sell any of the buildings, the land, or other assets. Supplies that the government could use were distributed to other Army posts.[2]

In March 1946, 195 buildings were transferred to the Federal Public Housing Authority, and were to be removed from the site.[3] That same month, the overhead and underground utilities (the water, sewage, and power systems) were put up for sale. The water system included 38,000 feet of pipes, valves, pumps, a gasoline engine, automatic controls, and the 100,000-gallon wooden water tank. The sewage system included 28,000 feet of clay pipe, 1,500 feet of cement culvert pipe, pumps, and a pump house. The power system included 100,000 feet of copper wire, 40 transformers, and 230 light

poles. For ten days, these utilities were offered to government agencies, the Reconstruction Finance Corporation, state and local governments, and nonprofit organizations, in that order of priority. If the utilities still were not sold after the ten days, then they would be offered to nonpriority holders for another ten-day period. All utilities had to be removed from the property.[4]

In June 1946, the Federal Land Bank acquired 95 of the buildings.[5] Other buildings were sold to private individuals. The nurses' quarters were moved to Miltonvale, Kansas, southeast of Concordia, and used by Miltonvale Wesleyan College.[6] Other barracks were moved into Concordia and converted into houses, some of which still are in use today. Others were bought by farmers and were used for barns, storage, and miscellaneous purposes. Part of building T-472 was moved to the Buss farm where it is still used as a tool shed. On the inside of this building, German writing is still visible. The camp's theater was torn down, and much of the material was used to build the Concordia Lutheran Church, including the boiler, which was used until it had to be replaced because of a crack in 1994.

∽∾∽

In late 1947 and early 1948, the original landowners exercised their option and purchased most of their acreage back from the government. In each case, the person paid less for the land than the government had paid them in 1943.[7] The land

The Officers Club, T916, as it appeared in May 1943. Later a bridge was built over the ditch and an awning was put up at the entrance. (Courtesy, National Archives)

The south end of the Officers Club, also called the Jayhawker Club. (Courtesy, Wayne E. Rosen)

was worthless, however, because in some cases the previous owner did not get back all of the property, and because there were now cement foundations on some areas, making farming impossible. The government sold some easements on the land for as little as $10.[8]

On October 24, 1947, the City of Concordia bought tract 101 for $5,800,[9] consisting of 20 acres at the entrance of the camp, on which was located the Officers Club, two warehouses of over 7,600 square feet each, and other buildings. The city planned to develop the area into a park, but this did not materialize, and in 1950, the tract was sold to the Veterans of Foreign Wars (VFW).[10] It was sold again in 1964. Since

The Rendezvous NCO Club. Besides the bar there were pool tables and a juke box. The club was opened to lower ranks on an associate membership basis. (Courtesy, Wayne E. Rosen)

The inside of the Rendezvous NCO Club. (Courtesy, Wayne E. Rosen)

that time, the tract has been divided into lots and is presently the site of private homes. Altogether, the city purchased 33 buildings and the sewage system.[11]

The VFW bought two buildings: the Officers Club, for which they paid $4,000, and Building T-9.[12] The Officers Club was left on the land, which was owned by the city. The building was used by several clubs, including the Knife and Fork Club, besides the VFW, which used the building until 1964, when it was sold.[13] It has changed hands since that time, but is still at its original location. Much of the interior has not been changed, and the original bar is still used by the owner. An overhead door has been put in the south end of the building, and cars are stored on what was once the dance floor.

Building T-9, which was the quartermaster and engineer warehouse, originally purchased by the city and then the VFW, is now owned by Donald Kerr, who had helped build the camp. Antique cars are stored in the 7,988 square-foot building.

A portion of the hospital was bought by the American Legion of Scandia, Kansas. It was moved there and is still in use as the Legion's post home.

The redwood from the 100,000-gallon water tank is now paneling inside some Concordia houses and businesses, according to Delmer Harris. The concrete base of the water tower, with its foot-thick cement walls, is still standing and dominates the surrounding countryside. Part of the metal ladder or

tower lies at the base. Other parts are still being used by at least one farmer.

The German prisoners had built two stone guard towers next to the highway and a stone entrance to the camp. The entrance and one guard tower have been restored and remain. The other guard tower was torn down in 1977, and the stone was used to restore the Brown Grand Theater in Concordia.[14]

In 1965, two Concordia businessmen built a one-half mile quarter-horse track and a 1,000-seat grandstand on the site of the original officers compound and hospital. Over the cement floors of what once had been enlisted men's barracks, horse barns were built. However, because betting was not legal in Kansas, the business only lasted for a year.[15] Cars raced on the track for a while, but that too failed, and the land was eventually returned to agricultural use.

The majority of the land bought back by the previous owners was eventually returned to some type of agricultural use. The elm trees planted in rows by the prisoners are gone, but scrub elms grow in cracks in the cement and in other areas. The cement floor of some of the barracks, latrines, and mess halls in the northwest corner of what was the enlisted compound are all that remain. Some waterways and terraces have been put in by the farmers. Today, except for the water tower base, the stone guard tower, and the two buildings, most signs of the once-busy camp have all but disappeared.

Notes

Chapter 1, pages 1-14.

1. Lieutenant Colonel George G. Lewis and Captain John Mewha, *History of Prisoner of War Utilization by the United States Army: 1776-1945*, Department of Army Pamphlet 20-213 (Washington, D.C.: Department of the Army, June 1955), chapt. 6, 73.

2. *Ibid.*, 83.

3. *Ibid.*, 88.

4. Letter dated May 15, 1948, in Camp Concordia File, Folder 254, National Archives, Washington, D.C., Record Group 389, Entry 434, Box 406, Administration Division, Mail & Records Branch, Technical Services.

5. Captain Karl C. Teufel, ed., *The History of Camp Concordia from Site Survey to Deactivation* (Washington, D.C.: National Archives, Record Group 389, unpubl., 1945), Chapt. 1, 7.

6. "No Defense Project for Concordia," *The Concordia Kansan*, July 16, 1942, 1.

7. Lewis and Mewha, *History of Prisoner of War*, chapt. 7, 85.

8. "U.S. to Build Camp Here," *The Concordia Press* (KS), Jan. 21, 1943, 1.

9. Teufel, *The History of Camp Concordia*. 6.

10. "Internment Camp Assured," *The Concordia Kansan*, Feb. 4, 1943, 1.

11. "Bids Open On Government Project," *The Concordia Kansan*, Feb. 11, 1943, 1.

12. Leslie A. Ward, *History of the Concordia Prisoner of War Camp* (Concordia, KS: The Kansan Printing House, Inc., 1969, 1992), 2.

13. "News Notes From Camp Concordia," *The Concordia Press*, Mar. 4, 1943, 1.

14. "Items of Interest From Our Internment Camp," *The Concordia Press*, Mar. 18, 1943, 1.

15. "Notice," *The Concordia Kansan*, Mar. 25, 1943, 1; "War Department," *The Concordia Press*, Mar. 25, 1943, 1; "Take Steps Curbing Absenteeism at Concordia Project," *The Concordia Blade-Empire* (KS), Mar. 24, 1943, 1.

16. "The Internment Camp," *The Concordia Kansan*, Apr. 29, 1943, 1.

17. Ward, *History of the Concordia Prisoner of War Camp*, 3.

18. "Camp Activity Still Goes On," *The Concordia Press*, May 13, 1943, 1; "Named Officers for Internment Camp," *The Concordia Press*, May 27, 1943, 1.

19. "Prisoners Arrive At Camp," *The Concordia Kansan*, July 15, 1943, 1.

20. "Prison Camp Notes," *The Concordia Kansan*, Aug. 26, 1943, 8.

21. Ward, *History of the Concordia Prisoner of War Camp*, 3.

22. Teufel, *The History of Camp Concordia*, 14.

23. *Ibid.*

❧

Chapter 2, pages 15-42.

1. "Change in Command," *The Concordia Kansan*, Dec. 9, 1943, 1; "Col. Lester Vocke New Prison Camp Commander Here," *The Concordia Blade-Empire* (KS), Dec. 9, 1943, 1.

2. "Camp Activity Still Goes On," *The Concordia Press* (KS), May 13, 1943, 1.

3. Captain Karl C. Teufel, ed., *The History of Camp Concordia from Site Survey to Deactivation* (Washington, D.C.: National Archives, Record Group 389, unpubl., 1945), chapt. 6, sect. F; "News of Concordia Internment Camp," *The Concordia Blade-Empire*, July 6, 1943, 1.

4. "Concordia USO Opens With Large Crowd," *The Concordia Press*, August 6, 1943, 1; "USO Notes," *The Concordia Kansan*, Apr. 6, 1944, 1.

5. "Prisoners Arrive At Camp," *The Concordia Kansan*, July 15, 1943, 1.

6. "Prisoners of War on the Kansas Prairie," *The Christian Science Monitor Weekly Magazine* (Oct. 16, 1943): 5.

7. "Prisoner of War Camp Notes," *The Concordia Kansan*, Sept. 2, 1943, 4; Teufel, *The History of Camp Concordia*, chapt. 4, sect. A, 36, 39.

8. Patrick G. O'Brien, *et al.*, "Stalag Sunflower: German Prisoners of War In Kansas," *Kansas History* (Autumn 1984)7, 3: 191.

9. "News of Concordia Internment Camp," *The Concordia Blade-Empire*, July 30, 1943, 1.

10. "German War Prisoners Are Good Farm Help," *The Concordia Blade-Empire*, July 23, 1943, 1.

11. "Set Maximum Wage For War Prisoner Labor," *The Concordia Press*, July 29, 1943, 1; "Wage of War Prisoners Set at $2.40 Per Day; May Work 7 to 8 Hours," *The Concordia Blade-Empire*, July 28, 1943, 1.

12. "Iron Crosses Are Dime-a-Dozen in New Prison Group," *The Concordia Blade-Empire*, Aug. 7, 1943, 1.

13. Glenn Thompson, *Prisoners on the Plains: German POWs in America* (Holdredge, NE: Phelps County Historical Society, 1993), 25.

14. This might have been the 47th Grenadier Regimental Band.

15. "Former P.O.W. in Concordia enjoying visit here," *The Concordia Blade-Empire*, June 22, 1976, 1.

16. Inspection Report, Lieutenant Colonel Edwards, Mar. 26, 1944, National Archives, Washington, D.C., Record Group 389, Provost Marshal General, POW Special Projects Division, Administrative Branch Decimal File 1943-1946, Box 1612.

17. "War Prisoners Not Unhappy Over Italian Comrades' Fall," *The Concordia Blade-Empire*, Sept. 9, 1943, 1, 4.

18. "Inmate at Prison of War Compound Takes Own Life," *The Concordia Blade-Empire*, Aug. 10, 1943, 1.

19. "Prisoner Gets Out of Bounds," *The Concordia Press*, Oct. 21, 1943, 1.

20. *Ibid.*

21. *Ibid.*; "Our Pampered War Prisoners," Robert DeVore, *Colliers*, Oct. 14, 1944, 59.

22. Teufel, *The History of Camp Concordia*, chapt. 4, sect. B.

23. "Fear Caused German Prisoner's Suicide," *The Concordia Kansan*, Jan. 13, 1944, 1.

24. Kramer is probably referring to the death of Captain Felix Tropschuh.

25. Inspection Report, Lieutenant Colonel Edwards.

26. "Accidentally Wounded," *The Concordia Kan-*

san, Oct. 28, 1943, 1; "Berserk Captain Shoots Wife of Col. Sterling," *The Concordia Blade-Empire*, Oct. 25, 1943, 1; Teufel, *The History of Camp Concordia*, chapt. 3, sect. A.

27. Teufel, *The History of Camp Concordia*, chapt. 2, sect. A, part 4; and sect. B, part 1.
28. *Ibid.*, chapt. 3, sect. F.
29. Inspection Report, Captain Robert B. Heinkel, Dec. 23, 1943, National Archives, Washington, D.C., Record Group 389, Provost Marshal General, Projects Division, Administrative Branch Decimal File, 1943-1946, Box 1612.
30. "Finds Pin-Up Girls Decorating Walls of German Prison Camps," *The Concordia Blade-Empire*, Oct. 26, 1943, 1.
31. Inspection Report, Lieutenant Colonel Edwards.
32. Teufel, *The History of Camp Concordia*, chapt. 3, sect. B.
33. "Christmas at Prisoner Camp," *The Concordia Kansan*, Dec. 23, 1943, 1; "News of Concordia Prisoner Camp," *The Concordia Blade-Empire*, Dec. 22, 1943, 1.
34. "Prisoners of War Big Farm Help, The Army Says," *The Concordia Blade-Empire*, Jan. 17, 1944, 1.

Chapter 3, pages 43-69.

1. "Captain Roberts Found Guilty," *The Concordia Kansan*, Jan. 6, 1944, 1; "Captain Roberts Convicted of Two Charges," *The Concordia Blade-Empire*, Jan. 6, 1944, 1.
2. "Food Delicacies Arrive Late For Nazi Prisoners," *The Concordia Blade-Empire*, Jan. 6, 1944, 1.
3. "Fear Caused German Prisoner's Suicide," *The Concordia Kansan*, Jan. 13, 1944, 1; Letter, Subject: Transfer of PW, dated 28 Dec. 1943, in National Archives, Washington, D.C., Record Group 389, Provost Marshal Enemy POW Information Bureau Reporting Branch Subject File 1942-1946, Box 2477.
4. "Fear Caused German Prisoner's Suicide," *The Concordia Kansan*, Jan. 13, 1944, 1.
5. "Fireplace at Officers' Club Causes Blaze," *The Concordia Blade-Empire*, Jan. 21, 1944, 1.
6. "German Officer Hangs Self at Prison Camp," *The Concordia Blade-Empire*, Jan. 29, 1944, 1.
7. "Prisoner of War Camp Notes," *The Concordia Kansan*, Feb. 10, 1944, 5; "News of Concordia Prisoner Camp," *The Concordia Blade-Empire*, Jan. 31, 1944, 2.
8. *Ibid.*, Feb. 8, 1944, 3; Feb. 3, 1944, 5; Jan. 28, 1944, 4.
9. *Ibid.*, Jan. 28, 1944, 4; Jan. 25, 1944, 4; Jan. 31, 1944.
10. *Ibid.*, Feb. 12, 1944, 4.
11. Captain Karl C. Teufel, ed., *The History of Camp Concordia from Site Survey to Deactivation* (Washington, D.C.: National Archives, unpubl., Record Group 389, 1945), chapt. 3, sect. F.
12. *Ibid.*, chapt. 6, sect. F.
13. "News of Concordia Prisoner Camp," *The Concordia Blade-Empire*, Jan. 31, 1944, 2; "Prisoner of War Camp Notes," *The Concordia Kansan*, Mar. 9, 1944, 4.
14. "Camp Here May Be Made Strictly an Officer Prison," *The Concordia Blade-Empire*, May 23, 1944, 1.
15. "German War Prisoner Labor No Longer Will Be Supplied To Farmers," *The Concordia Blade-Empire*, May 31, 1944, 1.
16. Teufel, *The History of Camp Concordia*, chapt. 2, sect. B, part 1.
17. "Nazi Prisoners Available for Farm Work Here," *The Concordia Blade-Empire*, June 13, 1944, 1.
18. "3 Nazi Captives Flee Camp After Tornado Strikes," *The Concordia Blade-Empire*, June 5, 1944, 1.
19. "Capture Escaped Nazi Prisoners Near Courtland," *The Concordia Blade-Empire*, June 8, 1944, 1; "Prisoners Returned to Camp," *The*

Concordia Kansan, June 8, 1944, 1.

20. "Officer Prisoners Here Lose Bets on Invasion," *The Concordia Blade-Empire*, June 6, 1944, 1.

21. Glenn Thompson, *Prisoners on the Plains German POWs in America* (Holdredge, NE: Phelps Co. Historical Society, 1993), 236. Former POW Karl Gassmann disputes this. He said that the instruments were provided later by the YMCA or Red Cross and that the men were medical orderlies of the 47th Infantry Regiment. "POW Camp News," *The Concordia Kansan*, June 22, 1944, 4.

22. *The National Sozialistich* (German spelling of the National Socialist Party) or the Nazi Party.

23. Teufel, *History of Camp Concordia*, chapt. 3, sect. F.

24. *Ibid.*, chapt. 3, sect. C.

25. *Ibid.*, chapt. 2, sect. F, part 2; Leslie A. Ward, *History of the Concordia Prisoner of War Camp* (Concordia, KS: The Kansan Printing House, 1992); "German's Liberty Short," *The Concordia Kansan*, Oct. 12, 1944, 1; Patrick O'Brien, *et al.*, "Stalag Sunflower: German Prisoners of War in Kansas," *Kansas History* (Autumn 1984), 7, 3: 185.

26. "POW Labor," *The Concordia Kansan*, Nov. 30, 1944, 1.

27. Teufel, *History of Camp Concordia*, chapt. 2, sect. F, part 1; Ward, *History of the Concordia Prisoner of War Camp*, 16; "German Prisoner a Suicide, *The Concordia Kansan*, Dec. 21, 1944, 1.

28. Teufel, *History of Camp Concordia*, chapt. 2, sect. B, part 1.

༺∾༻

Chapter 4, pages 70-87.

1. Red Cross Inspection of January 26-27, 1945, by M. Perret (Washington, D.C.: National Archives, Record Group 389, Box 1612).

2. *Ibid.*; Inspection Report, Captain Alexander Lakes, Feb. 17-18, 1945, National Archives, Washington, D.C., Record Group 389, Box 1618, Provost Marshal General, Prisoner of War Division.

3. Inspection Report, Captain Lakes.

4. "Prisoner of War Camp Notes," *The Concordia Kansan*, Feb. 22, 1945, 4.

5. Captain Karl C. Teufel, *The History of Camp Concordia from Site Survey to Deactivation* (Washington, D.C.: National Archives, unpubl., Record Group 389, 1945), chapt. 2, sect. B, part 1; "Transfer German Prisoners," *The Concordia Kansan*, Mar. 1, 1945, 1.

6. Teufel, *History of Camp Concordia*, chapt. 2, sect. F, part 1; Leslie A. Ward, *History of the Concordia Prisoner of War Camp* (Concordia, KS: The Kansan Printing House, 1969, 1992), 16; "German Prisoner Dead," *The Concordia Kansan*, Mar. 8, 1945, 1.

7. Arnold Krammer, *Nazi Prisoners of War in America* (Lanham, MD: Scarborough House,

1952), 240-241.

8. "War Prisoners Here to Eat Substitutes," *The Concordia Kansan*, Mar. 22, 1945, 4.

9. Teufel, *The History of Camp Concordia*; "German Prisoners Celebrate," *The Concordia Kansan*, Apr. 26, 1945, 1.

10. Teufel, *The History of Camp Concordia*.

11. "Concordia Prisoners Off KP Duty Again," *The Concordia Kansan*, May 3, 1945, 1.

12. "Model Camp Dispels Prisoner Pampering," *The Concordia Press*, June 7, 1945, 1.

13. "No War Prisoner Labor," *The Concordia Kansan*, April 26, 1945, 1.

14. "Prisoner Labor Available," *The Concordia Kansan*, June 14, 1945, 1.

15. "Nazi Salutes, Swastikas Are Out," *The Concordia Kansan*, May 10, 1945, 1.

16. Inspection Report, Captain Lakes.

17. "Prisoner of War Notes," *The Concordia Kansan*, June 21, 1945, 1.

18. Teufel, *History of Camp Concordia*, chapt. 2, sect. F, part 1; Ward, *History of the Concordia Prisoner of War Camp*, 16; "German Prisoner of War Dies," *The Concordia Kansan*, Aug. 23, 1945, 1.

19. Teufel, *The History of Camp Concordia*, chapt. 4, sect. D; "German Prisoners Leave," *The Concordia Kansan*, Sept. 6, 1945, 1.
20. Teufel, *The History of Camp Concordia*, chapt. 2.
21. "POW Camp Notes," *The Concordia Kansan*, Sept. 20, 1945, 1; Ward, *History of the Concordia Prisoner of War Camp*.
22. "Camp To Close Soon," *The Concordia Kansan*, Sept. 27, 1945, 1; *The Concordia Press* and *The Concordia Blade-Empire* also received telegrams from Senator Carlson.
23. Teufel, *The History of Camp Concordia*, chapt. 7.
24. "To Turn Over POW Camp to Civilian Crew on Nov. 5," *The Concordia Blade-Empire* (KS), Oct. 22, 1945, 1; "Town Talk," *The Concordia Blade-Empire*, Oct. 30, 1945, 1; "POW Camp Closing," *The Concordia Kansan*, Nov. 1, 1945, 1; "Last of German POWs Leave Concordia Camp," *The Concordia Blade-Empire*, Oct. 31, 1945, 1; "POW Camp Closing," *The Concordia Kansan*, Nov. 1, 1945, 1; "Town Talk," *The Concordia Blade-Empire*, Nov. 8, 1945, 1.

Chapter 5, pages 88-90.

1. Declaration of Surplus Property, Record Group 270, Box 78, National Archives, Central Plains Region, Kansas City, MO.
2. "Town Talk," *The Concordia Blade-Empire*, Oct. 26, 1945, 1.
3. Letter to Bernard L. Grove, Record Group 270, Box 78, National Archives, Central Plains Region, Kansas City, MO.
4. *Ibid.*, Surplus Government Overhead and Underground Utilities.
5. *Ibid.*, List of Buildings Concordia Prisoner of War, Federal Land Bank Acquired.
6. Leslie A. Ward, *History of the Concordia Prisoner of War Camp* (Concordia: The Kansan Printing House, Inc., 1969, 1992), 22.
7. Folders for Tracts 1,2,3,4, Record Group 270, Box 77, National Archives, Central Plains Region, Kansas City, MO.
8. *Ibid.*, Folder for Tract 13, Record Group 270, Box 77.
9. *Ibid.*, Folder for Tract 101, Record Group 270, Box 77.
10. Ward, *History of the Concordia Prisoner of War Camp*, 18.
11. Project Folder #2, Record Group 270, Box 76, National Archives, Central Plains Region, Kansas City, MO; Ward, *History of the Concordia Prisoner of War Camp*, 20-22.
12. Ward, *History of the Concordia Prisoner of War Camp*, 18.
13. *Ibid.*, 18, 20.
14. *Ibid.*, 20.
15. *Ibid.*, 24.

Bibliography

Arndt, Jessie Ash. "Prisoners of War on the Kansas Prairie," *The Christian Science Monitor Magazine* (Oct. 16, 1943): 5,15.

The Concordia Blade-Empire (KS).

The Concordia Kansan (KS).

The Concordia Press (KS).

DeVore, Robert. "Our Pampered War Prisoners," *Collier's* (Oct. 14, 1944): 14, 57-60.

Gansberg, Judith M. *Stalag: U.S.A.* New York: Cromwell, 1997.

The Kansas City Times (MO).

Krammer, Arnold. *Nazi Prisoners of War in America.* Lanham, MD: Scarborough House, 1993.

Lewis, George G., Lieutenant Colonel, and Mewha, John, Captain. *History of Prisoners of War Utilization by the United States Army: 1776-1945.* Department of Army Pamphlet 20-213. Washington, D.C.: Department of the Army, June 1955.

O'Brien, Patrick G., *et al.* "Stalag Sunflower: German Prisoners of War in Kansas," *Kansas History* (Autumn 1984): 182-198.

Teufel, Karl C., Captain, ed. *The History of Camp Concordia from Site Survey to Deactivation*, Unpubl., Record Group 389, Washington, D.C.: National Archives, 1945.

The Topeka Capital-Journal (KS).

Thompson, Glenn, *Prisoners on the Plains: German POWs in America.* Holdredge, NE: Phelps County Historical Society, 1993.

Ward, Leslie A. *History of the Concordia Prisoner of War Camp.* Concordia, KS: The Kansan Printing House, Inc., 1969, 1992.

Archival Sources

Cloud County Historical Museum, Concordia, KS.

Frank Carlson Library, Concordia, KS.

HNTB Architects, Kansas City, MO.

Kansas State Historical Society Library, Topeka, KS.

National Archives, Washington, D.C., Provost Marshal General's Office Records, Special Projects Division, 1943-1946, Record Group 389.

U.S. Corps of Engineers, Maps, Kansas City, MO.

War Assets Administration, Real Property Case Files, in Record Group 270, National Archives, Central Plains Region, Kansas City, MO.

Wichita State University Ablah Library, Wichita, KS.

Interviews and Correspondence

Baxa, Lorene, Concordia, KS, Feb. 6, 1995.

Blanke, Gustav H., Germersheim, Germany, Jan. 27, 1995.

Bloch, Joseph L., Chicago, IL, Dec. 23, 1994.

Blochlinger, Helen, Concordia, KS, Nov. 29, 1994.

Blosser, Isabell, Concordia, KS, Dec. 3, 1994.

Brooks, Letha Mae, Concordia, KS, Jan. 30, 1995.

Brumleve, Robert H., Louisville, KY, July 14, 1994.

Buss, Keith, Concordia, KS, Jan. 22, 1995.

Cool, Dale, Concordia, KS, Feb. 3, 1995.

Cool, Mary Jane, Concordia, KS, Feb. 3, 1995.

Cummings, Bernadine (Blochinger), Concordia, KS, Jan. 1, 1995.

Dixon, Ellen R., Concordia, KS, Jan. 31, 1995.

Erickson, Chester, Belleville, KS, Oct. 31, 1994.

Everett, Charles, Concordia, KS, Jan. 30, 1995.

Fahlstrom, Harriet, Concordia, KS, Feb. 5, 1995.

Forsberg, Rachel, Concordia, KS, Nov. 24, 1994.

Funk, Von E., Fruitland Park, FL, Apr. 18, 1994.

Garlow, Fern, Concordia, KS, Feb. 3, 1995.

Gassmann, Karl, Schweinfurt, Germany, Apr. 11, 1994; June 7, 1994; Jan. 20, 1995.

Gilkison, June (Avery), Winfield, KS, Feb. 17, 1995.

Gruenzig, Gerhard, Chemnitz, Germany, Feb. 20, 1995.

Harris, Delmer F., Jr., Concordia, KS, Jan. 12, 1995.

Harris, Rosella, Concordia, KS, Dec. 3, 1994.

Johnson, Wilma M., Concordia, KS, Jan. 30, 1995.

Kerr, Donald, Concordia, KS, Nov. 29, 1994; Dec. 22, 1994.

King, Al, Vining, KS, Oct. 29, 1994.

King, Jean, Vining, KS, Oct. 29, 1994.

Klein, Gunter, Dusseldorf, Germany, Dec. 19, 1994.

Kosin, Erik, Concordia, KS, June 1976.

Krager, Jack, Concordia, KS, Jan. 26, 1995.

Kramer, Franz, Gundelfingen, Germany, Nov. 17, 1994.

Krapf, Philipp, Schweinfurt, Germany, Jan. 22, 1995.

Lutzke, Martin H., Beaver Dam, WI, Oct. 5, 1994.

Metro, Mary, Concordia, KS, Feb. 7, 1995.

Oeser, Bernadette (Blochinger), Wichita, KS, Feb. 20, 1995.

Palmquist, Richard, Concordia, KS, Jan. 19, 1995.

Payton, Bessie, Concordia, KS, Feb. 7, 1995.

Pickering, Joseph W., New Castle, IN, June 23, 1994.

Purdy, Alfred W., Pennsauken, NJ, Dec. 2, 1994.

Roberts, Vicki, Concordia, KS, Jan. 23, 1995.

Rodel, Franz, Fraureth, Germany, Mar. 13, 1995.

Rosen, Wayne E., Jamestown, IN, Nov. 29, 1994.

Ross, James D., Redlands, CA, May 27.

Roy, Opal (Chaput), Clyde, KS, May 30, 1995.

Snodgress, Cleon, Mooreland, IN, June 23, 1994; June 25, 1994.

Stanford, Robert, Augusta, KS, Aug. 17, 1994.

Stangel, Casey, Concordia, KS, Feb. 2, 1995.

Stortz, Marvin L., Concordia, KS, Nov. 27, 1994.

St. Pierre, Elmo, Concordia, KS, May 23, 1992.

Swenson, Dorothy L., Concordia, KS, July 25, 1994.

Tucker, Vida N., Concordia, KS, Feb. 3, 1995.

Waechtler, Kurt, Denzlingen, Germany, Feb. 10, 1995.

Ward, Beryl E., Concordia, KS, Nov. 25, 1994.

Weber, Adolf, Bad Lasphe, Germany, Feb. 15, 1995.

Wendorff, Rudolf, Gutersloh, Germany, Jan. 28, 1995.

Wilson, Jane, Concordia, KS, Feb. 13, 1995.

Yaksich, Mike, Concordia, KS, Oct. 8, 1994.

Appendix

Abbreviations —Appendices A-J

Appendices are unedited, unrevised transcriptions of the originals.

AC	Air Corps
Adm Off	Administrative Officer
AGD	Adjutant General Department
ANC	Army Nurse Corps
Asst	Assistant
AUS	Army of the United States
AWOL	Absent Without Leave
Bn	Battalion
Br	Branch
CAC	Coast Artillery Corps
Capt	Captain
Cav	Cavalry
CE	Corps of Engineers
C&E	Carpenter and Engineers
ChC	Chaplain Corps
Ch Clk	Chief Clerk
Clk	Clerk
CMP	Corps of Military Police
CO	Commanding Officer
Col	Colonel
Co.	Company
Comp/Cpd	Compound
Contract	Contracting
Cp	Camp
Cpl	Corporal
DC	Dental Corps
Det/Dt	Detachment
Div	Division
EENT	Eye, Ears, Nose, and Throat
EM	Enlisted Men
Eng'r	Engineer
FC/FD	Finance Corps/Department
Fin Adv	Finance Adviser
Gd Det	Guard Detachment
1st Lt/ 1 Lieut/ 1 Lt	First Lieutenant
GO	General Order
HQ	Headquarters
INF/Inf	Infantry
KP	Kitchen Police
Lt Col	Lieutenant Colonel
MAC	Medical Administrative Corps
MC	Medical Corps
Med	Medical
Med HQ	Medical Headquarters
Med Off	Medical Officer
MP	Military Police
MPEG	Military Police Escort Guard
NCO	Noncommissioned Officer
O/Off/ Off'r	Officer

Off Asp	?
Op	Operations
ORD	Ordnance
QM	Quartermaster
QMC	Quartermaster Corps
P-2	Pay Grade 2
P-3	Pay Grade 3
Pers	Personnel
PFC	Private First Class
PM	Provost Marshal
PMG	Provost Marshal General
PMGO	Provost Marshal General Office
PMO	Provost Marshal Office
Pol	Police
Pris	Prison/Prisoner
Pub	Publicity
Purch	Purchasing
Pvt	Private
PW	Prisoner of War
PWCK	Prisoner of War Camp Concordia
PX	Post Exchange
Reg	Regiment
SA	*Sturmabteilungen*: Storm Troopers
SCU	Service Command Unit
SD	*Sicherheisdienst*: Security Service
Sect	Section
Serv D/ Sv Det	Service Detachment
Sgt	Sergeant
1/Sgt	First Sergeant
M/Sgt	Master Sergeant
S/Sgt	Staff Sergeant
T/Sgt	Technical Sergeant
SigC	Signal Corps
SnC	Sanitation Corps
Spec	Specialist/Special
Spec Proj	Special Project
SS	*Schutzstaffel*: Rifle Squadron
Sta	Station
SU	Service Unit
Sv/Svc	Service
SvC	Service Command
T/3	Technician 3rd Grade
T/4	Technician 4th Grade
T/5	Technician 5th Grade
VC	Veterinary Corps
WD AGO	War Department Adjutant General Offfice
Whse	Warehouse
WOJG	Warrant Officer Junior Grade

Appendix A
American Strength

From *The History of Camp Concordia from Site Survey to Deactivation*, edited by Captain Karl C. Teufel (Washington, D.C.: National Archives, Record Group 389, unpubl., 1945), chapt. 2, sect. A, parts 1 through 4:

This section is . . . purely statistical in character and is designed to serve as a reference section for those who may be concerned with the data given herein. . . .

Part 1: Officers

Name of Officer Arm or Service	Rank on Assignment and Departure	Date or Arrival and Departure	Duty Assignment
A. Colonel [John A.] Sterling's Administration:			
Devales, Samuel P., CE	Capt.	26Apr43-10Dec43	Post Engineer
Hummel, John N., AUS	2d Lt.-Capt.	4May43-	Adj., Asst. Prov. Mar., PW Pers., Off.
Wells, Hubbard W., FC	2d Lt.-1 Lt.	6May43-26Jul44	Finance Officer
Renfro, Donald M., INF	Capt.	7May43-13Mar44	Intelligence Off.
Mangiameli, Carl L., MC	Capt.-Major	10May43-15July44	CO Sta. Hosp., Post Surgeon
Sterling, John A., INF	Colonel	12May43-12Dec43	Post Commander
McShane, Kenneth J., QMC	1 Lt.-Capt.	13May43	Sales O., QM
Hansen, Clarence P., MAC	1 Lt.	15May43-9Sep44	Med. Supply Off.
Inbody, Roy N., INF	Major	24May43-3Apr44	Exec. O., Prov. Mar.
Austin, John J., INF	Capt.	11Jun43-14Apr44	Compound Commander
Rohn, George J., MAC	2nd Lt.-1 Lt.	24Jun43-9Jul44	Hospital Adjutant
Monson, Leigh, CMP	Capt.	1Jun43-16Aug43	Compound Commander
Charles, Earl S., AUS	Capt.	14Jun43-10Mar44	Personnel Officer
King, Josiah R., CMP	1 Lt.-Capt.	1Jul43-29Jan44	Transportation Off.
O'Connell, Wm. M., MC	Capt.	1Jul43-9Sep43	CO Station Hospital
Riniger, Harold, C., MC	Capt.	2Jul43-24Nov43	Medical Officer
Wright, Wilburn E., DC	1 Lt.	2Jul43-28Jul44	Dental Officer
Roberts, David, CMP	Capt.	3Jul43-11Feb44	CO 456th MPEG Co.
Sitzman, Phillip E., CMP	2 Lt.- 1 Lt.	3Jul43-15Jul44	CO 457th MPEG Co.
Carlson, Oke E., CMP	2 Lt.	5Jul43-8May44	Co. O. 457th MPEG Co.
Siegel, Joseph A., CMP	2 Lt.	6Jul43-29Jan44	Co. O. 456th MPEG Co.
Pollock, Bernice A., ANC	1 Lt.	10Jul43-28Dec44	Chief Nurse
Johnson, Paul L., CMP	Capt.	15Jul43-25Aug43	CO Officers' Compound
Harding, Richard D., INF	Capt.	15Aug43-4Jun44	CO Officers' Compound CO Minn. Br. Camps
Yockey, Jacob A., AUS	2 Lt.	27Jul43-13Jun44	CO Compound #2
Gentes, Chas., E. F., QMC	1 Lt.	28Jul43-11Mar44	Post Property Officer
Coverdale, Ralph T., INF	Capt. - Major	3Aug43-19Jun45	Labor Relations Off. Provost Marshal
Lutzke, Martin H., SigC	2 Lt. - Capt.	8Aug45 -	CO Compond #1 Stockade Commander
Ball, Marty, CMP	1 Lt. - Capt.	15Aug43-14Jun44	CO 480th MPEG Co.

Name of Officer Arm or Service	Rank on Assignment and Departure	Date or Arrival and Departure	Duty Assignment
Hughes, Vincent B., AUS	2 Lt. - 1 Lt.	12Aug43-14Jun44	CO Headquarters Det.
Strong, Giles, H., INF	Capt.	14Aug43-17Sept45	CO Officers' Comp. Stockade Commander
Broyles, Neal A. CMP	1 Lt.	15Aug43-17Jul44	Co. O. 480th MPEG Co.
Dietz, Carl I., INF	Capt.	25Aug43-14Jun44	CO Officers' Comp. Pol. & Prison Off.
Bergman, Carl J., ChC	1 Lt.	18Aug43-10Nov44	Chaplain
Simons, Max, MC	Capt.	13Aug43-14Apr44	Chief EENT Clinic
Schoeller, Ewald S., CMP	2 Lt. - Capt.	15Aug43-	Co. O. 480th MPEG Co. & Gd. Det, CO Serv. D.
Shipley, Angus M., MAC	2 lt. - 1 Lt.	1Sep43-22Apr45	Med. Lab. Off., CO Med. Det.
McCallister, Curtis S., DC	Capt.	1Sep43-	Dental Officer
Biehle, Wm. C., INF	Capt.	3Sep43-2Jun44	Personnel Officer
Compton, Russell L., CAC	1 Lt. - Capt.	8Sep43-8Apr45	Asst Comp. CO, Off'rs.
Mulder, Russell H., Cav	Capt.	8Sep43-31Jul44	Asst Executive Off. CO 457th MPEG Co.
Rawdon, Frederick E., CE	Capt.	12Sep43-	Post Engineer
Chambers, James W., MC	1 Lt.	16Sep43-15Apr44	Medical Officer
Bates, Robert R., MC	Capt.	27Sep43-25Apr44	Chief Surgical Serv.
Gomez, Frank D., VC	1 Lt.	28Sep43-23Nov44	Post Veterinarian
Strange, Bill M.., AUS	WOJG	18Oct43-5Feb44	Personnel Officer
Bracken, Harry G., CMP	1 Lt. - Capt.	2Nov43-19Jun44	CO 592nd MPEG Co. CO Br. Camp #404
Denicke, Clem J., CMP	2 Lt.	2Nov43-15Jan44	Co. O. 592d MPEG Co.
Doyle, Peter J., CMP	2 Lt.	5Nov43-26Jan44	Asst P. X. Officer
Johnson, Marvin C., AUS	Capt.	16Nov43-9May45	Post Exchange Officer
Vocke, Lester, CMP	Lt. Col.	24Nov43-31Aug44	Post Commander
Yeoman, Leo C., CMP	2 Lt.	2Nov43-11Nov43	Co. O. 592d MPEG Co.
Byrd, Byrum G., CMP	2 Lt.	2Dec43-22Apr44	Co. O. 592d MPEG Co., Co. O. Guard Det.

B. Lt. Colonel [Lester] Vocke's Administration:

Name of Officer Arm or Service	Rank on Assignment and Departure	Date or Arrival and Departure	Duty Assignment
Rogers, John W., CMP	1 Lt. - Capt.	8Dec43-22Sep44	Post Adjutant
Campbell, Arnold, CMP	2 Lt.	12Dec43-29Jan44	Co. O. 456th MPEG Co.
Lawyer, Charles, INF	Capt.	10Jan44-15Aug44	Asst. Provost Marshal
Folkenson, Paul V., QMC	2 Lt.	1Jan44-3Jul44	Asst. Transportation
Eastwood, Sherrill C., QMC	Capt.	1Jan44-4Aug45	Post Property Officer Director of Supply
Fanning, Roy C., QMC	2 Lt.	3Feb44-3Jul44	Salvage Officer
Groshardt, Norman L., AUS	2 Lt.	7Feb44-23Jul44	Personnel Officer
Hutchinson, Sam C., CMP	1 Lt. - Capt.	10Feb44-18Sep45	Co. O. 642 MPEG Co., CO Gd. Det., Asst. PM
McGovern, Joseph, CMP	2 Lt.	10Feb44-17Jul44	Co. O. 642d MPEG Co.
Nuss, John F., CMP	2 Lt.	10Feb44-16Jul44	Co. O. 642d MPEG Co.
Eggerss, George W., FA-CMP	Lt. Col.	18Feb44-	Provost Marshal Post Commander
Hooper, Melvin H., CMP	Capt.	20Mar44-8Apr44	CO 361st MPEG Co.
Wolf, Jerome E., QMC	1 Lt.	9Mar44-17Jun44	Post Exchange Officer
Cook, Oscar T. Jr., AUS-CMP	1 Lt. - Capt.	20Mar44-	Co. O. 361st MPEG Co. Post Adjutant

Name of Officer Arm or Service	Rank on Assignment and Departure	Date or Arrival and Departure	Duty Assignment
Sigler, Sigmund H., CMP	2 Lt.	1Apr44-17Jun44	Co. O. 361st MPEG Co.
Ickes, Kendall S., Cav	Major	1Apr44-	Executive Officer
Friend, Walter W., AUS-AGD	2 Lt. - 1 Lt.	2May44-	Dir. of Personnel
Jerich, Eli, CMP	2 Lt.	3May44-14Jun44	Asst. Pol. & Pris. O.
Karpas, Jules L., MC	1 Lt. - Capt.	3May44-	Chief Medical Service Post Surgeon, Hosp CO.
Dexter, Rodney S., CE	1 Lt.	8May44-25Aug44	Asst. Post Engineer
Ridge, Alfred J., CE	Capt.	12May44-26Jul44	Asst. Post Engineer
Montgomery, George P., ORD	Capt.	17May44-22Jul44	Ordnance Office
Turek, Lada J., DC	Capt.	3Jun44-22Jun44	Dental Officer
Schmitt, Clarence F., MC	1 Lt.	7Jun44-13Aug44	Chief Med & Surg Serv.
Entringer, Albert J., MC	Capt.	2Jun44-1Dec44	Post Surgeon
Kremens, Jack B., CMP	1 Lt.	15Jun44-20Sep44	Intell. O., Asst. PM

C. Lt. Colonel [George W.] Eggerss' Administration:

Mehlman, Joseph S., MC	1 Lt.	16Sep44-6Dec44	Medical Officer
Patrick, Melton H., MAC	Capt.	10Sep44-	Med. Supply O., Adj., Executive Off. (Hosp.)
Rooney, Vincent R., CAC	1 Lt.	13Oct44-18Sep45	Special Services Off.
Dexter, Rodney S., CE	1 Lt.	10Nov44-27Dec44	Purch. & Contract. O
Carner, Wilford R., ChC	Capt.	9Nov44-17Jul45	Chaplain
Cleveland, Winifred, ANC	1 Lt.	16Nov44-12May45	Chief Nurse
Paalman, Russell J., MC	1 Lt.	18Nov44-13Feb45	Chief Surgical Serv. CO Station Hospital
Abrams, William W., MC	Capt.	20Nov44-5Feb45	Post Surgeon
Long, Elmer I., VC	Major	27Nov44-17Jan45	Post Veterinarian
Teufel, Karl C., AC	Capt.	2Dec44-	Asst. Executive Off.
Martin, Melvin C., MC	Major	3Dec44-20Jun45	Post Surgeon, CO Station Hospital
Felenstein, James M., FC	2 Lt - 1 Lt.	24Dec44-	Finance Officer
McCormick, Edmund B., VC	Capt.	17Jan45-	Post Veterinarian
Baker, Joseph H., MC	Capt.	12Feb45-27Jul45	Post Surgeon, CO Station Hospital
Fishel, Elliott R., SnC	1 Lt.	24Apr45-	Med., Lab. Off., Station Hospital Adjutant
Schoen, Irwin D., QMC	2 Lt. - 1 Lt.	5May45-	Post Exchange Officer
Dietrich, John R., CMP	2 Lt.	9May45-18Jun45	Co. O., Guard Dt.
Leiser, Helen L., ANC	1 Lt.	11May45-	Chief Nurse
Mowry, Patrick W., CMP	2 Lt.	4Jul45-17Sep45	Co. O. Service Det.
Johnson, Bertha L., ANC	2 Lt.	12Jul45-	Nurse
Culbertson, Harry E., MAC	1 Lt.	4Sep45-	Med., Supply Officer

EDITOR'S NOTE: Information contained above was obtained from Special Order files at Headquarters, Prisoner of War Camp, Concordia, Kansas, and from other personnel files pertaining thereto.

These statistics were prepared and stenciled for mimeographing on 1 October 1945, and do not show data subsequent to that date.

Part 2: Enlisted Men

Sgt. Robert A. McKinley, Telephone Operator, is the oldest enlisted man in point of service on the Post. He was on temporary duty with the Area Engineer during the construction period, arriving 6 March 1943, and then was permanently assigned here on 10 May 1943, and remains to this date.

The following statistics are given only on those enlisted men who are and have been regarded by the Director of Service as key personnel:

Name of Officer Arm or Service	Rank on Assignment and Departure	Date or Arrival and Departure	Duty Assignment
McKinley, Robert A., (Hq)	T/5 — Sgt.	10May43-	Telephone Operator
Hoxie, Karl E. (Hq)	1/Sgt.	10May43-31Jul44	1/Sgt. P.W.Compound
Minton, Richard L. (Hq)	T/4 — S/Sgt.	10May43-9Apr45	Chief Signal Clerk
Carpenter, Wilbur W. (Hq)	1/Sgt.	14May43-2Mar44	1/Sgt.
McBride, Earl J. (Hq)	Cpl. — T/Sgt.	11May43-2Mar44	Personnel Sgt/Major
McQueen, Malcolm L. (Hq)	T/5 — S/Sgt.	11May43-27May44	Ch. Clerk P.W. Pers.
Hobson, Millard E. (Hq)	T/5 — M/Sgt.	11May43-	Post Sergeant-Major
Bearman, Merritt L. (Hq)	Cpl. — 1/Sgt.	11May43-2Mar44	1/Sgt. Hq. Det.
Schade, Walter E. (Hq)	1/Sgt.	11May43-1Jul44	1/Sgt P.W. Compound
Newkirk, Clarence (Hq)	T/5 — Sgt.	11May43-2Jun45	Postal Clerk
Molz, Johann G.. (Med., Hq)	Sgt. — M/Sgt.	11May43-27Aug45	Hosp. Sgt./Major Ch. Clk. Sp. Proj.
Pando, Joseph P., (Med.)	Sgt. — T/Sgt.	11May43-12Jun44	Hosp. Mess Sgt.
Nichols, Oscar E. (Med.)	T-5 — S/Sgt.	11May43-15Sep45	Pharmacist
Musser, Joseph V. (Med.)	Pvt. — Sgt.	11May43-	Lab. Technician
Walker, John C., (Hq)	T/4 — S/Sgt.	11May43-27May44	QM Stock Records
Floyd, Simon (Hq)	1/Sgt.	14May43-5Mar44	1/Sgt.
Dyer, Cecil O., (Hq)	S/Sgt.	14May43-2Mar44	Compound Supply/Sgt.
McClay, St. Elmo (Hq)	S/Sgt.M/Sgt.	14May43-12Jun44	Ordnance
Munro, John L. (Hq)	S/Sgt.	14May43-6May45	Motor Sergeant
Schwartz, Walter J. (Hq)	Sgt. — M/Sgt.	14May43-27Dec43	Post Sergeant/Major
Roberts, James E. (Hq)	T/5 — Sgt.	14May43-19Sep44	Chief Publ. Clerk
Herthel, Richard J. (Hq)	Pfc. — Cpl.	14May43-18Apr44	Mess Ctr. Chief
Siders, Clyde L. (Hq)	Sgt.	14May43-10Mar44	Officers' Mess
Fugate, Oakley (Hq)	Sgt. — S/Sgt.	14May43-20Dec44	Clk., Sgt/Major's O. Labor Foreman
Tracy, Hugh E. (Hq)	Pfc. — S/Sgt.	14May43-1Jul44	Ch. Clk. Mil. Pers.
Meyer, Elmer C. (Hq)	T/Sgt. — M/Sgt.	20May43-17Mar44	Ch. Clk., Finance
Morgan, Bert (Hq)	S/Sgt.	23May43-8Aug44	Veterinary Asst.
Aughton, Harold (Hq)	T/Sgt. — M/Sgt.	23May43-17Sep44	Stockade Sgt./Major
Nolan, Roy M. (Hq)	Pvt. — S/Sgt.	23May43-9Jun45	C. & E. Shop
Warren, Charles L. (Hq)	T/Sgt.	23May43-9Feb44	Motor Sergeant
Koski, Louis (Hq)	S/Sgt.	23May43-9Jun45	QM Whse, Stable Sgt.
McClure, Kenneth E. (Hq)	M/Sgt.	23May43-	QM Chief Clerk
Rosen, Wayne E. (Hq)	Pvt. — Sgt.	3Jul43-	Pers. Clk., Fin. Clk.
Shubert, Joseph Jr. (Hq)	Pvt. — Cpl.	3Jul43-21Apr44	Pers. Classif'n Clk.
Richey, Ralph V. (Hq)	T-5 — T/Sgt.	26Aug43-	Rec. & Rpts. Sect. Personnel Sgt/Major
Seymour, Alfred Jr. (Hq)	Pvt. — S/Sgt.	26Sep43-3Oct44	Spec. O. Sect.
West, James Jr. (Hq)	Pfc. — T/4	15Aug43-	Co. Clk. Hq. Det., Finance Clerk
Hayward, Orville (Hq)	Pvt. — Sgt.	23Sep43-	Subsistence Clerk
Stover, Glenn (Hq)	Pvt. — Sgt.	12Oct43-	Clk. Stockade Hq.
Nash, Walter (Hq)	Pvt. — Cpl.	18Oct43-	Interpreter, Spec. Proj
Mann, Richard (Hq)	S/Sgt-T/Sgt.	6Dec43-1Jul44	Personnel Sgt./Major
Prudhon, Dale (Hq)	Sgt. — S/Sgt.	6Dec43-	Compound Chief Clerk
Nee, Edward J. (Hq)	Pfc. — Sgt.	29Dec43-21Sep44	Clk, 1/Sgt., Hq. Det.

Name of Officer Arm or Service	Rank on Assignment and Departure	Date or Arrival and Departure	Duty Assignment
Loewen, Arthur (Hq)	Pvt. — S/Sgt.	4Jan44-	Labor foreman
Workman, Floyd (Hq)	Cpl. — Sgt.	13Jan44-1Jul44	Clerk Stockade Hq.
Stanton, Kenneth (Hq)	Pvt. — S/Sgt.	15Jan44-	Sgt/Major Stockade Hq.
Burger, Clarence (Hq)	Pfc. — Cpl.	11Feb44-	Dispatcher, Motor Sgt.
Proscia, Rocco (Hq)	Pvt. — Cpl.	11Feb44-	Theater Manager
Kwiatkowski, Ray (Sv.Det)	Cpl.	11Feb44-	Company Clerk
Fredericks, Morton (Hq)	Pfc. — Sgt.	9Feb44-	Officers' Mess Steward
Jepson, Jack (Hq)	Pfc. — Sgt.	20Jul44-	Stockade records
Simpson, Frederick (Med. Hq)	Pfc. — Cpl.	22Jul44-	Classif'n Spec., Hosp. Sergeant-Major
Taddeo, John A. (Sv. Det)	Sgt. — 1/Sgt.	1Apr44-	Supply Sgt., 1/Sgt.
Slade, Virgil (Sv. Det)	T-5 — S/Sgt.	1Apr44-	Supply Sgt.
Giuffre, Dominick (Sv. Det)	Pfc. — T/5	1Apr44-5Sep45	Company Clerk
Bruno, Dominick (Sv. Det)	Pvt. — Cpl.	1Apr44-	Compound Clerk
Norgard, Lorenzo (Hq)	Pvt. — Sgt.	24Jun44-	Stenographer to C.O.
Schuler, Louis (Hq)	Pvt. — T/5	15Dec44-	Postal Clerk

The first authorization for enlisted men for this Post, June 1943, permitted 12 Grade 1, 6 Grade 2, 144 Grade 3, 28 Grade 4, 39 Grade 5, 23 Grade 6, and 0 Grade 7. The last authorization, September 1945, also authorized 158 men as follows: 2 Grade 1, 2 Grade 2, 7 Grade 3, 22 Grade 4, 25 Grade 5, 46 Grade 6, and 54 Grade 7. The coincidence of 158 and the contrast are interesting.

Part 3: Civilian

Name	Date of Arrival and Departure	Duty Assignment	Org.
Bonnett, Clarence W.	16May43-	Chief Engineer, P-3	Post Eng'r.
Bethel, John W.	20May43-28Sep45	Civil Engineer, P-2	Post Eng'r.
Harrison, Arthur M.	1Jul43-31Oct45	Chief Clerk	Post Eng'r.
Horan, Virginia R.	1Dec44-22Dec45	Chief Clerk	Post Eng'r.
Phipps, Rose M.	23Sep45-	Chief Clerk	Post Eng'r.
Crawford, Ira B.	16Jul43-23May44	Agricultural Aide	Post Eng'r.
Hanson, Theodore E.	16Jul43-1Apr44	Coal Yard Supt.	Post Eng'r.
Jensen, James P.	16Jun43-15Feb45	Fire Chief	Post Eng'r.
Wright, Judd P.	16Jun44-15Feb45	Fire Chief	Post Eng'r.
Rheault, Leo A.	17May43-	Fireman, Fire Chief	Post Eng'r.
Vance, Neal V.	1June43-31Dec43	Assoc. Eng'r., Supt. of Construction	Post Eng'r.
Kimbrough William A.	6May43-	Carpenter Foreman	Post Eng'r.
Thompson, Claude B.	7Jun43-	Chief Op. Engineer	Post Eng'r.
Pearce, Chester J.	8May43-	Electrician Foreman	Post Eng'r.
Husselman, Charles H.	28May43-	Painter Foreman	Post Eng'r.
Morrow, Mathias H.	24May43-	Plumbing Foreman	Post Eng'r.
Johnson, Walter C.	22May43-	Roads Labor Foreman	Post Eng'r.
Stevenson, George H.	14May43-	Operating Engineer	Post Eng'r.
Warren, Charles L.	9May44-29Sep45	Truck Drive, Fireman	Post Eng'r.
Caw, John J.	11May43-	Purch. & Contr. Clerk	Post Eng'r.
Dehner, Lela H.	14Jun43-21Mar45	Chief Clerk	Finance
Mangiameli, Josephine	16Jul43-16Mar45	Chief Clerk	Sta. Hosp.
VanGoor, Margaret E.	1Jul43-29Feb44	Chief Clerk	Quartermast.

Name	Date of Arrival and Departure	Duty Assignment	Org.
McNamara, Ethel V.	24May43-29Jun45	Chief Clerk	Quartermast.
Schroth, Fred J.	1Jun43-	Chief Storekeeper	Quartermast.
Blochlinger, Bernadine	1Jun43-	Transportation Clerk	Quartermast.
Zumbrun, Lola A.	1Jul43-	Chief Clerk	Civ. Pers.
Droege, Opal R.	28Sep43-	Payroll Clerk	Civ. Pers.
Blochlinger, Helen M.	24May43-10May44	Payroll Clerk	Civ. Pers.
Dunn, Lynette C.	28Sep43-	Classification Clerk	Mil. Pers.
Farrell, Vera M.	16Sep43-	Chief Clerk	P.W. Pers.
Richey, Elizabeth L.	24Jan44-	Chief Clerk	Pub. & Rec.
Havel, William	1Sep43-	Ch. Clk, Storek'p'r.	Ordnance.
Abbey, Fred A.	20Sep43-19May45	Auto Mech. Foreman	Ordnance.
Tucker, Oliver B.	1Jul43-	Auto Mech. Foreman	Ordnance.

Part 4: Personnel Strength

	Month	Officers	Enl. Men	Civilians	Total
1943					
	June	18	160	169	347
	July	31	437	160	628
	Aug.	42	573	164	779
	Sept.	49	593	174	816
	Oct.	39	616	179	834
	Nov.	39	754	171	964
	Dec.	45	788	128	961
1944					
	Jan.	45	618	122	785
	Feb.	45	717	123	885
	Mar.	49	686	115	850
	Apr.	44	801	104	949
	May	50	658	121	829
	June	42	445	107	594
	July	27	279	108	414
	Aug.	25	265	97	387
	Sept.	24	249	93	366
	Oct.	25	251	98	374
	Nov.	30	345	101	496
	Dec.	27	335	99	461
1945					
	Jan.	27	313	95	434
	Feb.	26	286	94	406
	Mar.	26	240	91	357
	Apr.	25	234	93	352
	May	25	232	90	347
	June	23	168	92	281
	July	22	166	91	279
	Aug.	21	164	80	265
	Aver.	33	421	117	571

(Information compiled by 1st Lt. Walter W. Friend, Jr., AGD, 0-1004006)

Appendix B
German Strength

From *The History of Camp Concordia, from Site Survey to Deactivation*, edited by Captain Karl C. Teufel (Washington, D.C.: National Archives, Record Group 389, unpubl., 1945), chapt. 2, sect. B, part 1:

Section B: German
Part 1: Strength and Movement Data

The following statistics are not designed to form a continuity or a story, but merely to relate facts to those who may be interested therein. Some of the movements and the reasons therefore are described in other sections of this volume, but here are just so many entries.

Strength Figures

Date	Prisoners of War E.M.	Off'rs	Total	Date	Prisoners of War E.M.	Off'rs	Total
1 Aug. 43	702	90	792	1 Sep. 44	602	944	1546
1 Sep. 43	2583	1001	3584	1 Oct. 44	619	1833	2452
1 Oct. 43	2962	1015	3977	1 Nov. 44	673	1893	2566
1 Nov. 43	3012	1015	4027	1 Dec. 44	663	1886	2549
1 Dec. 43	3012	996	4008	1 Jan. 45	613	1864	2477
1 Jan. 44	2929	997	3926	1 Feb. 45	622	1760	2382
1 Feb. 44	2248	995	3243	1 Mar. 45	617	1713	2330
1 Mar. 44	2226	997	3223	1 Apr. 45	621	1716	2337
1 Apr. 44	1943	969	2912	1 May 45	621	1701	2322
1 May 44	1945	969	2914	1 Jun. 45	609	1693	2302
1 Jun. 44	1938	961	2899	1 Jul. 45	284	1613	1897
1 Jul. 44	788	940	1728	1 Aug. 45	309	1540	1849
1 Aug. 44	607	945	1552	1 Sep. 45	309	1534	1843

On 2 October 1945 (date of writing), there were 323 prisoners of war in the Concordia Compounds, 17 Officers and 306 Enlisted Men [EM].

Appendix C
Morale Factors

From *The History of Camp Concordia from Site Survey to Deactivation*, edited by Captain Karl C. Teufel (Washington, D.C.: National Archives, Record Group 389, unpubl., 1945), chapt. 2, sect. E, parts 1 and 2:

Morale Factors
Part 1: American

The morale of the soldiers on any military post will determine in almost exact proportion the efficiency of that Post, providing, of course, that a capable Commanding Officer is in charge. Perfectly appointed posts can be operated poorly because morale is poor; or, a side camp, possessed of a minimum of creature comforts, can operate amazingly well because efforts of a serious sort have been taken to build up morale. At Concordia, the spirit of the soldiers has been extraordinarily good, and this is despite the fact that a goodly proportion of the Post personnel have had to perform guard duty at a prisoner-of-war camp, a deadly monotonous and yet responsible activity. How good morale has been here is indicated by the fact that no soldier has been absent without leave [AWOL] here for more than twenty months, a most exceptional record.

On 20 February 1945, we received a letter from the Headquarters of the Seventh Service Command, commenting on the fact that our AWOL rate had been persistently below the Service Command average for many months, and requesting that we explain our procedure in combatting low morale. In the first indorsement to that letter, the factors entering into our excellent experience here were detailed, basically as follows:

Furlough and Pass Policy: This Post has done its best to prevent the cancellation of passes and leaves because of such difficulties as personnel shortages and temporary emergencies. Since such cancellation is the prerogative of the Officers in authority, it is not infrequent at other posts to have all enlisted personnel restricted to duty in order to play completely safe. Although passes and furloughs have occasionally been very sparingly issued, no blanket restriction has ever been employed. Men work harder, longer, and more willingly when they are assured that this foundational privilege is being sympathetically and fairly handled.

Special Services: This program is extension at Concordia. Prior to October 1994, the Special Services assignment was an additional duty, but since that time has occupied the total time of one Officer. While not all facilities of the national set-up are feasible here, every one which is appropriate has been developed to the fullest. This has proceeded through the closest possible association between this Officer and his charges, and the program here was built on the expression of the wishes of the enlisted men. . . .

Non-Commissioned Officers' [NCO] Club: In as much as the city of Concordia is a small town of less than 6,000 population, it does not offer a great deal in the line of entertainment for the Camp's personnel. In order to compensate for this fact, the commanding Officer permitted the inauguration of a Non-Commissioned Officers' Club here, and proceeded considerable beyond the normal organization of this type by authorizing associate-member status for the enlisted men below NCO standing. The Club has its own Board of Governors, while an Officer serves it as liaison with the Commanding Officer. A fine program of varied social events have marked its career, while its facilities have made it a frequent gathering place for a good time for men who otherwise would have little of interest to do with their leisure.

The Chaplain at Concordia has served most effectively. The enlisted men gave him a large measure of their confidence, and received in return wise counsel and advice. Undoubtedly, the Chaplain, through devoted human understanding and the appeal of religious reason, did much to block AWOL intentions and other acts which would have reflected on the military reputation of the Post.

Last, but probably most important for high morale, has been the existing Post regulation that married enlisted men of all grades, if their behavior merited it, were permitted to ration separately. Particularly in the cases of enlisted men who were formerly overseas, or who are on limited service, this privilege has done a great deal, through the stabilizing influences of family, to create the right attitude toward the work to be done here. In all cases where enlisted men have been permitted to ration separately, the psychological effect has resulted in the production of a better soldier of the type needed here. . . .

Morale Factors
Part 2: German

. . . In this section, we are not concerned with schooling or cosmic phenomena — only with those interior facilities and arrangements which defied *barbed-wire-itis* and made Camp Concordia as bearable as prisoner-of-war camps are ever likely to be. Relatively speaking, morale from the beginning, to establish ways and means of amusing themselves as well as to train themselves academically for the future.

Within a very short time after their arrival, the prisoners had constructed a simple open-air stage, from which all types of entertainments were given. It was possible to replace this stage with one of more permanent and desirable construction in early 1944 through the arrival of $10,126.00, of which $800.00 came from the Vatican, and the balance was a gift of the German government. This fund also accomplished many other essential entertainment purposes. Later on, after dividends were paid from the profits of the canteens (Feb. 1945), it was possible to spend a sum equivalent to one dollar ($1.00) per capita each month for such activities from the Prisoner-of-War Fund thus established. In addition, on another occasion, due to financial difficulties caused by the large decrease in canteen profits, a grant of $1,282.00 was received from the Central Prisoner of War Fund.

. . . The most important expenditure was for club-rooms and gardens. Every Company took pride in building a "Casino" (a miniature Officers' Club), and these buildings became the center of social life in the compounds. The Casinos gave the Officers opportunity to entertain their friends outside their cramped living quarters. They were the arenas for Bridge, Skat, and Chess tournaments. Birthdays and military "reunions" were celebrated in them, and at all times they enabled the prisoners to assemble under an atmosphere where it was possible to forget the dreariness of their positions. Although built entirely out of scrap and salvage materials, the workmanship was excellent, art work, sculpturing and carvings plentiful, and even the unupholstered chairs were cunningly designed to give a maximum of comfort. Under the circumstances, the beauty and utility of the Casinos constituted a decided achievement.

A great deal of effort also was put into beautifying the camp grounds. Both the American commandant and the Senior German Spokesman cooperated in securing the planting of trees, shrubbery, flower beds and grass. Each barracks was thus landscaped, and in addition, most of the prisoners kept what they called "little defeat gardens" in which tomatoes and other vegetables were raised for between-meal snacks and to supplement and vary regular rations. Through these efforts, the Camp was as externally beautiful as the rather drab "temporary-construction" barracks would permit.

A constantly increasing number of dogs and cats become pets of the internees. They finally became so numerous that it was necessary to call a halt. Pigeons, snakes, turtles and other species too numerous to mention became endeared to their owners. Probably the prize pet of all was a hive of bees which had swarmed on the athletic field and been captured by one of the prisoners who was an experienced bee-man. These were installed in a specially-constructed hive with lots of glass which permitted their private lives to be studied.

The theater was one of the main morale-building installations during the colder months, when it was possible for crowds to assemble in the barrack-like building without benefit of artificial ventilating devices. Classical dramas and comedies were performed, recitals and concerts given, while vaudeville and magic performances rounded out a versatile program.

A great deal of time was devoted to music in the Camp. Symphony orchestras gave concerts and numerous smaller circles of musically inclined friends practiced on chamber music. The influence of American films and radio resulted in the formation of a dance band on the American model. A choir was also organized to cultivate appreciation of German folk-songs. Recorded music, usually of a classical variety, was played several times each week in the theater, and a great deal more for individuals and small groups. Much time was also consumed in listening to the music on the radios, as well as to the news broadcasts and other programs.

The fine arts were extensively practiced in the Camp. More than forty art students busied themselves with the Kansas landscape or other suitable subjects. Classes in water-color painting, modelling and drawing were part of the university's curriculum. The artists were frequently permitted to take walks into the surrounding country-side after giving their paroles and when accompanied by an American. The Casinos and private quarters were profusely decorated with these objets d'art, and did much to make them cozy and liveable. On the departure of most of the Officers from the Camp, the majority of these pictures were dispatched to the International Red Cross in Geneva, Switzerland, for safekeeping.

The Camp was very well equipped with athletic facilities, both in grounds and paraphernalia. Soccer fields, fistball courts, tennis courts and a quartermile track were the scenes of many a contest, both organized and unorganized. The prisoners who did not indulge in the more strenuous forms of exercise took walks, and occasionally, a large group of them, on parole, and accompanied by an American guard, took hikes beyond the Camp, a practice which had to be discontinued in the late Spring of 1945.

Appendix D
The Station Hospital

From *The History of Camp Concordia from Site Survey to Deactivation*, edited by Captain Karl C. Teufel (Washington, D.C.:National Archives, Record Group 389, unpubl., 1945), chapt. 6, sect. D:

Station Hospital

Early History: Station Hospital [Service Unit] SU 4750, Prisoner of War Camp, Concordia, Kansas, was officially opened on 1 August 1943, when twenty-six (26) German prisoner-of-war transferees arrived from Halloran General Hospital. Major Carl L. Mangiameli, [Medical Corps] MC, was the first Post Surgeon and Hospital Commander. However, a great deal of ground-work had been accomplished prior to the official opening. Major Mangiameli (then a Captain) arrived with fifteen (15) enlisted men from Fort Leonard Wood, Missouri, on 12 May 1943, and was confronted with empty buildings, unfinished floors, incomplete plumbing and complete lack of equipment. A short time later, he was joined by additional "medics" from Fort Snelling, Minnesota, and Camp Carson, Colorado.

Between 12 May and the activation date, life at Concordia was somewhat rugged for the new detachment. Service walks and roads had not yet been completed, and due to the exceptionally inclement weather at that time, there was constant danger of miring down when outside. No recreational facilities had yet been set up, and to pile unaccustomed jobs on top of acts of God and dearth of entertainment, the enlisted men found themselves occupied at odd jobs in behalf of the Quartermaster and the Post Engineer, and even descended, after the first week, to doing Kitchen Police [KP] for the entire Post. They were spared this latter duty the first week inasmuch as no messhalls had yet been activated, and all meals were being obtained in Concordia. To round out the versatility of their labors, they even endured guard duty and fire details. About the middle of July, they began shifting equipment and supplies into the Hospital, and otherwise prepared for the opening day, which arrived and passed without fanfare. In the interim, all medical service on the Post was rendered in Dispensary Building No. T-57. At the time of activation, twenty-six enlisted men and 2nd Lt. George J. Rohn, Commanding Officer, composed Medical Detachment SU 4750. By the end of August, the Detachment had reached its maximum strength, never again attained, of thirty (30) enlisted men.

The Hospital's Facilities: From the beginning, the Hospital was well equipped with both medical facilities and the number of its services. A large administration building housed a Registrar's Office, a Sergeant-Major's Office, the Medical Adjutant, Post Surgeon, a Medical Library (doubling as a sort of Day Room), and the Out-Patient Clinic in its West Wing. The East Wing, which was completely air-conditioned, contained the Pharmacy, the X-Ray Service, and the Operating Rooms. The Pharmacy was well supplied with drugs and chemicals, and was under the control of the Pharmacy Officer, assisted by an American Sergeant and a German enlisted man, both with previous pharmaceutical training. The X-Ray Service was housed in two rooms, the one containing a radiographic and fluoroscopic machine, a portable X-Ray machine and two shadow boxes, while the other, the dark room, contained a developing and fixing tank, a field dryer and a shadow box. Chief of X-Ray was an American Medical Officer, assisted by an American Noncom Chief Technician and a German enlisted man.

At the far end of the East Wing were the Operating Rooms, one for major surgery and one for minor. A scrub room and an office separated the two, while adjacent to them was the sterilizing room and store rooms. These rooms ware exceptionally well equipped. The Chief of Surgical Service was an American Medical Officer, assisted by a civilian Surgical Nurse, and two German enlisted men who had formerly been surgical technicians of the *Wehrmacht*.

The main corridor of the Hospital runs directly south from the Administration Building. Branching out to the West of the corridor is Building T-501 which houses the Laboratory, the E.E.N.T. Clinic, Physiotherapy and the Dispensary. The Laboratory is under the charge of a Laboratory Officer, assisted by an experienced American Sergeant, a German Officer pharmacist, and a German enlisted men, and is fully equipped to perform routine blood, urine, serology, water, and milk tests. More elaborate laboratory work is sent to the Service command Laboratory in Omaha. The E.E.N.T. Clinic is controlled by an American Medical Officer, assisted by a German Officer Optometrist. Physiotherapy contains a massage table, two infra-red lamps, an ultra-violet lamp, a Baker Light lamp, and is operated by two trained German enlisted men masseurs, under the direction of an American Officer. An American Medical Officer also has charge of the Dispensary which is housed in this Building likewise, and it is here that sick call is held for American personnel. An American Sergeant assists at sick call and keeps the records. (Prior to 28 June 1945, this facility was outside in Building T-57.)

On the opposite end of this east-west corridor is the East Wing which contains the air-conditioned Dental Clinic. It is supervised by an American Dental Officer, who directs two German dentists and a German dental technician. The Clinic has six chairs and a dental X-Ray machine, as well as dark rooms for development work.

The main north-south corridor is bisected south of the above installations by another and much longer east-west corridor, which leads to three wards to the east and three to the west. Wards B-1, B-2, and B-3 contain ten (10) private rooms, a large ward room, a kitchen, two latrines, a utility room, two (2) store rooms, a medical officer's office and a nurse's office. Wards B-4, B-5, and B-6 are practically identical except that they have but one private room each, and the ward room is substantially larger therefore. The first three have a capacity of 27 beds, and the last three, 332 beds. Total bed capacity is 177. All kitchens are equipped with an electric stove, a refrigerator, a hotwater dish-washer, eating utensils and a food cart, but most of the meals are prepared in the central kitchen and transported to the wards by food cart. However, special diets and midnight meals for personnel on duty are prepared in the ward kitchen, as are between-meal liquids for the patients. Each ward is under the jurisdiction of an American Medical Officer (although only one is in operation at the moment of writing), and he has been customarily assisted by a civilian nurse, an American wardman and a German wardman. An Army nurse supervises the ward nurses in the capacity of Chief Nurse. (In July 1945, all civilian nurses were discharged, and their work taken over by an additional Army Nurse.)

The wards, as originally intended, handle the following cases:

Ward B-1 is a locked ward for mental and guardhouse cases. Its private rooms are especially constructed, having no open pipes, and being equipped with screened windows and radiators, and with a heavy "peep-hole" door.

Ward B-2 was a German Officers' ward. It was closed in July 1945.

Ward B-3, which is air-conditioned, was originally intended for American personnel, but after July 1945 served all the Hospital's patients. Americans are treated in the private rooms and the prisoners-of-war in the ward room.

Ward B-4 was originally for enlisted man prisoners-of-war. It has been closed since June 1945.

Ward B-5 was used for the overflow cases and respiratory diseases.

Ward B-6 was never used.

Along the main-south corridor, south of the wards, another corridor lends off to the west. Two buildings, lying to the south of it, are reached by this walkway. The first houses a very attractive dining room, behind which is an exceptionally well-appointed kitchen. The establishment is under a Mess Officer, assisted by two (2) American enlisted men, who in turn exercise direct control over eight (8) German cooks, bakers and general kitchen personnel. A mess office, a shower and a locker room adjoin the kitchen.

At the extreme end of the north-south corridor is the Medical Supply Building. In addition to supplies, it also is concerned with the Hospital records. The Medical Supply Officer is assisted by a Supply Sergeant, a Private First Class, and two (2) German enlisted men serving as a clerk and a utility man respectively.

The Hospital grounds are very attractive. They are kept meticulously neat by a crew of German enlisted men. Flower gardens are numerous, and to the east of the surgical wing of Building T-500 is a vegetable garden which provides a large proportion of the messhall's vegetables in Summer.

There are also four external buildings under Hospital jurisdiction. Each of the prisoner-of-war compounds (two for Officers and one for Enlisted Men) is equipped with a Dispensary under the charge of German medical officers and enlisted men. The fourth is Building T-57, originally used for sick call, but now serving solely as a prophylaxis station.

Hospital Personnel: Turn-over in the Hospital's Officer personnel has been rather large. In its little more than two years of history, thirty Officers, including Nurses, have served here. Six of them were Post Surgeons and Hospital Commanders, serving as follows:

Major Carl L. Mangiameli, MC
    1 Aug. 1943 - 14 July 1944
Capt. Albert J. Entringer, MC
    15 July 1944 - 30 November 1944
Capt. William W. Abrams, MC
    1 December 1944 - 3 December 1944
Major Melvin C. Martin, MC
    4 December 1944 - 18 June 1945
Capt. Joseph H. Baker, MC
    19 June 1945 - 27 July 1945
Capt. Jules L. Karpas, MC
    28 July 1945

. . . The Hospital's Officer personnel, . . . [are] as follows, exclusive of the above:

Capt. William M. O'Connell, MC
1st Lt. Wilburn E. Wright, MC
2nd Lt. George J. Rohn, MAC
Capt. Max Simons, MC
Capt. Robert R. Bates, MC
1st Lt. James W. Chambers, MC
1st Lt. Clarence F. Schmitt, MC
Capt. Melton H. Patrick, MAC
1st Lt. Winifred W. Cleveland, ANC
Major Elmer I. Long, VC
1st Lt. Elliott R. Fishel, SnC

2nd Lt. Bertha L. Johnson, ANC
Capt. Harold C. Rininger, MC
2nd Lt. Clarence P. Hansen, MAC
1st Lt. Bernice A. Pollock, ANC
Capt. Curtis S. McCallister, DC
2nd Lt. Angus M. Shipley, MAC
Capt. Lada J. Turek, DC
1st Lt. Frank D. Gomez, VC
1st Lt. Joseph S. Mehlman, MC
1st Lt. Russell J. Paalman, MC
Capt. Edmund B. McCormick, VC
1st Lt. Helen L. Leiser, ANC
1st Lt. Henry E. Culbertson, MAC

Capt. Benjamin F. Markowitz, MC, was on Temporary Duty here from Fort Riley for 30 days starting 15 November 1944, while Capt. Eugene Van Epps, MC, spent ten days here in a like capacity beginning on 10 September 1945.

As described in the account of Hospital facilities, German personnel has been extensively used here, and have proven very efficient. Outstanding among them are Capt. Johannes Hass and Capt. Hans Schreiber, both Medical Officers of the German Army.

Branch Camp Facilities: From September 1943 until August 1944, Concordia operated side camps in Kansas, Nebraska and Minnesota. Peabody, Kansas, had an American enlisted man technician assigned as a medical aid man, while sick call and emergency were handled by a contract surgeon from the town. The situation at Hayes [*sic*], Kansas, was identical. Hebron, Nebraska, had no medical aid man, and being only forty (40) miles from the base camp, came here for treatment when necessary. Bena, Remer, Deer River and Owatonna (Minnesota) Camps were equipped with seven-bed hospitals, medicines and surgical instruments, and were operated by a German Medical Officer and two German enlisted men. Major cases were handled by contract surgeons and hospitalization. The Bena Camp used a government hospital originally set up for the Indians. Cases requiring extended hospitalization were sent to Fort

Shelling, Minnesota. The Minnesota Camps, excepting Owatonna were also equipped with ambulances.

Sanitary Services: The Medical Inspector and the Post Sanitary Officer have been also responsible for the command when outside the Hospital Area. Inspections have been made regularly of Concordia's eating establishments which, as a whole, do not meet Army standards. Post eating installations are also inspected periodically, and have always been excellently maintained and fully up to the dietary requirements.

Problems: There have been no serious medical problems at Camp Concordia. Insects and rodents are present, particularly the former, and considerable difficulty has been experienced in eradicating roaches. Methods employed are fumigation and DDT-spraying performed by the Post Engineer, but have not been completely successful. Rodents are easily controlled by the use of Red Squill offered in meat patties. Fly traps are in use at each of the Post's messhalls, and in addition, DDT-Saturated linen strips have been hung in all eating places, and in some other buildings as well.

The Medical Detachment: The first Detachment Commanding Officer, Lt. Rohn, was relieved by 2nd Lt. Angus M. Shipley on 9 July 1944, and the latter was, in turn, relieved by Captain Melton H. Patrick. 1st Lt. Elliott R. Fishel succeeded Capt. Patrick on 12 September 1945. The Detachment's history is in no wise extraordinary. However, it has been marked by an exceptional esprit-de-corps, and this has been fostered by frequent social events in which all Hospital personnel have participated heartily.

A Detachment of Patients, activated on 28 July 1944, originally contained five Americans and thirty-one prisoners-of-war. Its strength peak was reached in October of that year with eight Americans and eighty-eight prisoners. It was deactivated on 13 January 1945.

Summary: The Hospital has always functioned well. The two nationalities serving it have proceeded very harmoniously, and all service has been performed in the full spirit of medical ethics. Its routine has been effective and the health of all concerned has been duly safe-guarded.

Appendix E
Enlisted Men Detachments

From *The History of Camp Concordia from Site Survey to Deactivation*, edited by Captain Karl C. Teufel (Washington, D.C.: National Archives, Record Group 389, unpubl., 1945), chapt. 4, sect. F:

Enlisted Men Detachments

1. The Concordia Internment Camp Serv C Unit No.4750, was activated 1 May 1943, per General Order [G.O.] #35, Hq. [Headquarters] 7th SvC. [Service Command], dated 1 May 1943. By virtue of General Order #6, this Hq., dated 23 July 1943, the Unit was redesignated as Serv C Unit #4750, Prisoner of War Camp, Concordia, Kansas.

2. Det. Med. Dept., Prisoner of War Camp, SCU #4750, Concordia, Kansas was activated as of 1 August 1943, per Sect., 1, G. O. #8, this Hq., dated the same date. 2nd Lt. George J. Rohn was named Commanding Officer.

3. Hq. Det., Prisoner of War Camp, SCU 4750, Concordia, Kansas was activated on 1 May 1943, per Sect. II, G. O. #8, this Hq., same date. 2nd Lt. Wilkie B. Dye was Commanding Officer [CO].

4. The 456th MPEG Co., arrived at this Station on 3 July 1943 from Ft. Custer, Mich., with 132 enlisted men and 3 officers, 1st Lt. David Roberts, Commanding Officer, and 2nd Lts. Herbert J. Ellis and Joseph A. Siegel, Company Officers.

5. The 457th MPEG Co. arrived at this Station on 3 July 1943 from Ft. Custer, Mich., with 129 enlisted men and 3 officers, 2nd Lt. Philip E. Sitzman, Commanding Officer, and 2nd Lts. Oke E. Carlson and Sol Zaretzki, Company Officers.

6. The 480th MPEG Co. arrived at this Station on 12 August 1943 from Ft. Custer, Mich., with 134 enlisted men and 3 officers, 1st Lt. Marty Ball, Commanding Officer, and 2nd Lts. Eqald S. Schoeller and Neal A. Broyles, Company Officers.

7. The 592nd MPEG Co. arrived at this Station in November 1943 from Ft. Custer Mich., with 134 enlisted men and 3 officers, 1st Lt. Harry G. Bracken, Commanding, and 2nd Lts. Clem J. Denicke and Leo O. Yeoman, Company Officers.

8. The 642nd MPEG Co. arrived at this Station on 11 February 1944 from Ft. Custer, Mich., with 126 men and 3 officers, 1st Lt. Sam C. Hutchinson, Commanding, and 2nd Lts. Joseph McGovern and John F. Nuss, Company Officers.

9. The 361st MPEG Co. arrived at this Station from Scotts Bluff, Nebraska, on 29 Mar 1944 with 135 enlisted men and 3 officers, Capt. Melvin C. Hooper, Commanding, and 1st Lt. Oscar T. Cook, Jr. and 2nd Lt. Sigmund H. Sigler, Commanding Officers.

10. The 456th MPEG Co. was transferred from this Station to Provost Marshal General Unit, Training Center, Ft. Custer, Mich., on 29 January 1944, with 135 enlisted men and 2 officers, 2nd Lt. Arnold Campbell, Commanding, and 2nd Lt. Joseph A. Siegel, Company Officer.

11. All MPEG Companies were deactivated on 15 April 1944, and SCU 4750 Guard Detachment was activated per G. O. #27, this Hq. The approximate strength of the MPEG Companies on deactivation averaged 129 enlisted men and 3 Officers. Strength of the Guard Detachment as of 15 April 1944 was 644 enlisted men and 17 Officers.

12. The 4750 SCU Gd. Det., PW Cp., Concordia, Kansas and the 4750 SCU, Hq. Det., PW Cp, Concordia, Kansas, were discontinued on 7 August 1945 per G.O. #34, this Hq., dated 2 August 1945.

13. The 4750 SCU PW Cp., Service Detachment was organized 7 August 1945 per G. O. #34, this Hq., dated 2 August 1945, with a strength of 152 enlisted men and 2 officers, Capt. Eqaldd S. Schoeller, Commanding Officer, and 2nd Lt. Patrick W. Mowry, Company Officer.

At this date of the discontinuance of the Guard Detachment, the strength was 106 enlisted men and two officers. Strength of Headquarters Detachment at that time was 46 enlisted men and one Officer (1st Lt. Walter W. Friend, Jr., Commanding Officer).

Appendix F
POW Roster, 1943

The following 1943 POW roster is compiled from the National Archives, Washington, D.C., from WD AGO Form R-5179, 2 October 1945.

POW Camp
Concordia, Kansas

Full Name Last, First, Middle	Internment Serial No.	Date of Birth mo/day/yr	Rank/ Grade	Organi- zation	Reg. Bn.	Co.	Date of Capture mo/day/yr	Affiliation with SS, SD, SA, or other secret police organizations
47th Grenadier Regt.								
Knejski, Horst	120578	9/11/20	Sgt	Gr. 47	—	—	5/8/43	—
Goetze, Herbert	120579	3/23/21	Sgt	Gr. 47	—	—	5/8/43	—
Hillermann, Gerhard	120587	1/1/13	Sgt	Gr. 47	—	—	5/8/43	SA
Hoffmann, Willi	120567	11/2/14	Sgt	Gr. 47	—	—	5/8/43	—
Huebl, Rudolf	120576	3/20/20	Sgt	Gr. 47	—	—	5/8/43	—
Kanzenbach, Ernst	143036	2/28/12	Sgt	Gr. 47	—	—	5/8/43	—
Machleb, Reinhold	184516	9/30/20	Cpl	Gr. 47	—	—	5/11/43	—
Albert, Heinz	143057	10/22/17	Sgt	Gr. 47	—	—	5/8/43	SA
Bade, Hans	120582	11/24/14	Sgt	Gr. 47	—	—	5/8/43	—
Bergstede, Otto	120826	10/26/13	Sgt	Gr. 47	—	—	5/7/43	—
Bostelmann, Hermann	120564	11/8/17	Sgt	Gr. 47	—	—	8/11/43	—
Brandt, Adolf	120570	6/1/14	Sgt	Gr. 47	—	—	5/8/43?	—
Feuerstacke, Kurt	120572	11/3/11	Sgt	Gr. 47	—	—	5/8/43?	—
334th Division								
Rube, Adolf	7WG 12672	1/14/11	Cpl	334	4	—	5/9/43	—
Osterbauer, Hans	7WG 16370	11/8/05	1st Lt	Mot Trop	—	—	5/26/43	—
Renz, Werner	7WG 16384	1/12/13	2nd Lt	756 Pan Jaeger	—	—	5/10/43	—
Bierwagen, Erich	7WG 15178	7/26/08	Pfc	754	—	14	5/9/43	—
Edlbauer, Ernst	7WG 15167	5/4/23	Pfc	754	—	—	5/9/43	—
Kassner, Max	7WG 14267	11/4/10	Pfc	PI	334	—	5/9/43	SA
Klupatschek, Josef Sepp	7WG 13407	11/20/13	Pfc	756	Geb Jag	—	5/9/43	—
Knoblach, Fridolin	7WG 14988	3/9/13	Pfc	754 Inf	—	—	5/9/43	—
Koschin, Erich von	7WG 15309	1/28/23	Pfc	756 Albine Troop	—	—	5/9/43	—
Kruechten, Franz	7WG 14883	9/20/13	Sgt	754 Inf	—	—	5/9/43	—
Messner, Leo	7WG 12838	5/19/11	Pfc	—	—	—	5/9/43	—
Muehlinger, Josef	7WG 15285	11/12/23	Pfc	756	0	—	5/9/43	—
Muehlmann, Peter	7WG 13778	11/4/23	Pfc	334	I/Pi	—	5/9/43	—
Mueller, Franz	7WG 12837	11/28/22	Pfc	334	I. Nachr	—	5/9/43	—
Muser, Karl	7WG 15168	11/20/08	Pvt	754	—	—	5/9/43	—
Nowak, Ludwig	7WG 12963	6/13/13	Pfc	334	Schw Art Mot	—	5/9/43	—
Pallesche, Willi	7WG 12989	9/25/08	Cpl	334	—	—	5/9/43	—
Papst, Gottfried	7WG 15079	10/4/14	Cpl	334	—	—	5/5/43	—

Full Name Last, First, Middle	Internment Serial No.	Date of Birth mo/day/yr	Rank/ Grade	Organi- zation	Reg. Bn.	Co.	Date of Capture mo/day/yr	Affiliation with SS, SD, SA, or other secret police organizations
Pawletta, Leonhard	81G 40011 PP	9/15/11	Sgt	St. KP	—	—	5/9/43	—
Rothschedl, Franz	7WG 12734	9/24/23	Pfc	Gebrgs	0	—	5/9/43	—
Rueger, Paul	7WG 12760	10/2/14	F/Sgt	754	—	Schuetzen	5/9/43	—
Spachmueller, Christian	7WG 15359	10/11/06	Sgt	754	—	14	5/9/43	—
Slopianka, Werner	7WG 12700	7/12/21	Pfc	Nach Abt	—	—	5/9/43	—
Siedermann, August	7WG 14884	4/17/11	Sgt	754	—	Stabs	5/9/43	—
Schwarz, Anton	7WG 16969	2/2/02	Sgt	Nachsh	—	Schlaeht	5/9/43	—
Schneider, Gottfried	7WG 16962	6/7/06	Sgt	Mot 334	—	—	5/9/43	—
Schmitz, Willi	7WG 50989	10/21/19	Cpl	754	—	7	5/12/43	—
Sillmann, Werner	7WG 15006	8/5/20	Pvt	754	—	Stabs	5/9/43	—
Wiesen, Albert	7WG 13250	2/3/22	5/10/43[sic] Palansladt	—	—	5/10/43	—
Wallach, Viktor	7WG 13326	10/16/22	Pfc	754	—	—	5/8/43	—

164th Division

Full Name Last, First, Middle	Internment Serial No.	Date of Birth mo/day/yr	Rank/ Grade	Organi- zation	Reg. Bn.	Co.	Date of Capture mo/day/yr	Affiliation with SS, SD, SA, or other secret police organizations
Bemuth, Wilhelm	7WG 16761	7/1/19	1st Lt			1/220	5/6/43	—
Dobeneck, Henning von	7WG 16556	4/9/12	2nd Lt	Staff			5/13/43	SS
Hunstorfer, Hans	7WG 14131	6/11/22	Cpl	125th		7th	5/13/43	SA
Kloth, Gerhard	7WG 14127	6/28/21	Pfc	433th		7th	5/13/43	—
Koehler, Horst	7WG 14034	4/20/21	Cpl	125th			5/13/43	—
Kromer, Walter	7WG 14106	11/12/18	Cpl	433th			5/13/43	—
Lorenz, Siegfried	7WG 16343	10/29/11	2nd Lt				5/11/43	SA
Neumann, Paul	7WG 14419	4/28/10	Pfc	125th			5/13/43	—
Roeschel, Franz	7WG 12725	10/22/10	Cpl			1/220	5/11/43	—
Romankowitz, Rudolf	7WG 14326	12/30/18	Pfc	125th			5/13/43	—
Schlareta, Ottokar	7WG 14274	5/15/23	Pfc	125th			5/13/43	—
Schmeir, Erich	7WG 22243	10/24/19	Cpl				5/12/43	SA
Steinert, Arno	7WG 14094	10/19/09	Cpl	125th		7th	5/13/43	—
Thaler, Hans	7WG 14181	12/2/17?	Pfc	433th		7th	5/13/43	—
Wenger, Fritz	7WG 50990	1/18/27	Cpl	125th			5/13/43	—
Wuensch, Kamill	7WG 15481	10/20/14	Sgt			1/220	5/11/43	—
Zilger, Hans	7WG 14087	8/19/09	Pfc	433th		8th	5/11/43	—

15th Panzer Division

Full Name Last, First, Middle	Internment Serial No.	Date of Birth mo/day/yr	Rank/ Grade	Organi- zation	Reg. Bn.	Co.	Date of Capture mo/day/yr	Affiliation with SS, SD, SA, or other secret police organizations
Boehmler, Paul	7WG 15813	2/13/23	Pvt	8	—	—	5/11/43	—
Fladt, Wolfgang	7WG 14894	9/16/19	I/Sgt	8	—	—	5/9/43	—
Ihrig, Anton	81G 25943	5/6/20	Cpl	—	—	—	5/9/43	—
Karstens, Heinrich	7WG 33974	2/22/11	Pvt	—	33	—	5/7/43	—
Kreide, Guenter	7WG 15894	5/3/13	Pvt	78	—	—	5/23/43	—
Loeher, Erich	7WG 14732	1/16/22	Pvt	8	—	—	5/11/43	—
Mueller, Walter	7WG 14905?	6/1/17	Cpl	775	1	11	5/9/43	—
Rudolph, Theodor	7WG 13037	3/7/21	Pfc	33	—	33	11/5/43	SA
Wirtz, Willi	7WG 13728	9/4/11	Cpl	—	—	—	9/5/43	—
Steinbauer, Armin	7WG 16428	11/23/09	Major	115	2	—	5/13/43	—

19th Flak Division

Full Name Last, First, Middle	Internment Serial No.	Date of Birth mo/day/yr	Rank/ Grade	Organi- zation	Reg. Bn.	Co.	Date of Capture mo/day/yr	Affiliation with SS, SD, SA, or other secret police organizations
Degen, Hermann	7WG 13097	8/8/20	Sgt	135	—	—	5/9/43	—
Fuengeling, Hans-Gerd	7WG 15794	4/28/22	Pfc	—	9?	—	11/5/43	—
Hackspiel, Heribert	7WG 13304	5/11/20	Cpl	135	—	—	5/11/43	—
Hornung, Johannes	7WG 12666	10/17/16	M/Sgt	I/43	—	—	5/9/43	—
Jonas, Heinrich	7WG 13913	4/17/20	Cpl	135	—	—	5/13/43	—
Kamp, Guenther	7WG 13797	4/30/22	Pvt	102	4	—	5/13/43	—

Full Name Last, First, Middle	Internment Serial No.	Date of Birth mo/day/yr	Rank/ Grade	Organi- zation	Reg. Bn.	Co.	Date of Capture mo/day/yr	Affiliation with SS, SD, SA, or other secret police organizations
Kopycick, Georg	120769	3/17/20	Sgt	135	I/43	2	5/7/43	—
Leitenberger, Helmut	7WG 15616	6/1/21	Pfc	25	7	—	5/12/43	—
Pfaffinger, Franz	7WG 13165	10/10/19	Pvt	43	—	—	5/11/43	—
Rebholz, Toni	7WG 13734	2/23/20	Sgt	—	—	—	5/11/43	—
Roiko, Geza	7WG 13760	5/1/17	Pvt	—	Stab	—	5/13/43	—
Sanow, Kurt	7WG 13495	10/18/23	Cpl	102	—	—	5/11/43	—
Schaefer, Georg	7WG 15791	4/9/21	Cpl	354	2	—	5/10/43	SS
Wirtz, Hubert	7WG 13443	11/14/14	Cpl	102	—	—	5/11/43	—
Hausmann, Kurt	7WG 13216	1/23/22	Pfc	105	—	—	11/5/43	—

20th Flak Division

Full Name Last, First, Middle	Internment Serial No.	Date of Birth mo/day/yr	Rank/ Grade	Organi- zation	Reg. Bn.	Co.	Date of Capture mo/day/yr	Affiliation
Antons, Nikolaus	7WG 13214	5/30/22	Pfc	66	—	—	5/11/43	—
Beckers, Heinz	7WG 13607	6/15/17	M/Sgt	14	—	—	5/11/43	—
Birnkammer, Josef	7WG 15754	10/3/13	Sgt	2025	sbv	—	5/7/43	—
Burghoff, Gustav	7WG 14141	11/19/08	Cpl	78	503	—	5/9/43	—
Eschey, Nikolaus	7WG 12853	8/13/08	Pfc	—	—	—	5/9/43	—
Froebel, Erhardt	7WG 12796	6/1/19	Pvt	52 Mot	9 Flak	—	5/9/43	—
Hoffmann, Fritz	7WG 14898	6/9/06	Sgt	—	—	—	5/9/43	—
Hohmann, Hermann	7WG 15160	9/8/06	Cpl	Unbekannt	—	—	5/9/43	—
Iwanow, Fritz	7WG 14929	6/22/23	Pvt	—	—	—	5/9/43	—
Kopp, Johann	7WG 15017	12/16/12	Pfc	I I 54	—	—	5/9/43	—
Luetkehoelter, August	7WG 15231	4/17/06	Cpl	9 Flak	—	—	5/9/43	—
Nicolai, Hans	7WG 15900	7/10/13	Sgt	644 ABt	—	—	5/11/43	—
Oehring, Karl	7WG 15179	2/9/01	Cpl	Nicht Mehr bekannt		—	5/9/43	—
Paris, Heinrich von	7WG 15373	11/13/10	Sgt	503	—	—	5/9/43	—
Penner, Arno	7WG 15380	12/8/04	Sgt	—	—	—	5/8/43	—
Pothmann, Bernhard	7WG 14912	11/1/07	Sgt	—	—	—	5/10/43	—
Richtsenhain, Bernhard	7WG 14880	12/4/13	Sgt	—	—	—	5/9/43	—
Soboll, Alfred	7WG 12847	2/25/17	Cpl	10.1 Flak.	52 Mot	—	5/9/43	—
Schmitt, Wolfgang	7WG 13124	2/8/14	F/Sgt	Unbekannt	—	—	5/9/43	—
Willing, Adalbert	7WG 13175	1/18/13	Sgt	54	—	—	5/13/43	—
Thimm, Wolfgang	7WG 12686	6/4/22	Cpl	52	—	—	5/9/43	—
Walker, Franz	7WG 15229	5/13/12	Cpl	66	—	—	5/9/43	—

21st Panzer Division

Full Name Last, First, Middle	Internment Serial No.	Date of Birth mo/day/yr	Rank/ Grade	Organi- zation	Reg. Bn.	Co.	Date of Capture mo/day/yr	Affiliation
Dudziak, Rudolf	7WG 12861	1/8/14	Sgt	—	220	—	5/12/43	—
Freytag, Martin	7WG 15899	5/1/11	Sgt	5	—	—	5/11/43	—
Gerhards, Heinrich	7WG 15329	7/25/08	Pfc	—	—	I/200	5/11/43	—
Juckel, Kurt	7WG 13376	6/4/24	Pfc	5	—	—	5/11/43	—
Katzler, Bogislav von	7WG 16626	10/26/16	1st Lt	—	—	—	5/11/43	—
Klein, Guenter	7WG 13840	8/26/23	Pfc	5	—	—	5/9/43	—
Krusch, Fritz	7WG 15422	10/2/22	Pfc	3	—	—	5/11/43	—
Pallutz, Kurt	7WG 13220	3/31/22	Pfc	200	—	—	5/11/43	—
Pfeiffer, Paul	7WG 15782	2/7/22	Pfc	—	—	—	5/13/43	—
Reimann, Werner	7WG 14635	12/21/22	Cpl	104	—	—	5/11/43	—
Riegel, Hermann	7WG 15445	7/22/18	Cpl	104	—	7	5/12/43	SA
Sander, Ottfried	7WG 15456	1/31/19	F/Sgt	—	200?	—	5/12/43	—
Schubert, Werner	7WG 15448	3/6/20	Cpl	—	—	—	5/12/43	—
Sebastian, Herbert	MBS-40032 PP	5/20/09	Pvt	I/220	—	—	5/10/43	—
Spiegelhauer, Ernst	7WG 12877	2/10/20	Pfc	220	—	—	5/12/43	—
Troesch, Reinhard	7WG 13242	12/27/21	Pfc	200	—	—	5/11/43	—

Full Name Last, First, Middle	Internment Serial No.	Date of Birth mo/day/yr	Rank/ Grade	Organi- zation	Reg. Bn.	Co.	Date of Capture mo/day/yr	Affiliation with SS, SD, SA, or other secret police organizations
10th Panzer Division								
Baisch, Eugen	7WG 13366	1/6/09	M/Sgt	7th			5/11/43	
Bast, Walter	7WG 15500	1/22/09	Pfc			1/90	5/13/43	
Brandt, Alfred	7WG 13983	7/3/07	Cpl			1/90	5/11/43	
Dienstdorf, Johannes	7WG 13993	6/28/11	Cpl				5/12/43	
Eckerlish, Nikolaus	7WG 15499	4/30/10	Cpl			1/90	5/13/43	
Fenchel, Karl	7WG 15507	7/31/09	Cpl			1/90	5/13/43	SA
Gahlen, Helmuth	7WG 15527	11/13/10	Cpl			1/90	5/13/43	
Goedde, Edmund	7WG 15525	2/26/12	Sgt			1/90	5/12/43	
Hansen, Carston [Kersten]	7WG 16293	8/15/14	1st Lt	90			5/10/43	SA
Hecht, Ernst	7WG 13600	8/19/16	Sgt	7th			5/11/43	
Herzig, Erhard	7WG 50990	9/1/12	Pfc				5/12/43	
Hochstein, Franz	7WG 15516	11/8/12	Cpl			1/90	5/12/43	
Juroitsch, Mattias	7WG 13232	3/10/20	Cpl	7th			5/11/43	
Kaiser, Ferdinand	7WG 13997	7/3/18	Cpl				5/9/43	SA
Knoche, Theodor	7WG 15504?	12/5/16	Cpl			1/90	5/13/43	
Kraller, Josef	7WG 13226	3/9/23	Pfc	7th			5/11/43	
Kuehn, Richard	7WG 13367	5/22/06	M/Sgt	7th			5/11/43	SA
Lambrecht, Albert	7WG 13994	11/24/13	Cpl	86th			5/13/43	
Mueller, Hans Georg	7WG 50987	6/23/17	Cpl				5/11/43	
Mueller, Heinz	7WG 13255	12/7/19	Cpl	7th			5/11/43	
Muellers, Hubert	7WG 13991	2/7/10	Cpl			1/90	5/13/43	
Otto, Johann	7WG 15412	4/28/12	Sgt			1/90	5/13/43	
10th Panzer Division								
Perndl, Hermann	7WG 13837	2/24/22	Cpl	7th			5/11/43	
Senn, Eckhard	7WG 14685	4/25/18	Cpl	69th			5/12/43	
Unschlag, Josef	7WG 15461	8/14/14	Cpl				5/12/43	
Weber, Gustav	7WG 50992	7/21/15	Sgt	7th			5/11/43	
Weisebredt, Ewald	7WG 15482	11/27/20	Cpl				5/13/43	
Woditschka, Rudolf	7WG 13244	10/22/20	Cpl	7th			5/11/43	
Zanitzer, Karl	7WG 13580	1/9/08	Cpl				5/9/43	
Miscellaneous								
Preussker, Alfred	7WG 14796	7/17/02	Pfc	686th			5/11/43	—
Sander, Eduard	31G 11712	10/12/02	Pvt				8/2/44	SA
Schwarz, Anton	31G 11628	6/24/05	Pvt	15th Flak	Division 13		8/4/44	—
Wende, Walter	31G 11647	12/14/09	Pvt	441th Flak	Division 23		8/4/44	—
Buchholz, Helmut	7WG 15526	8/28/21	Sgt		Division 18		5/12/43	—
Buchholz, Hans-Guenter	8WG 12490	1/15/19	Sgt		Division 16		5/9/43	—
Blohm, Werner	7WG 15511	5/28/19	Sgt				5/12/43	—
Greiner, Hermann Otto	7WG 16844	5/21/11	1st Lt				5/11/43	—
Diettrich, Walter	7WG 15892	7/15/07	F/Sgt				5/7/43	SA
Spengler, Walter Kurt	7WG 14628	4/7/21	Cpl	Luftgau 7			5/8/43	—
Kraus, Josef	7WG 14601	1/3/21	Cpl	Luftgau 7			5/8/43	—
Huebner, Walter	7WG 14629	7/27/22	Pfc	Luftgau 7			5/8/43	—
Kossiedowski, Franz	7WG 13872	8/17/21	Cpl	LN	Air Corps	13	5/17/43	—
Koch, Helmuth	7WG 13402	2/17/21	Sgt	LN	Air Corps		5/15/43	—
Koehn, Siegfried	7WG 13400	9/17/21	Cpl	LN	Air Corps		5/15/43	—
Liebermann, Martin	7WG 15888	1/1/16	M/Sgt	LN	Air Corps		5/11/43	—
Wassmann, Heinz	7WG 13730	6/26/07	Cpl	LN	Air Corps	2nd Div	5/13/43	—

Full Name Last, First, Middle	Internment Serial No.	Date of Birth mo/day/yr	Rank/ Grade	Organi- zation	Reg. Bn.	Co.	Date of Capture mo/day/yr	Affiliation with SS, SD, SA, or other secret police organizations
Kalb, Martin	7WG 13655	10/12/07	Cpl	LN	Air Corps		5/13/43	—
Wehr, Hans	7WG 13731	3/17/22	Cpl	62nd Luftnachrichten			5/13/43	—
Strunk, Friedrich	7WG 15551	1/12/06	Sgt				5/11/43	—
Schubert, Walter Arno	7WG 15809	11/15/19	Cpl		Air Corps		5/11/43	—
Niewelt, Walter	7WG 13157	3/20/23	Cpl	4th Luftgau			5/13/43	—
Dernbach, August	31G 9811	9/4/01	Pvt				8/7/44	—
Froh, Werner	7WG 12876	9/18/07	Pfc	Division Manteuffel			5/9/43	SS
Liebermann, Hans	MBS 197 Mi	10/31/23	Pvt				3/10/43	—
Fitter, Albert	7WG 13112	3/17/23	Sgt				5/9/43	—
Heja, Bruno	7WG 16612	7/16/10	S/Sgt	Division Manteuffel			5/9/43	—
Hummel, Anton	7WG 13253	5/10/17	Cpl				5/12/43	—
Schaper, August	7WG 12723	6/23/20	Cpl	Division Manteuffel			5/9/43	—
Wunsch, Fritz	7WG 16472	3/17/06	Pvt	4th Luftgau			5/13/43	—
Garske, Fosef	7WG 15136	8/21/02	Cpl	11th Luftgau			5/11/43	—
Fischer, Wolfgang	7WG 15748	10/25/24	Pvt				5/10/43	—
Zimmermann, Konrad	7WG 12936	11/1/08	F/Sgt	541st			5/12/43	—
Zechert, Adolf	81G 9178	12/7/19	Cpl				5/12/43	SA
Scheler, Manfred	81G 260929	5/27/25	Pvt	16th Division			7/8/44	—
Mueller, Helmut	7WG 13418	9/28/19	Pfc	501st Panzer			5/9/43	—
Beierlein, Ernst	31G 11698	2/28/04	1st Lt	709 Division			6/26/44	—
Dingler, Kurt	7WG 16264	5/31/06	1st Lt	501st Panzer			5/9/43	—
Doering, Heinz Walter	7WG 16537	5/31/10	Capt				5/12/43	—
Haller, Dr. Wilhelm	7WG 16073	3/24/01	Lt Col				5/11/43	—
Landgrebe, Erich	7WG 16653	1/18/08	2nd Lt				5/11/43	—
Czaika, Siegfried	7WG 15518	8/20/14	Sgt	11th Flak			5/11/43	—
Weber, Roman	7WG 14212	5/31/12	Pfc		334th		5/9/43	—
Bobowk, Theo	7WG 15895	1/3/19	Sgt		Air Corps		5/8/43	—
Kern, Artur	7WG 13138	10/16/19	Cpl		Air Corps		5/13/43	—
Herrmann, Josef	7WG 13593	2/16/22	Cpl	475th		1st	5/12/43	—
Neumann, Helmut	7WG 13860	1/31/17	F/Sgt	Luft	17th Div		5/13/43	—
Thun, Herbert	7WG 13722	10/25/13	F/Sgt	Luft	17th Div		5/13/43	SA
Meixner, Rudolf	7WG 13150	6/28/22	Pfc				5/13/43	—
Jaeger, Peter	31G 10661	9/17/03	Pvt				8/9/44	SA
Blume, Kurt	7WG 15541	9/18/19	Sgt	155th Panzer	90th Div		5/12/43	—
Florreck, Kurt	7WG 16566	11/1/09	2nd Lt		90th Div		5/13/43	SA
Wojciechowski, Heinz	7WG 15455	8/30/21	Cpl		90th Div		5/13/43	—
Ihrig, Heinrich	7WG 14761	6/7/21	Pfc		90th Div		5/13/43	—
Zettel, Johann	7WG 15433	12/26/08	Pvt		90th Div		5/12/43	—
Hicthammer, Karl	7WG 14763	2/11/20	Cpl		90th Div		5/13/43	—
Lukas, Wilhelm	7WG 14756	1/11/15	Cpl		90th Div		5/12/43	—
Lenz, Heinrich	31G 11708	7/10/10	Pvt				8/3/44	SA
Markert, Arthur	31G 11582	2/2/99	Pvt				8/6/44	SA
Zieker, Karl	31G 11742	8/17/11	Pvt	Oberbauleitung Cherbourg			6/8/44	SA
Hochstein, Hans	31G 11755	5/27/08	Pvt	Oberanleitung Cherbourg			6/26/44	SS
Rothfuss, Georg	31G 11753	8/26/10	Pvt	Oberbauleitung Cherbourg			6/26/44	—
Helbing, Frithjof	31G 11516	9/29/99	Pvt	Oberbauleitung Cherbourg			6/26/44	—
Ehrlich, Ewald	31G 11392	11/3/09	Pvt	1st	64th Div		8/16/44	—
Mueller, Ludwig	31G 11747	12/22/08	Pvt	Oberbauleitung Cherbourg			6/8/44	—
Ost, Fritz	7WG 12876	6/3/20	Sgt	4th Panzer	475 Div		5/12/43	—
Kirches, Walter	7WG 13193	9/23/21	Pfc	4th Panzer	475 Div		5/11/43	—
Goriup, Lorenz	7WG 13989	11/25/14	Cpl				5/12/43	—
Laiminger, Josef	7WG 14070	7/7/13	Cpl	756th			5/9/43	—
Zimmermann, Felix	7WG 13345	8/28/07	Pfc				5/11/43	SA

Full Name Last, First, Middle	Internment Serial No.	Date of Birth mo/day/yr	Rank/ Grade	Organi- zation	Reg. Bn.	Co.	Date of Capture mo/day/yr	Affiliation with SS, SD, SA, or other secret police organizations
Mikolajozak, Stanislaus	31G 3808	8/16/98	Pvt				8/7/44	—
Nicol, Georg	7WG 15865	6/7/06	Cpl				5/11/43	—
Kalbach, Otto	7WG 15751	1/15/05	Pfc			2nd	5/8/43	—
Borshert, Walter	7WG 15761	5/15/20	Pfc				5/11/43	—
Fratzke, Georg	7WG 15552	11/23/20	Sgt				5/11/43	—
Litz, Andreas	7WG 15587	8/18/20	Cpl				5/11/43	—
Vagt, Ernst	7WG 15429	6/25/21	Pfc				5/11/43	—
Gottwald, Adolf	7WG 15085	1/1/02	Cpl	264th Flak			5/9/43	—
Franek, Hans-Ullrich	7WG 14889	3/22/13	Sgt	511st			5/9/43	SA
Flick, Karl	7WG 15852	6/22/22	Pfc	1st			5/2/43	—
Kohn, Wilhelm	7WG 13917	6/27/18	Cpl	504th		1st	5/9/43	—
Keilhofer, Wolfgang	7WG 13189	3/23/21	Sgt				5/13/43	—
Waschulewsky, Karl	31G 5826?	1/26/96	Pvt				8/9/44	—
Schimmel, August	7WG 12867	10/30/21	Cpl				5/11/43	—
Raeger, Karl	7WG 15621	11/18/22	Cpl				5/11/43	—
Hitschke?, Erich	7WG 15467	3/21/21	Cpl				5/9/43	—
Elter, Leo	7WG 14607	9/3/19	Cpl	5th			5/11/43	—
Wagner, Otto	7WG 13729	5/19/21	Cpl				5/11/43	—
Bendorf, August	7WG 15566	2/27/09	Cpl	Flak			7/17/43	—
Lamprecht, Erich	7WG 13320	10/14/18	Cpl				5/12/43	—
Knauer, Gottfried	7WG 14095	9/29/20	Cpl	125th Panzer Division			5/13/43	—
Frieser, Peter	7WG 15238	11/9/03	Pfc	503rd Flak	21st Division		5/9/43	—
Hupka, Heinz	7WG 15932	4/12/18	F/Sgt	17th Division			5/11/43	—
Steiding, Heinrich	31G 125352	5/19/10	Pvt	709th Div., 84th Reg			6/26/44	—
Mathis, Inver Franz	7WG 15717	12/19/14	Cpl				5/12/43	—
Babiek, Richard	7WG 13233	1/1/15	F/Sgt				5/12/43	—
Babenzien, Horst	7WG 13501	12/29/19	Cpl				5/12/43	—
Wolter, Karl	7WG 13524	10/5/21	Cpl				5/12/43	—
Seifert, Helmut	7WG 13234	11/10/17	F/Sgt				5/12/43	—
Tittel, Erich	7WG 13123	4/24/10	Pvt	999 Div, 999 Reg			5/9/43	—
Hille, Wilhelm von	31G 9751	10/5/98	Pvt	266th Div			8/9/44	—
Gaertner, Walter	31G 9732	12/11/96	Pvt	266th Div			8/9/44	—
Grimm, Erich	7WG 15536	8/1/08	Sgt	Goering Div			5/13/43	—
Kunnemann, Gerhard	7WG 13371	4/1/22	Pvt	Goering Div, 2nd Reg			7/13/43	—
Mueller, Gottfried	7WG 15931	7/2/14	Pvt	Goering Div, 2nd Reg			7/15/43	—
Wendt, Oskar	7WG 14254	4/1/24	Pfc	580th	21st Div		5/11/43	—
Raimer, Anton	7WG 13522	11/15/05	Cpl	66th	20th Div		5/11/43	—
Schaffaszezyk, Rudolf	7WG 13559	12/20/14	Sgt	66th	20th Div		5/13/43	—
Weiss, Erich	7WG 13726	9/8/10	Sgt	1st			5/11/43	—
Rudolph, Willy	7WG 12701	5/7/16	Sgt		22nd		5/12/43	SA
Klein, Otto	7WG 15137	5/14/16	Sgt	47th	22nd Div		5/9/43	—
Rommert, Richard	7WG 12732	1/5/10	Cpl	43rd	15th Div		5/12/43	SA
Klein, Alois	7WG 15296	2/15/10	Pvt	47th	22nd Div	3rd Co.	5/9/43	—
Boller, Anton	7WG 12733	4/15/15	Cpl	22nd	22nd Div	6th Bat	5/9/43	—
Bittner, Heinz	7WG 15166	10/26/10	Sgt	47th	22nd Div		5/9/43	—
Pladwig, Heinz	7WG 13434	11/19/21	Pfc	115th			5/9/43	—
Rokos, Ludwig	7WG 12724	11/6/15	Sgt	3rd	77th Div		5/11/43	—
Rudolph, Ernst	7WG 12695	3/14/20	Pfc	27th	2nd Flak Div		5/11/43	—
Rudolph, Willi Georg	7WG 12693	10/17/22	Pfc	4th Flak			5/11/43	—
Weiss, Georg	7WG 12802	12/6/06	Sgt	20th	192nd	Flak	5/9/43	—
Gossmann, Heinz	7WG 14623	2/22/20	Pfc				5/11/43	—
Wunn, Heinz Friedrich	31G 15489	11/27/21	1st Lt	9th Panzer Div. 102nd Reg			9/6/44	—
Hoge, Herbert	7WG 22074	8/31/12	Cpl				7/15/43	—
Betke, Walter	7WG 15544	8/24/18	Sgt				5/12/43	—

Full Name Last, First, Middle	Internment Serial No.	Date of Birth mo/day/yr	Rank/ Grade	Organi- zation	Reg. Bn.	Co.	Date of Capture mo/day/yr	Affiliation with SS, SD, SA, or other secret police organizations
Schlenkrich, Kurt	31G 11634	12/13/08	Pvt	15th	441st Flak Div		8/7/44	—
Becker, Hubert	7WG 14972	5/8/07	Cpl	51st	511th Flak Div		5/9/43	—
Jeergens, Karl	7WG 14896	2/18/6	Sgt	21st Panzer Div		1/200	5/11/43	—
Fischer, Wilhelm	7WG 22369	5/5/21	Pvt	143rd	6th Div		10/16/43	—
Schlemm, Richard	7WG 14621	2/24/03	Pfc	16th Div			5/8/43	—
Bombrowski, Rudi	7WG 15889	6/17/14	F/Sgt	686th Div			5/11/43	—
Lampe, Erich	7WG 15658	10/14/14	Sgt				5/11/43	—
Dinse, Herbert	7WG 15640	7/22/06	Pfc				5/7/43	—
Mertha, Alfons	7WG 12863	8/26/11	Sgt	10th	1 Div		5/12/43	—
Kornek, Anton	31G 11688	6/13/99	Pvt	7th Div			8/2/44	—
Seitz, Friedrich	7WG 14336	9/15/18	Cpl	1.4.54th	Flak Div		5/11/43	SA
Struemper, Lothar	7WG 12832	3/6/22	Pfc	2nd	52nd Flak Div		5/9/43	—
Biergann, Werner	7WG 15369	2/7/14	Sgt	47th	22nd Div		5/9/43	—

Appendix G
POW Roster, 1945

The following 1945 POW roster was provided by Bernardine Cummings of Concordia, who worked in the Transportation Office at the camp:

STATION HOSPITAL
Prisoner of War Camp
Concordia, Kansas

File No. 383.6   20 August 1945

SUBJECT: Physical Condition of Prisoners of War.

TO: Provost Marshal, PW Camp, Concordia, Kansas.

The following prisoners of war are physically capable of performing heavy work:

Company #3

Aichner	Bruno	2nd Lt	16512	Heitmeyer	Eberhard	Lt Col	16075
Auerswald	Wilhelm	1st Lt	16513	Hitzentaler	Hans	1st lt	16307
Baehr	Wilhelm	Major	17018	Hoennekes	Heinz	Major	15970
Boldt	Alfons	Lt Col	16060	Von Hoffmann	Wilfried	1st Lt	15971
Brechmann	Bernd	1st Lt	245906	Horn	Fritz	1st Lt	16297
Breitenbach	Ernst	1st Lt	15962	Jackisch	Manfred	1st Lt	15972
Brix	Ernst	Lt Col	16061	Kegel	Erwin	1st Lt	16627
Burk	Klaus	2nd Lt	15964	Kerth	Emil	2nd Lt	15973
Chilian	Erich	1st Lt	16544	Kirchlehner	Willi	2nd Lt	16493
Dallinger	Hermann	2nd Lt	16546	Kirschner	Eugen	Major	16984
Eberhardt	Heinz	2nd Lt	15965	Koellenberger	Heinrich	2nd Lt	16636
Edeling	Helmut	2nd Lt	17022	Koller	Friedrich	2nd Lt	37874
Enderle	Max	1st Lt	16276	Kopf	Wolfgang	1st Lt	17036
Endres	Hans	Major	16065	Korff	Guenter	2nd Lt	256709
Eurisch	Richard	1st Lt	232650	Kraemer	Rudi	Lt Col	16086
Feige	Richard	Major	16066	Krahnke	Herbert	Major	16087
Feuerstein	Heinz	2nd Lt	15966	Kramer	Dieter	2nd Lt	16126
Fischbeck	Walter	2nd Lt	16124	Kraus	Siegfried	2nd Lt	15976
Geisenheyner	Ernst	1st Lt	17025	Krueger	Hans	1st Lt	16644
Gellmroth	Josef	1st Lt	9743	Kurzai	Erich	Major	16088
Gernand	Georg	2nd Lt	16575	Kuso	Fritz	1st Lt	16335
Gleiss	Garlieb	2nd Lt	16576	Lang	Heinrich	1st Lt	15980
Gnatzy	Helmut	2nd Lt	15968	Leiber	Hans	1st Lt	16134
Graeser	Werner	2nd Lt	17026	Von Lewinski	Volker	Lt Col	16090
Gramlich	Erich	1st Lt	16582	Lewandowski	Donald	2nd Lt	16901
Von Grundherr	Erich	1st Lt	16590	Littmann	Hans	1st Lt	36988
Haller	Wilhelm	Lt Colonel	16073	Lorenzen	Hans	2nd Lt	15982
Hammel	Siegfried	Lt Col	16074	Michaelsen	Hermann	1st Lt	16357
Hansen	Gerd	1st Lt	15969	Moesler	Reinhold	Major	16094
Harder	Hans	2nd Lt	16125	Molzahn	Hans	2nd Lt	15983
Hehle	Erwin	Capt	17029	Moritz	Gerhard	2nd Lt	245903
Heise	Heinrich	Major	16076	Mueller	Eberhard	1st Lt	15985

Mueller	Edmund	1st Lt	15986
Mueller	Leopold	1st Lt	16361
Mueller	Horst	1st Lt	15987
Musal	Ernst	2nd Lt	16053
Mutze	Werner	1st Lt	15988
Neubauer	Hans	1st Lt	16498
Novotny	Alois	Major	16098
Ottomann	Hans	1st Lt	17040
Patterson	Heinz	2nd Lt	15990
Petzmeyer	Hans	1nd Lt	16054
Pilger	Fritz	Major	16100
Plohmann	Ernst	1st Lt	15991
Ploog	Heinz	2nd Lt	17041
Pottgiesser	Karl	2nd Lt	16499
Prael	Wolfgang	2nd Lt	767412
Von Rantzau	Heino	2nd Lt	15992
Von Restorff	Cord	1st Lt	15993
Richter	Georg	Major	16104
Riedel	Hilmar	Major	16105
Rothley	Helmut	2nd Lt	16702
Rupp	Heinz	2nd Lt	15994
Russegger	Friedrich	2nd Lt	17044
Saueressig	Rudolf	2nd Lt	16127
Schaller	Volkmar	2nd Lt	775902
Schafhauser	Erwin	1st Lt	257721
Schaper	Karl	1st Lt	16707
Schauer	Hans	1st Lt	258163
Scheinert	Willi	1st Lt	16401
Schlafke	Bruno	1st Lt	15996
Schmidt	Gerhard	1st Lt	16957
Schmidt	Paul	1st Lt	16997
Schmidt	Willi	2nd Lt	16129
Schnell	Rudolf	1st Lt	256718
Schoeffel	Kurt	1st Lt	16128
Schreinert	Hermann	Capt	37040
Schuth	Erwain	2nd Lt	16402
Schwarzenberg	Willi	1st Lt	16403
Seeliger	Ulrich	Colonel	16112
Seip	Heinz	2nd Lt	16130
Sichra	Karl	1st Lt	15998
Sirot	Erich	Major	16113
Staroste	Karl	2nd Lt	16728
Steinmann	Hans	2nd Lt	15999
Stoehr	Otto	2nd Lt	16001
Von Stosch	Albrecht	1st Lt	16002
Stuempfl	Karl	2nd Lt	16131

Stuenkel	Hans	1st Lt	256722
Szeszat	Hans	2nd Lt	16132
Thiem	Werner	1st Lt	16734
Trapp	Herbert	2nd Lt	16005
Uebel	Gerhard	2nd Lt	16007
Uetz	Herbert	2nd Lt	16008
Umbreit	Peter	2nd Lt	16010
Urmersbach	Fritz	2nd Lt	16011
Valk	Kurt	1st Lt	16049
Vogel	Werner	2nd Lt	16012
Vogt	Rudolf	1st Lt	16013
Wagner	Georg	Capt	16014
Weibel	Kurt	2nd Lt	16015
Waltenberger	Eduard	Colonel	16116
Walter	Friedrich	2nd Lt	16016
Wartenberg	Konrad	1st Lt	16018
Wecke	Werner	2nd Lt	16021
Weiken	Konrad	1st Lt	16022
Weiler	Sebastian	2nd Lt	16048
Weiser	Maximilian	1st Lt	16453
Welteke	Karl	1st Lt	16023
Wendt	Heinz	1st Lt	16024
Wenzel	Kurt	2nd Lt	16025
Wernicke	Klaus	1st Lt	16026
Wettig	Werner	Major	16027
Winnefeld	Helmut	Capt	16029
Winter	Harald	2nd Lt	16030
Wittkopp	Willi	2nd Lt	16031
Witzmann	Friedrich	2nd Lt	16032
Wodege	Helmut	2nd Lt	16033
Wolff	Dieter	2nd Lt	16034
Wurm	Konrad	2nd Lt	16035
Zeh	Fritz	2nd Lt	17053
Zeise	Heinz	2nd Lt	16037
Zillert	Karl	2nd Lt	16040
Zimmermann	Georg	2nd Lt	16041
Zimmermann	Herbert	1st Lt	16042
Zipfel	Friedrich	1st Lt	16044
Zuza	Walter	Major	16046
Zwickler	Hermann	2nd Lt	16045
Brennig	Hubertus	2nd Lt	15953
Horbach	Eberhard	1st Lt	16614
Weber	Heribert	Major	16020
Woehlert	Karl	Capt	16465
Weinhold	Rudolf	1st Lt	16747

Company #4

Adler	Lorenz	2nd Lt	16478
Andres	Bruno	2nd Lt	16235
Asche	Fritz	1st Lt	16236
Baesler	Otto	2nd Lt	16241
Bathelt	Fritz	2nd Lt	16240
Bauer	Hans	Capt	16238
Bessrich	Karl	1st Lt	16242

Biermann	Julius	2nd Lt	16342
Biernath	Gerhard	1st Lt	16244
Birk	Heinz	2nd Lt	16488
Blau	Arno	2nd Lt	16245
Blobel	Herbert	1st Lt	16485
Blume	Wilhelm	Capt	16246
Bonin	Walter	Capt	16248

Borchert	Fritz	1st Lt	16251
Borges	Werner	1st Lt	16250
Bostelmann	Hermann	1st Lt	16253
Bourmer	Karl	2nd Lt	256727
Bracher	Karl	2nd Lt	16487
Brandt	Hermann	1st Lt	16486
Brandt	Ulrich	Capt	16254
Braunschweig	Richard	Capt	16255
Burkert	Franz	2nd Lt	16256
Danjes	Martin	Major	16259
Dehne	Joachim	1st Lt	16260
Desch	Egon	2nd Lt	16261
Dichmann	Willi	1st Lt	16263
Dickopp	Otto	1st Lt	16262
Dingler	Kurt	1st Lt	16264
Driver	Helmut	Capt	16267
Duschenek	Alex	2nd Lt	16268
Ebertshaeuser	Karl	1st Lt	16270
v. Eisenhart-Rothe	Sigismund	2nd Lt	16825
Eschbach	Rudolf	2nd Lt	16253
Feix	Hermann	1st Lt	16407
Fenster	Wilhelm	1st Lt	16278
Fischer	Walter	Capt	16280
Fleck	Friedrich	2nd Lt	16491
Frey	Anton	2nd Lt	11549
Friedrich	Werner	1st Lt	16492
Frost	Erich	1st Lt	256724
Gillitzer	Karl	1st Lt	16286
Gonnermann	Bernhard	1st Lt	16288
Grosse	Werner	Capt	16289
Guss	Heinrich	1st Lt	16291
Hansen	Kersten	1st Lt	16293
Hartitz	Werner	Capt	16479
Hechler	Gerd	2nd Lt	16304
Heitz	Johann	1st Lt	16302
Henne	Johannes	2nd Lt	16303
Herzer	Karl	2nd Lt	16306
Hoeltze	Ernest	2nd Lt	16295
Hoeppner	Walter	2nd Lt	16299
Hoeres	Hans	2nd Lt	16303
Jandt	Hans	2nd Lt	16309
Kalke	Bernhard	1st Lt	16328
von Kappeller	Walter	1st Lt	16312
Katzenberger	Helmut	1st Lt	16313
Kerschowski	Karl	1st Lt	16314
Kieninger	Wilhelm	1st Lt	256728
Kienle	Hans	1st Lt	16316
Kissing	Eberhard	2nd Lt	16318
Kittelberger	Karl	2nd Lt	16317
Klunker	Friedrich	2nd Lt	260042
Kneisner	Hans	2nd Lt	16319
Koch	Guenter	1st Lt	16321
Koehler	Kurt	2nd Lt	16324
Koester	Erich	2nd Lt	16494
Koerbel	Willi	2nd Lt	16322
Kolmorgen	Hans	1st Lt	16323
Kraft	Otto	Capt	16326
Kremp	Fritz	Capt	16330
Kubsch	Wilhelm	Major	16333
Kuehn	Heinz	1st Lt	16495
Kumm	Herbert	1st Lt	16334
Lang	Manfred	1st Lt	16337
Lange	Karl	1st Lt	16338
Lebmann	Fritz	2nd Lt	16496
Lelle	Willi	2nd Lt	16340
Loechelt	Joachim	1st Lt	16344
Lorenz	Siegfried	2nd Lt	16343
Ludwig	Joachim	2nd Lt	16346
Maessen	Karl	2nd Lt	16348
Magnus	Heinz	2nd Lt	16349
Mai	Helmut	1st Lt	16352
Maier	Willi	1st Lt	16353
Mairguenther	Ludwig	1st Lt	16350
Meissner	Heinz	Major	16355
Mertens	Kurt	1st Lt	16356
Mueller	Heinrich	1st Lt	16359
Mueller-Frank	Ulrich	1st Lt	16358
Muenchmeyer	Hans	Capt	16363
Naegele	Fritz	2nd Lt	16364
Neidhardt	Wilhelm	1st Lt	16366
Niessner	Kurt	2nd Lt	16367
Oehlschlaegel	Richard	1st Lt	16369
Ossenbrueggen	Johann	2nd Lt	16371
Panzer	Johann	2nd Lt	256728
Penzel	Helmut	Capt	16373
Pilgrim	Franz	1st Lt	16374
Pohl	Johannes	1st Lt	16376
Purrmann	Max	Capt	16357
Rauch	Erich	2nd Lt	16383
Rave	Gerhard	2nd Lt	16381
Rehage	Guenter	2nd Lt	16500
Rentzsch	Herbert	Capt	16382
Richter	Heinz	Capt	16387
Rischanek	Walter	2nd Lt	16388
Rode	Werner	1st Lt	16390
von Roemer	Heinrich	Capt	16393
Roemer	Dietrich	2nd Lt	16391
Roepcke	Hermann	Capt	16395
Romeick	Gerhard	1st Lt	16394
Rosshirt	Kurt	Capt	16396
Rzepka	Walter	1st Lt	16380
Sachse	Alfred	1st Lt	16397
Segler	Rudolf	1st Lt	16398
Sigges	Franz	1st Lt	16502
Sigmund	Jakob	2nd Lt	16480
Schad	Heinrich	2nd Lt	254845
Schaepe	Wilhelm	2nd Lt	16421
Scheuermann	Horst	2nd Lt	16424
Schiffmann	Josef	Capt	16406
Schleith	Walter	2nd Lt	16409
Schmoelz	Andreas	1st Lt	16412

Schneider	Waldemar	2nd Lt	16503
Scholz	Willi	Capt	16414
Schorer	Erwin	2nd Lt	16426
Schroedter	Wilhelm	1st Lt	16410
Schroer	Theodor	1st Lt	16405
Schwab	Georg	1st Lt	16413
Schwarzer	Franz	1st Lt	16440
Schweiger	Karl	1st Lt	16420
Staeuber	Wilkin	2nd Lt	16431
Stahl	Fritz	1st Lt	16432
Steffens	Hans	1st Lt	16436
Steinbach	Fritz	1st Lt	16435
Steinbauer	Arnim	Major	16428
Stock	Helmut	2nd Lt	260620
Stoffregen	Karl	1st Lt	16427
Struve	Karl	1st Lt	16429
Spengemann	Heinrich	1st Lt	16434
Tank	Guenter	1st Lt	16439
Tanneberger	Ernst	1st Lt	16440
Thiede	Erich	1st Lt	16441
Trampe	Ewald	2nd Lt	16443
Vogel	Walter	2nd Lt	16481
Vogelsang	Rudolf	1st Lt	16504
Vogelsang	Franz	Major	16444
Voigt	Werner	1st Lt	16446
Walk	Max	1st Lt	16449
Wegener	Werner	1st Lt	16455
Welzel	Fritz	2nd Lt	16454
Wiebus	Norbert	Capt	16464
Winkel	Joachim	Capt	16463
Wilms	Willi	1st Lt	16460
Wollmann	Rudolf	2nd Lt	16467
Wollny	Fritz	Capt	16470
Wopp	Guenter	Capt	16471
Zeuner	Heinz	1st Lt	16475
Frey	Wilhelm	2nd Lt	16282
Gatz	Alfons	1st Lt	16285
Kornfeld	Josef	1st Lt	16332
Leitert	Kurt	1st Lt	16339
Loesche	Helmut	2nd Lt	16345
Pollak	Paul	1st Lt	16376
Woldsen	Edward	2nd lt	16466

Company #5

Ahlborn	Hubert	2nd Lt	16784
Von Alten	Konrad	Capt	16785
Albrecht	Udo	2nd Lt	16786
Aeissen	Harm	2nd Lt	16787
Ankersen	Hans	1st Lt	16788
Andrasch	Guenter	2nd Lt	16789
Apisch	Erich	2nd Lt	16790
Asbach	Artur	2nd Lt	17012
Baumann	Gottfried	1st Lt	16791
Baenerle	Volker	2nd Lt	17019
Behrend	Georg	2nd Lt	16793
Beims	Wilhelm	2nd Lt	16795
Bellon	Paul	2nd Lt	16796
Berg	Erich	1st Lt	16797
Blank	Helmut	2nd Lt	16799
Blume	Gerhard	2nd Lt	17020
Bobe	Willi	Capt	16801
Boenig	Helmut	1st Lt	16802
Boese	Felix	1st Lt	16803
Borrman	Gerhard	2nd Lt	16804
Brauner	Oskar	2nd Lt	16805
Brending	Dieter	Capt	17021
Broenner	Josef	Capt	16807
Buchholz	Fritz	1st Lt	16808
Bueckmann	Anton	1st Lt	16809
Burkard	Eberhard	2nd Lt	254796
Christern	Alfred	1st Lt	16812
Crone	Kurt	2nd Lt	16813
Czichon	Karl	2nd Lt	16814
Czock	Wilhelm	2nd Lt	16815
Daeumling	Karl	2nd Lt	16817
Doeffinger	Herbert	2nd Lt	16818
Driemann	Karl	1st Lt	16819
Dipper	Heinz	Capt	16821
Dylla	Guenter	1st Lt	16822
Eckardt	Ullrich	2nd Lt	16823
Eichhorn	Otto	1st Lt	16824
Endlich	Karl	2nd Lt	16826
Enhuber	Karl	1st Lt	16827
Ewald	Otto	2nd Lt	260862
Feuerriegel	Karl	2st Lt	16829
Fingerle	Theodor	2nd Lt	16830
Franz	Robert	1st Lt	16833
Frister	Kurt	2nd Lt	16834
Fromm	Fritz	Capt	16833
Frost	Johann	Capt	16836
Funk	Georg	2nd Lt	16837
Gambeck	Max	1st Lt	254848
Gaul	Hartwig	2nd Lt	16839
Gerisch	Hans	1st Lt	16842
Goeppert	Albert	2nd Lt	254827
Groengroeft	Otto	2nd Lt	16845
De Groot	Ernst	2nd Lt	16846
Guehler	Johannnes	2nd Lt	16847
Gutzeit	Herbert	1st Lt	16851
Hantelmann	Oskar	2nd Lt	16852
Haefner	Otto	2nd Lt	17208
Hartung	Kurt	2nd Lt	16853
Haeusser	Hermann	2nd Lt	254828
Heiner	Herbert	1st Lt	16857
Heinl	Walter	2nd Lt	16858
Heinsch	Max	1st Lt	16859
Hesse	Ernst	1st Lt	16862
Hesse	Frido	2nd Lt	16863

Hilscher	Heinz	2nd Lt	16865		Peters	Hermann	1st Lt	16929
Hofmann	Walter	2nd Lt	16868		Philipp	Rudolf	2nd Lt	16931
Hofmann	Otto	Capt	17031		Platte	Hermann	Major	16932
Hofmann	Arnd	1st Lt	17014		Pracht	Emil	2nd Lt	16933
Hoehne	Wolfgang	2nd Lt	16869		Rackebrandt	Walter	2nd Lt	17042
Hotzel	Hans	2nd Lt	16871		Rathje	Hermann	2nd Lt	16935
Hoeppner	Heinz	2nd Lt	17033		Rauwolf	Ernst	1st Lt	254825
Hummel	Hans	2nd Lt	16872		Reinecke	Hans	2nd Lt	16937
Honig	Helmut	Capt	17032		Reinhold	Hans	2nd Lt	16938
Horn	Rudolf	2nd Lt	254838		Reiss	Helmut	1st Lt	17043
Jaspert	Hans	1st Lt	16874		Riess	Heinrich	1st Lt	16939
Jessen	Karl	1st Lt	16875		Risch	Artur	1st Lt	16940
Kampe	Otto	2nd Lt	16877		Ritgen	Kurt	2nd Lt	16941
Kaestle	Anton	Capt	16878		Rixen	Christian	2nd Lt	16942
Karnath	Siegfried	2nd Lt	17034		Roeder	Karl	2nd Lt	16944
Keck	Paul	1st Lt	16879		Roeder	Bruno	1st Lt	16945
Klor	Hermann	1st Lt	16880		Roevekamp	Heinrich	2nd Lt	37247
Konert	Erich	2nd Lt	16884		Rohner	Bernhard	1st Lt	16947
Koschel	Erich	1st Lt	16885		Ruppert	Heinrich	1st Lt	16949
Koenig	Hans	2nd Lt	16886		Schaefer	Karl	2nd Lt	254815
Koestenbach	Hans	1st Lt	16887		Schaerfe	Wolfgang	2nd Lt	16954
Kuke	Friedrich	1st Lt	16888		Schaube	Friedrich	2nd Lt	16955
Kuepa	Herbert	1st Lt	16889		Schutovits	Erich	2nd Lt	16956
Lang	Dieter	2nd Lt	16891		Schmidt	Guenter	1st Lt	16958
Lang	Walter	2nd Lt	16892		Schmidtborn	Herwig	2nd Lt	16960
Langner	Heinz	2nd Lt	16895		Schulze	Bruno	1st Lt	16963
Lehmann-Doerfel	Werner	1st Lt	16897		Schwabel	Karl	1st Lt	16967
Leibold	Josef	2nd Lt	16898		Seibert	Guido	1st Lt	16970
Leitzke	Martin	1st Lt	17037		Seyfert	Erich	1st Lt	16971
Loebus	Fritz	1st LT	16900		Siegel	Wilhelm	2nd Lt	16973
Lezim	Erich	1st Lt	16902		Sichart	Adolf	2nd Lt	253586
Link	Heinrich	1st Lt	16904		Sodidt	Manfred	2nd Lt	16974
Lochmann	Hermann	Major	16092		Straub	Fritz	2nd Lt	16979
Mattheis	Artur	1st Lt	16905		Thimm	Otto	2nd Lt	16980
Meiler	Herbert	2nd Lt	16907		Thomas	Ernst	2nd Lt	254805
Michell	Fritz	1st Lt	16908		Troche	Martin	1st Lt	16982
Mittermann	Herbert	2nd Lt	254836		Ueckermann	Heino	2nd Lt	16983
Moellmann	Viktor	1st Lt	16910		Unger	Rolf	Major	16984
Monski	Alexander	2nd Lt	16911		Urhahn	August	1st Lt	16985
Moerwald	Sepp	1st Lt	16912		Vogt	Wilhelm	1st Lt	37656
Moos	Karl	1st Lt	16913		Vogt	Hubert	2nd Lt	254831
Moser	Hans	2nd Lt	16914		Vogelsaenger	Walter	2nd Lt	16987
Muehlhaeuser	Gerhard	Major	16915		Wagner	Herbert	1st Lt	16988
Nestmann	Heinz	1st Lt	37225		Walther	Hans	1st Lt	16989
Neumann	Hans	1st Lt	16918		Walther	Karl	1st Lt	17050
Neuber	Gerhard	2nd Lt	16919		Von Wartenberg	Klaus	2nd Lt	16990
Nitsche	Paul	1st Lt	17038		Wallner	Alfons	1st Lt	16991
Noffke	August	Capt	16920		Werner	Hans	1st Lt	16995
Oexle	Joachim	2nd Lt	16921		Weiser	Hans	2nd Lt	16997
Oppermann	Horst	2nd Lt	16922		Waechtler	Kurt	2nd Lt	16998
Oppmann	Norbert	1st Lt	16923		Willert	Paul	1st Lt	16999
Orschel	Siegfried	2nd Lt	16925		Wien	Hans	1st Lt	17000
Pallas	Karl	1st Lt	16926		Wiechert	Richard	1st Lt	17002
Paulus	Lutz	2nd Lt	16927		Winkelmann	Wilhelm	1st Lt	17052
Papa	Hinrich	1st Lt	16928		Wittig	Heinz	2nd Lt	17003
					Wolber	Matthias	2nd Lt	17005

Wonneberger	Walter	2nd Lt	17006		Greiner	Hermann	1st Lt	16844
Wuelfing	Klaus	2nd Lt	17007		Haunschildt	Friedrich	2nd Lt	16856
Zeyss	Andreas	Major	17009		Schulze	Georg	Major	16964
Foernges	Kurt	1st Lt	254835		Stark	Alwin	1st Lt	16976
Ganster	Friedrich	2nd Lt	16838		Budig	Herbert	1st Lt	16810

Company #6

Darwig	Hans	1st Lt	16547		Full	Hans	1st Lt	16571
Ackermann	Ernst	2nd Lt	16510		Gassler	Guenter	2nd Lt	16572
Adams	Leo	2nd Lt	16511		Gassmann	Karl	2nd Lt	16573
Arndt	Hermann	2nd Lt	254798		Gideon	Fritz	1st Lt	16763
Bauer	Axel	2nd Lt	16515		Giegold	Christian	2nd Lt	258161
Becker	Horst	2nd Lt	16516		Goetz	Willi	1st Lt	16578
Behrens	Karl	2nd Lt	16517		Gohritz	Reinhard	1st Lt	16579
Bergami	Hermann	2nd Lt	16520		Goossen	Hans	1st Lt	16580
Bergmann	Karl	1st Lt	16521		Graeb	Werner	2nd Lt	16581
Berck	Fritz	1st Lt	16522		Gravert	Fritz	2nd Lt	16583
Berthold	Klaus	2nd Lt	16523		Grimmeisen	Werner	Major	16585
Beutel	Werner	1st Lt	16525		Grossmann	Walter	Capt	16588
Beyerl	August	1st Lt	16527		Hambrock	Emil	1st Lt	16591
Bickes	Hans	2nd Lt	16528		Hasse	Helmut	1st Lt	16855
Biedermann	Egon	Capt	16529		Heinitz	Werner	1st Lt	16595
Blumstaengl	Helmut	2nd Lt	254832		Hengesbach	Siegfried	2nd Lt	16598
Boeckmann	Werner	1st Lt	16531		Henk	Kurt	2nd Lt	16599
Bork	Gerhard	1st Lt	16533		Herrmann	Werner	1st Lt	16601
Brandenburger	Hans	2nd Lt	254792		Hermes	Guenter	2nd Lt	16602
Brandes	Guenter	Major	775004		Herzog	Robert	Capt	16603
Brandes	Werner	2nd Lt	16535		Hille	Hans	1st Lt	16605
Braun	Siegfried	1st Lt	16536		Hinnenthal	Hans	1st Lt	16606
Breitbarth	Walter	1st Lt	16537		Hoeht	Paul	2nd Lt	16607
Brendel	Anton	2nd Lt	16538		Helmig	Ernst	2nd Lt	16596
Brenner	Herbert	2nd Lt	16539		Hofbauer	Hans	Capt	16608
Broetzmann	Karl	1st Lt	254840		Hofer	Heinz	2nd Lt	16609
Brueckner	Werner	1st Lt	16540		Hofer	Rudolf	2nd Lt	16610
Bunjes	Johann	1st Lt	16541		Hoffmann	Jakob	2nd Lt	253591
Busse	Fritz	2nd Lt	16542		Hohmeier	Friedebert	2nd Lt	16611
Crasemann	Horst	2nd Lt	16545		Hopf	Rudolf	Major	11528
Dedie	Kurt	1st Lt	16548		Huegel	Wilhelm	1st Lt	16615
Dieck	Harry	2nd Lt	16551		Idelberger	Walter	Capt	16616
Diefenbach	Johannes	2nd Lt	16552		Ihrig	Fritz	2nd Lt	16617
Distelkamp	Heinz	1st Lt	16554		Jaeger	Erich	1st Lt	16619
v. Dobeneck	Henning	2nd Lt	16556		Jenninger	Alfred	2nd Lt	16550
Doering	Heinz	Capt	16557		Kaiser	Hermann	2nd Lt	16766
Dummann	Bruno	1st Lt	16558		Kalle	Gert	1st Lt	16623
Eggert	Georg	2nd Lt	16559		Katzenmeier	Eduard	2nd Lt	16625
Ehlich	Johannes	1st Lt	16560		v. Katzler	Bogislav	1st Lt	16626
Endriss	Karl	1st Lt	16562		Keller	Karl	2nd Lt	16628
v. Etthofen	Karl	2nd Lt	16274		Kerger	Rudolf	2nd Lt	16631
Etzold	Rudolf	1st Lt	16563		Klischat	Hans	2nd Lt	16634
Fellner	Karl	1st Lt	16564		Knoblach	Horst	1st Lt	16635
Fischer	Rudolf	2nd Lt	16565		Koertge	Guenter	2nd Lt	16637
Florreck	Kurt	2nd Lt	16566		Korpis	Rudolf	1st Lt	16638
Frank	Rudolf	2nd Lt	16567		Kowalewski	Willi	1st Lt	16639
Friedrich	Hans	2nd Lt	254811		Krabbes	Rudolf	1st Lt	16640
Frohwein	Karl	1st Lt	16569		Krause	Kurt	2nd Lt	16641

Kruegel	Willi	2nd Lt	16643	Pufahl	Karl	Capt	16695
Krupp	Herbert	2nd Lt	16645	Rasek	Horst	2nd Lt	16696
Kuehne	Hans	1st Lt	16648	Reichardt	Helmut	2nd Lt	16698
Kuhnke	Horst	2nd Lt	16649	Reiter	Kurt	1st Lt	16699
Kuska	Erhard	2nd Lt	16651	Risse	Willi	2nd Lt	254864
Kwoczek	Erhard	2nd Lt	16652	Roedel	Richard	2nd Lt	16701
Laker	Wilhelm	2nd Lt	256720	Rottmann	Gerhard	1st Lt	16703
Lanzendoerfer	Rudolf	2nd Lt	16654	Rumpl	Hans	2nd Lt	16775
Lauer	Albert	2nd Lt	16655	Sasse	Otto	1st Lt	11454
Lehmann	Guenter	1st Lt	16656	Schaht	Claus	Capt	16706
Lenzner	Helmut	Capt	16658	Schauenburg	Heinz	1st Lt	16708
Liebelt	Ernst	2nd Lt	16659	Schindler	Norbert	2nd Lt	16710
Lohbauer	Fritz	2nd Lt	16662	Schneider	Karl	Capt	16712
Luedecke	Wenzel	2nd Lt	16347	Schnorrbusch	Erisch	1st Lt	16713
Marticke	Hans	1st Lt	16666	Schoenfelder	Franz	1st Lt	16714
Matt	Eugen	2nd Lt	16760	Scholz	Willi	2nd Lt	16716
Matzat	Robert	1st Lt	16768	Schrade	Erich	Capt	16717
Meinhardt	Hans	2nd Lt	255550	Schroeder	Ernst	2nd Lt	16718
Meister	Ernst	2nd Lt	16668	Schubert	Erwin	2nd Lt	16719
Meistring	Rudolf	2nd Lt	16669	Schwarz	Ernst	2nd Lt	16723
Menzefricke	Guenter	Capt	16670	Splittgerber	Herbert	1st Lt	16727
Merlet	Eberhard	1st Lt	16770	Stenzel	Hans	1st Lt	16731
Menzell	Reinhold	1st Lt	21461	Treffenstedt	Willi	1st Lt	16735
Michall	Reinhold	2nd Lt	16674	Ulmer	Egon	1st Lt	16738
Mohn	Reinhard	2nd Lt	16675	Veil	Georg	1st Lt	16739
Mueller	Arno	1st Lt	16771	Vieth	August	2nd Lt	16740
Nagel	Albert	1st Lt	16667	Voss	Hermann	2nd Lt	37473
Neugirg	Max	1st Lt	16772	Wagentrotz	Lothar	2nd Lt	16743
Niggl	Karl	2nd Lt	16679	Waldraff	Heinrich	1st Lt	16778
Oestreich	Hans	1st Lt	16682	Wallenstein	Heinrich	2nd Lt	16745
Ohm	Walter	1st Lt	16683	Welter	Arnim	2nd Lt	16748
Pape	Wilhelm	1st Lt	16684	Wernitz	Erich	Capt	16750
Peters	Guenter	2nd Lt	16687	Wauer	Joachim	2nd Lt	16751
Pfeiffer	Horst	1st Lt	16688	Willert	Joachim	1st Lt	16752
Pfuetzenreiter	Ludwig	2nd Lt	16689	Willert	Manfred	1st Lt	37702
Philipp	Otto	1st Lt	16690	Wettig	Albert	2nd Lt	16754
Pickrahn	Heinz	Capt	16691	Wittmer	Hans	2nd Lt	16755
Plinke	Otto	2nd Lt	16692	Wolff	Kurt	2nd Lt	16757
Press	Herbert	1st Lt	16693	Wurche	Georg	2nd Lt	16758
Pruemers	Rudolf	1st Lt	16694	Merkle	Eberhard	Major	16671

Company #7

Abel	Walter	2nd Lt	9754	Eckert	Alfred	2nd Lt	11387
Achleitner	Josef	2nd Lt	9719	Egner	Ludwig	1st Lt	11420
Althoff	Heinrich	2nd Lt	11779	Eisele	Emanuel	1st Lt	11250
Anhut	Alfons	1st Lt	9804	Emmich	Adolf	1st Lt	9726
Beck	Stefan	2nd Lt	11789	Feder	Alwin	1st Lt	11775
Belgard	Hans	1st Lt	11240	Felder	Max	2nd Lt	11762
Berning	Helmut	1st Lt	9834	Fischer	Hans	1st Lt	9769
Bluemler	Werner	2nd Lt	11559	Fruth	Ewald	2nd Lt	11622
de Boer	Johann	1st Lt	11274	Giessler	Martin	2nd Lt	11576
Büchler	Kurt	2nd Lt	11606	Grabow	Guenter	2nd Lt	11450
Buerger	Hermann	1st Lt	11246	Grimm	Josef	1st Lt	212256
Burkhardt	Otto	1st Lt	11408	Hahn	Herbert	1st Lt	11649
Dormehl	Ernst	1st Lt	11253	Haller	Robert	1st Lt	11529

Hawner	Wilhelm	2nd Lt	11592	Pirchl	Ludwig	1st Lt	11695
Hempeler	Werner	1st Lt	11499	Potengowski	Hermann	1st Lt	10674
Henningsen	Helmut	2nd Lt	11577	Rambach	Alois	1st Lt	11388
Herold	Karl	2nd Lt	11574	Rauscher	Otto	1st Lt	9810
Hildebrand	Hans	2nd Lt	11615	Reichardt	Wilhelm	2nd Lt	11716
Hinz	Emil	Capt	11500	Reichert	Emil	1st Lt	9729
Hoener	Rudolf	2nd Lt	9702	Reimers	Erwin	1st Lt	11673
Hoffmann	Wilhelm	2nd Lt	11248	Reinhardt	Hemann	1st Lt	11655
Huebner	Kurt	2nd Lt	10223	Reiss	Fritz	2nd Lt	11306
Huettlin	Friedrich	2nd Lt	11689	Rocholl	Willi	2nd Lt	11676
Indlekofer	Friedrich	Capt	11496	Roehrkasten	Hans	2nd Lt	258162
Ingenhoven	Josef	2nd Lt	11729	Rothvoss	Karl	2nd Lt	11614
Insel	Werner	2nd Lt	11688	Rube	Bernt	1st Lt	10696
Jacobi	Juergen	2nd Lt	16618	Schaeffer	Erwin	2nd Lt	11612
Janu	Franz	1st Lt	9768	Schmidt	Hans	2nd Lt	11432
Jaehn	Friedrich	Capt	11268	Schneider	Friedrich	1st Lt	9748
Jessberger	Franz	Capt	10687	Schober	Walter	2nd Lt	11759
Kaese	Walter	Capt	11362	Schwab	Robert	2nd Lt	11568
Kastner	Albert	2nd Lt	11705	Simianer	Alfred	2nd Lt	11687
Kaufmann	Franz	2nd Lt	10444	Simon	Heinrich	1st Lt	11424
Kauke	Walter	2nd Lt	11682	Simons	Alfred	2nd Lt	10679
Keller	Erich	2nd Lt	11588	v.d. Smissen	Karl	2nd Lt	10258
Kernreiter	Robert	2nd Lt	11694	Speiser	Ernst	1st Lt	9746
Kiefel	Franz	1st Lt	11778	Staeble	Heinrich	2nd Lt	9805
Kiefer	Hans	2nd Lt	11672	Steffens	Herbert	2nd Lt	256712
Kietz	Richard	2nd Lt	11602	Sterner	Heinrich	2nd Lt	11353
Klar	Alfred	1st Lt	10251	Stienen	Bernd	2nd Lt	11605
Kleier	Rudolf	1st Lt	11523	Stoeckmann	Helmut	2nd Lt	16977
Kohlschuetter	Richard	2nd Lt	11583	Stoessel	Gottlieb	1st Lt	11348
Kramer	Max	1st Lt	10649	Summersberger	Hermann	2nd Lt	10647
Kraus	Otto	2nd Lt	31176	Thannhauser	Joachim	2nd Lt	11428
Kuckuk	Alfred	2nd Lt	9759	Thummert	Hans	1st Lt	11320
Kuester	Helmut	2nd Lt	11616	Thumser	Gerhard	1st Lt	11769
Kodytek	Josef	1st Lt	15979	Traub	Wilhelm	2nd Lt	9703
Lamby	Philipp	2nd Lt	11585	Uhlig	Werner	2nd Lt	11770
Lamp	Karl	1st Lt	20176	Walter	Horst	2nd Lt	16133
Laubis	Ulrich	2nd Lt	11670	Walter	Adolf	1st Lt	11504
Lehnert	Paul	1st Lt	10675	Weiss	Fritz	2nd Lt	11728
Lienau	Walter	Capt	11536	Wimmer	Heinz	2nd Lt	10236
Luginsland	Eugen	1st Lt	11446	Wimmer	Josef	2nd Lt	11406
Lutter	Hans	Capt	256707	Windisch	Johann	2nd Lt	11355
Matt	Max	2nd Lt	9790	Witteweg	Wilhelm	Capt	800667
Matthiesen	Alfred	1st Lt	11494	Woelfel	Johann	1st Lt	800467
Mosemann	Emil	2nd Lt	11342	Wukasch	Walter	2nd Lt	113448
Muck	Berthold	2nd Lt	11765	Zelzer	Kurt	1st Lt	15763
Muecke	Kurt	2nd Lt	11265	Zernikow	Gerhard	1st Lt	15679
Mueller	Karl	2nd Lt	11584	Zitzmann	Guenter	1st Lt	11393
Nolte	Otto	2nd Lt	11270	Zobel	Otto	Capt	800114
Obenhack	Raimond	1st Lt	11567	Meyer	Ortwin	2nd Lt	11731
Oelschlegel	Gerhard	2nd Lt	11378	Jebsen	Rolf	2nd Lt	11656
Ott	Willi	1st Lt	11328	Kracht	Hans	1st Lt	11631
Otto	Bruno	1st Lt	11679	Martin	Herbert	2nd Lt	9710
Palous	Franz	Capt	11503	Muerre	Erich	2nd Lt	10713
Paulus	Walter	2nd Lt	11677	Neumeister	Kurt	1st Lt	11400
Pfeiffer	Otto	2nd Lt	9818	Niess	Wilhelm	1st Lt	11402
Pforr	Albin	1st Lt	11427	Rosteck	Ernst	2nd Lt	10667

Schade	Lothar	1st Lt	11262	Wolter	Herbert	1st Lt	11304
Schmidt	Karl	2nd Lt	11370	Hentschel	Helmut	2nd Lt	11613
Troebelsberger	Karl	1st Lt	10254				

Company #8

Abba	Hans	2nd Lt	9502	Kammer	David	2nd Lt	11581
Amling	Robert	1st Lt	9733	Karl	Josef	Capt	11281
Arnold	Gustav	1st Lt	9740	Kettner	Fritz	1st Lt	10734
Ascherl	Hubert	2nd Lt	11690	Kiel	Fritz	Capt	10206
Bauer	Georg	1st Lt	11596	Kimmich	Fritz	2nd Lt	11739
Bauer	Willi	1st Lt	9787	Klein	Albert	2nd Lt	40948
Baumann	Werner	Capt	11738	Kleiner	Walter	1st Lt	11561
Baur	Willi	1st Lt	11334	Koch	Paul	2nd Lt	10266
Beck	Heinz	2nd Lt	11591	Kochlett	Heinz	1st Lt	10253
Becker	Erwin	2nd Lt	10680	Koenig	Herbert	2nd Lt	11434
Beisswaenger	Karl	1st Lt	10664	Kuegler	Ernst	1st Lt	10231
Boelt	Bernhard	2nd Lt	9775	Kuehnemund	Konrad	1st Lt	11751
Bogendoerfer	Eugen	Major	11397	Kuester	Franz	2nd Lt	11425
Brandt	Adolf	2nd Lt	11785	Laue	Wolfgang	2nd Lt	11654
Brauner	Fritz	2nd Lt	11345	Lieb	Karl	2nd Lt	9735
Braunstein	Karl	1st Lt	11340	Luschnat	Walter	2nd Lt	9827
Buchsbaum	Hugo	2nd Lt	9824	Mannheim	Wilhelm	Capt	10216
Christmann	Theo	2nd Lt	9712	Mattausch	Fritz	2nd Lt	11254
Conrad	Gerhard	1st Lt	11410	Matthis	Julius	Capt	11736
Dittrich	Kurt	2nd Lt	11531	Meissner	Ernst	2nd Lt	11326
Ellinger	Friedrich	Capt	9799	Mende	Helmut	2nd Lt	9785
Engler	Rudolf	2nd Lt	10226	Mikula	Fritz	1st Lt	11529
Ewig	Wilhelm	2nd Lt	10642	Miska	Ernst	1st Lt	8474
Fiedler	Paul	Capt	11380	Mohr	Paul	2nd Lt	10271
Finke	Erich	2nd Lt	263305	Moosmann	Erich	Capt	10639
Flaemig	Gerhard	2nd Lt	11297	Narr	Karl	2nd Lt	10682
Foltz	Rolf	2nd Lt	10219	Oechslein	Karl	1st Lt	9806
Freise	Helmut	1st Lt	10217	Oehmke	Guenter	2nd Lt	11255
Fricke	Herbert	2nd Lt	9803	Paasch	Alfred	Capt	10638
Froechling	Heinrich	2nd Lt	9734	Poelka	Otto	2nd Lt	9733
Froehlich	Kurt	2nd Lt	9782	Porzelt	Alfred	2nd Lt	11227
Furcht	Helmut	2nd Lt	10232	Prager	Fritz	2nd Lt	11291
Gayer	Hans	1st Lt	11564	Preuss	Heinz	2nd Lt	11624
Gistl	Walter	2nd Lt	10269	Raab	Josef	2nd Lt	11572
Goder	Bruno	Capt	10669	Rueberg	Horst	2nd Lt	9503
Grajetzki	Johann	1st Lt	10698	Schilling	Hans	2nd Lt	9791
Gruenberg	Helmut	2nd Lt	10719	Schmidt	Kurt	2nd Lt	11364
Guembel	Martin	2nd Lt	9837	Schober	Hans	2nd Lt	11696
Guenther	Erich	2nd Lt	9716	Schuchard	Heinrich	Capt	10728
Hartke	Kurt	Capt	9745	Schuesseler	Bernhard	2nd Lt	9802
Auf d. Heide	Hermann	2nd Lt	9714	Schuff-Werner	Paul	1st Lt	11667
Heidel	Rolf	2nd Lt	11777	Schulze	Werner	Capt	11229
Henke	Hubert	2nd Lt	9744	Schild	Hans	2nd Lt	11369
Henning	Ernst	1st Lt	11665	Schwarze	Robert	2nd Lt	9737
Herrmann	Gerhard	1st Lt	10668	Seelaender	Ewald	1st Lt	11329
Hippchen	Peter	1st Lt	11567	Stoeber	Volkmar	2nd Lt	9781
Hirn	Karl	2nd Lt	9738	Syrowy	Friedrich	2nd Lt	9783
Hoette	Karl	2nd Lt	11790	Tasch	Josef	2nd Lt	9757
Jakobs	Paul	1st Lt	9715	Thoeren	Hermann	2nd Lt	11787
Kaeufer	Albert	2nd Lt	11788	Thoms	Ludwig	1st Lt	11325

Tietz	Hermann	1st Lt	10727		Cordes	Fritz	2nd Lt	11580
Traber	Gerhard	2nd Lt	9728		Dublinski	Konrad	1st Lt	212147
Twellmann	Georg	Major	11633		Engelhardt	Erich	Capt	9721
Verbeck	Johannes	1st Lt	11562		Franke	Heinrich	1st Lt	10665
Wegener	Karl	2nd Lt	11681		Geissler	Bernhard	2nd Lt	9819
Wehrmann	Fredy	2nd Lt	10695		Gostischa	Herbert	1st Lt	11439
Weith	Alois	2nd Lt	15563		Heinrich	Gerhard	Capt	11242
Werner	Rudolf	1st Lt	15516		Kattermann	Wilhelm	1st Lt	11782
Werntgen	Helmut	2nd Lt	704258		Kronberg	Paul	2nd Lt	11579
Wiesenhoefer	Otto	Capt	11436		Kuestermeyer	Aloys	2nd Lt	11552
Winkler	Gerhard	1st Lt	9795		Mohren	Ernst	2nd Lt	9792
Wittke	Otto	1st Lt	15485		Popp	Alfred	2nd Lt	11625
Wohlfahrt	Theodor	2nd Lt	10252		Rischer	Walter	1st Lt	10730
Wuelfing	Walter	2nd Lt	15529		Stolze	Fritz	2nd Lt	11267
Wunderlich	Alfred	Capt	15432		Uebelmesser	Konrad	1st Lt	11403
Wunsch	Georg	2nd Lt	9821		Waibel	Julius	1st Lt	10694
Zorn	Paul	2nd Lt	9624		Wismar	Franz	2nd Lt	15745
Bock	Kurt	2nd Lt	10268		Zahn	Kurt	Capt	15238
Bornebusch	Joern	2nd Lt	9820		Zebrowski	Hans	2nd Lt	11346

Company #9

Augner	Willi	2nd Lt	253595		Haslberger	Walter	2nd Lt	259508
Barth	Rudolf	2nd Lt	254781		Haslingen Graf v.	Eckbrecht	1st Lt	11745
Baumgart	Paul	2nd Lt	11767		Hausberg	Dietrich	Capt	11501
Bechinka	Johann	1st Lt	10641		Heimbach	Heinrich	2nd Lt	11617
Beierlein	Ernst	1st Lt	11698		Heidmann	Albert	2nd Lt	260053
Bertenburg	Helmut	2nd Lt	11702		Hepp	Fritz	Capt	10744
Boetticher	Eckhardt	2nd Lt	264141		Hild	Hans	2nd Lt	245904
Bruhn	Karl	2nd Lt	253579		Hoffmann	Werner	Capt	11743
Brueggemann	Heinrich	1st Lt	11566		Hoi	Rudolf	1st Lt	11407
Conrad	Erich	2nd Lt	253585		Hopfensitz	Heymo	2nd Lt	248630
Damm	Karl	Capt	11505		Jaegers	Anton	2nd Lt	9786
Denninghaus	Friedrich	2nd Lt	261735		Juergener	Julius	2nd Lt	9747
Deussen	Helmut	2nd Lt	254829		Kattnig	Hans	2nd Lt	11543
Dickel	Ernst	Capt	254807		Kelz	Karl	2nd Lt	254809
Dockweiler	Josef	2nd Lt	260047		Kies	Karl	1st Lt	10662
Dollinger	Paul	2nd Lt	11586		Kindling	Horst	2nd Lt	11722
Doerfer	Herbert	2nd Lt	248155		Kinzler	Horst	2nd Lt	11453
Droesser	Peter	1st Lt	40493		Kitzler	Gerhard	Capt	11739
Elfgang	Josef	1st Lt	254862		Klindtworth	Walter	1st Lt	11298
Esker	Ernst	Capt	11514		Kloberg	Paul	2nd Lt	260041
Fenzel	Heinrich	2nd Lt	253581		Kloss	Konrad	2nd Lt	11593
Flamme	Leberecht	2nd Lt	253598		Koch	Wilhelm	2nd Lt	260054
Freynhagen	Walter	1st Lt	9777		Kosterhofer	Rommald	2nd Lt	10643
Friederich	Rudolf	2nd Lt	257221		Kraft	Guenter	2nd Lt	11669
Friedt	Friedrich	2nd Lt	10255		Kraemer	Kurt	Capt	254850
Graffenberger	Horst	1st Lt	11243		Kreutzer	Gerd	1st Lt	11640
Grittmann	Eugen	2nd Lt	245912		Krohn	Alfred	1st Lt	11282
Gross	Erich	2nd Lt	9807		Kruft	Guenter	1st Lt	10244
Gutbrod	Karl	1st Lt	253853		Laue	Helmut	2nd Lt	11735
Haaf	Friedrich	2nd Lt	253601		Lechner	Josef	2nd Lt	11423
Haberland	Kurt	Major	16072		Lehmann	Max	1st Lt	11284
Hafemeister	Hans	Major	11219		Lieke	Willi	2nd Lt	11573
Harnau	Ernst	Capt	11389		Liebhaber	Karl	2nd Lt	254822
Harrer	Karl	1st Lt	10193		Linder	Hermann	2nd Lt	11331

Lukowski	Leo	1st Lt	253377
Madach	Anton	2nd Lt	254812
Maleika	Anton	2nd Lt	11363
Maennel	Konrad	2nd Lt	257907
Martin	Heinrich	2nd Lt	258164
Melahn	Karl	2nd Lt	254837
Meyer	Karl	2nd Lt	11703
Meyer zu Spelbrink	Ernst	Capt	11398
Mohr	Hermann	1st Lt	11653
Mueller	Walter	1st Lt	9763
Mueller	Willi	2nd Lt	261736
Naehlen	Egon	2nd Lt	11678
Nussbaum	Gerhard	2nd Lt	258159
Oellerich	Ludwig	Capt	11386
Onken	Horst	2nd Lt	254226
Ortmann	Ernst	2nd Lt	11557
Passie	Waldemar	2nd Lt	254846
Rabe	Rudolf	2nd Lt	40947
Regmann	Willi	2nd Lt	257906
Reichstein	Robert	Capt	11257
Reimer	Kurt	2nd Lt	264140
Renners	Anton	1st Lt	11686
Richter	Gotthold	1st Lt	253594
Riese	Guenter	2nd Lt	11619
Roehle	Walter	1st Lt	10194
Segieth	Johannes	2nd Lt	253584
Seibold	Josef	1st Lt	11257
Scheding	Willi	2nd Lt	253602
Schimps	Heinrich	2nd Lt	11672
Schlenker	Rudolf	2nd Lt	11247
Schlossbauer	Adolf	1st Lt	256729
Schmid	Heinz	2nd Lt	261202
Schmidt	Ludwig	1st Lt	11302
Schmitz	Paul	2nd Lt	254847
Schneider	Kurt	2nd Lt	256711
Schoedl	Alfred	2nd Lt	254860
Schroeder	Robert	2nd Lt	11734
Schulz	Erich	1st Lt	256707
Schwering, Graf v.	Joachim	2nd Lt	254810
Schwinge	Werner	2nd Lt	253597
Schymeinsky	Anton	2nd Lt	10242
Solle	Bernhard	2nd Lt	10697
Stauffer	Oskar	1st Lt	11379
Steiner	Artur	1st Lt	259507
Stoeber	Walter	2nd Lt	254508
Stueber	Werner	1st Lt	11741
Szatkowski	Rudi	Capt	11660
Telsnig	Theodor	1st Lt	245908
Trexler-Walde	Eberhard	2nd Lt	254844
Tschistakowski	Peter	2nd Lt	253589
Voigt	Eberhard	1st Lt	259506
Vollert	Heiner	2nd Lt	11244
Wagner	Erwin	1st Lt	10263
Wagner	Klaus	2nd Lt	258157
Walter	Hermann	2nd Lt	260863

Wayand	Otto	2nd Lt	15678
Weber	Walter	2nd Lt	Weber
Weigel	Erhard	2nd Lt	704234
Weitz	Erich	2nd Lt	800450
Welle	Hubert	1st Lt	15492
Wenske	Albert	2nd Lt	11715
Westerhausen	Karl	2nd Lt	704269
Wiedok	Erich	1st Lt	11786
Wiegel	Detlef	2nd Lt	704158
Willemsen	Rudolf	1st Lt	11560
Willert	Rolf	2nd Lt	800278
Willutzki	Heinz	2nd Lt	800085
Wittek	Willi	1st Lt	15716
Witz	Julius	2nd Lt	11550
Wocelka	Adolf	2nd Lt	800636
Wolff	Heinrich	1st Lt	15749
Wollschlaeger	Otto	1st Lt	15490
Wunder	Paul	1st Lt	800417
Wurster	Walter	2nd Lt	222737
Wuttig	Heinz	2nd Lt	11376
Wycisk	Wilhelm	1st Lt	10295
v. Zastrow	Reiner	1st Lt	704177
Zoberst	Werner	2nd Lt	800298
Haarhoff	Hans	2nd Lt	9796
Bachmair	Heinz	2nd Lt	11721
Biessmann	Oskar	2nd Lt	253582
Brackhane	Bernhard	1st Lt	11539
Doerfler	Hans	1st Lt	261733
Furherr	Karl	2nd Lt	40544
Gottschling	Willi	2nd Lt	256714
Harramhof	Gottfried	2nd Lt	254841
Herrmann	Gerhard	2nd Lt	254794
Unruh	Karl	1st Lt	254816
Wendel	Fritz	2nd Lt	253578
Wickmann	Friedrich	2nd Lt	11726
Widmann	Adolf	2nd Lt	15481
Wortmann	Anton	2nd Lt	15729

signed, Jules L. Karpas, 1st Lt MC
Post Surgeon

A POW work detail. (Courtesy, Beryl Ward)

STATION HOSPITAL
Prisoner of War Camp
Concordia, Kansas

File No. 383.6   31 August 1945

SUBJECT: Physical Condition of Prisoners of War.

TO: Provost Marshal, PW Camp, Concordia, Kansas.

The following prisoners of war are physically capable of performing heavy work:

Company #3

Rapp	Heinrich	1st Lt	256716	Inders	Hans	1st Lt	17023
Lewicki	Hans-Bertr.	1st Lt	248871	Rode	Heinz	1st Lt	16943
Staedtler	Walter	1st Lt	16975				

Company #4

Gemassmer	Karl	1st Lt	16482	Wilhelm	Otto	2nd Lt	16461
Busche	Walter	1st Lt	16258	Oeser	Johannes	1st Lt	16368
Thal	Oskar	2nd Lt	16483	Boerner	Georg	2nd Lt	16249
Moellermann	Rolf	2nd Lt	16497	Rumbach	Berthel	2nd Lt	16501
Kessler	Rudolf	1st Lt	16320	v. Buehler	Hans-Eberh.	2nd Lt	16257
Schultz	Werner	Capt	16423	Ahlmann	Hans	2nd Lt	16234
Bachmann	Ernst-Heinz	1st Lt	16237	Krohn	Gerd	2nd Lt	16331
Gruettner	Lambert	1st Lt	16290				

Company #5

Hoffman	Erwin	2nd Lt	16867	Dallinger	Wilhelm	2nd Lt	16816
Ilse	Wilfried	2nd Lt	16873	Fischer	Hans August	2nd Lt	16831

Company #6

Fritz	Dieter	2nd Lt	16568	George	Helmut	2nd Lt	16574
Benning	Wilhelm	1st Lt	16519	Kappler	Ernst	2nd Lt	16630
Henze	Ludwig	1st Lt	16600	Dr. Schreiber	Hans	Capt	37680
Meyerholz	Theodor	1st Lt	16673	Dr. Hass	Johannes	Capt	16522
Lorenz	Ludwig	2nd Lt	16663				

German officer-prisoner compound from Guard
Tower T-368. (Courtesy, National Archives)

OFFICER'S COMPOUND
Prisoner of War Camp
Concordia, Kansas

29 February 1944

TO: Commanding Officer, Prisoner of War Camp, Concordia, Kansas

Following are the recommended personnel for the Officers' Compound as authorized by Memo #11:

German Spokesman	Colonel Waltenberger	
Adjutant	Lt. Zander	
Adm. Off.	Lt. Florreck	
Asst. Adm. Off.	Lt. Uebel	
Fin. Adv.	Capt. Winnefeld	
Med. Off	Capt. Ritter	
2 Med. 1st Aid	1st Sgt. Goebel (O.A.)	
	Sgt. Schwenninger	Cpd. #1
1 Mail orderly	1st Sgt. Fertig	Cpd. #3
1 Supply Sgt	1st Sgt. Diettrich	Cpd. #1
1 Ration Sgt. and overseer	1st Sgt. Fickel	Cpd. #3

Companies:

Co. #13
Major Schroedter — C.O.
1st Lt. Trapp — Asst. Co.
1st Sgt. Hesse — (Off. asp.) clerk

Co. #14
Major Leibl — C.O.
Lt. Hoeppner — Asst. Co.
M. Sgt. Springer — (Off. Asp.) clerk

Co. #15
Major Lorenz — C.O.
1st Lt. Pape — Asst. Co.
Lt Huegel — clerk

Co. #16
Major Lochmann — C.O.
Capt. Brending — Asst. Co.
1st Ltr. Nerreter — clerk

————

2 clerks adm. (German)
1st Sgt. Hupks — Cpd. #1
Sgt. Kalicki — Cpd. #3

Appendix H
American Rosters

The following American rosters are taken from Christmas menus.

From menu, Christmas Day 1943. (Courtesy, Alfred W. Purdy)

480TH MILITARY POLICE ESCORT GUARD CO.
PRISONER OF WAR CAMP
CONCORDIA, KANSAS
Captain Marty Ball — Commanding Officer
First Lieutenant Neal A. Broyles
Second Lieutenant Ewald S. Schoeller

First Sergeant
Sackett, Elton S.

S-Sergeants
Rogers, Arland I.
Vidmosko, John

Sergeants
Arcoleo, Frank
Mattord, Ernest L.
Parker, Hugh M.
Piette, Edward A.

Tech-4ths
Adelman, Philip
Berryman, Edward L.
Eicher, Janes R.

Corporals
Benson, Meyer C.
Best, Willis J.
Fisher, Charles S.
Hobza, Edward J.
Karuzas, Walter P.
Malone, James A.
Millican, James O.
Osswald, Lawrence E.
Pena, Joseph R.
Prather, Alex J.
Pruett, George M.
Purdy, Alfred W.
Treat, Charles F.

Tech-5ths
Cafantaris, George
Cohen, Jack
Moucha, Frank J.

Null, William R.
Pattek, Irwin
Pizzinski, Edmund E.
Siegel, Hyman H.
Solie, Dean H.
Tobin, Thomas H.

Privates First Class
Bailey, Walter A.
Barrett, Joseph J.
Besant, Martin F.
Bonkowski, Alexander J.
Book, Veryl S.
Broderick, Frank J.
Clougher, Robert J.
Cullen, John J.
DiLorenzo, Maurice J.
Ely, Robert W.
Evans, Vernal T.
Fischoff, Louis
Fish, Joseph E.
Fitzgerald, David A.
Guerci, John M.
Gumer, Ben
Harrison, Myron
Holmes, William F.
Kruk, John I.
Lee, Howard E.
Luck, Max M.
McGuire, Edward T.
Megginson, Edward B.
Mentall, Arthur C.
Minor, Kenneth C.
Moncello, Daniel
Ninni, James, V.
Olivieri, Michael J.

Olson, Ervin J.
Overmann, Raymond J.
Owen, Claude M.
Pearson, Stanly R.
Piero, William
Roenish, Charles H.
Romain, Martin
Rose, Simon
Rowan, John W.
Samuel, Leo L.
Scalia, Russell L.
Schmotzer, Orville W.
Schumann, Howard
Scrudato, Leonard T.
Sierchio, Girard A.
Sloan, Samuel J.
Speed, Robert C.
Steinberg, Charles
Sucharzewski, Henry A.
Taylor, Brant H.
Tiemann, Robert A.
Trilsch, Edward J.
Ursetti, Thomas S.
Vail, Donald B.
Vinig, Samuel J.
Wagner, Charles
Weglarz, Joseph J.
West, James, Jr.
Woolf, George

Privates
Andrzejewski, Alex J.
Benson, Lewis F.
Brimberg, Jacob S.
Brown, David J.
Candjoun, Dimitrie

Carlisle, Robert C.
Carney, Charles L.
Carrigan, Edward F.
Coy, Donald H.
Eckstein, Sol
Engel, Louis J.
Gardner, Charles S.
Gray, Harry P.
Greenberg, Harold P.
Hamrick, Douglas H.
Hardigree, Fred
Hinshaw, Rex M.
Jorgensen, Christopher A.
Keller, Ivan W.

List, George
Mears, Candler
Morezzi, Aristide C.
Morgan, Daniel R.
Nanoski, Michael
Norquist, Charles O.
Occhiuto, Joseph
Phillips, Robert H. S.
Polirstok, Joseph
Prest, John F.
Ricker, Kenneth E.
Ross, Douglas J.
Roth, Arnold
Rowe, Edward W.

Scherer, Eugene R.
Seminoff, Richard R.
Settle, Vernon V.
Seymour, Christopher T.
Shoaf, Floyd S.
Sibole, John H.
Simcox, Daniel F.
Speth, Harry E.
Takes-the-Horse, John
Thomas, Warren G.
Turner, David P.
Urban, Ernest P.
Yerges, Harold C.
Zitolo, Joseph J.

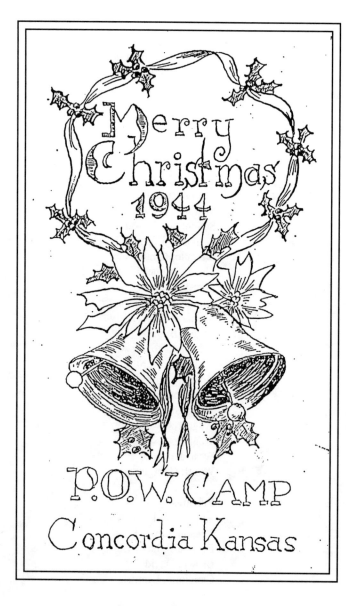

The following roster is from the menu, Christmas, 1944. (Courtesy, Wayne E. Rosen)

OFFICER PERSONNEL
Lt. Col. George W. Eggerss
Major Elmer I. Long
Major Melvin C. Martin
Major Kendall S. Ickes
Captain Ralph T. Coverdale
Captain Curtiss W. McAllister
Captain Melton H. Patrick
Captain William W. Abrams
Captain Frederick E. Rawdon
Captain Sherrill C. Eastwood
Captain Marvin C. Johnson
Captain Wilford R. Carner
Captain Giles H. Strong
Captain Kenneth J. McShane
Captain Russel L. Compton
Captain Martin H. Lutzke
Captain San C. Hutchinson
Captain John N. Hummel
Captain Karl C. Teufel
1st. Lt. Rodney S. Dexter
1st. Lt. Vincent R. Rooney
1st. Lt. Jules L. Karpas
1st. Lt. Oskar T. Cook, Jr.
1st. Lt. Ewald S. Schoeller
1st. Lt. Winifred W. Cleveland
1st. Lt. Angus M. Shipley
1st. Lt. Russel J. Paalman T.
2nd. Lt. Walter W. Friend, Jr.
continued on next page

GUARD DETACHMENT

First Sergeants
Taddeo

Staff Sergeants
Bittlingmeyer
Larkin
Randa
Rutkowski
Slade
Walser

Sergeants
Foster
Oliver
Yaksich

Technicians 4th Grade
Bolin
Crady
Douglas
Huck

Corporals
Amabile
Beardon
Berish
Bono
Broderick
Carr
Carrado
Colbert
Cummo
Davis
Kostner
Kwiatkowski
Mazza
McGill
Medsker
Pace
Testardi

Technicians 5th Grade
Brown
Copeland
Demmy
Elliott
Giuffre
Hardin
Nelligan
Peters
Read
Tidquist
Wilson

Privates First Class
Anderlay
Barnett
Bates
Bauermeister
Blohm
Blue
Bogner
Bricker
Brassel
Brouwer
Candjoun
Carney
Carrara
Carter
Cataldo
Cecil
Clement
Clougher
Cota
Coulonbe
Crane
Crist
De Matteo
De Trolio
Dixon
Donadeo
Dumboski
Edge
Ely
Hardy
Hildebrand
Hill
Hogue
Huser
Hoppis
Iaccino
Jerelle
Jones, H. J.
Jones, W.
Kanaby
Kaposta
Keller
Kenning
Kight
Kisielewski
Klonowski
Knowles
Kralj
Larson
Leimbeck
Loden
Long
Malloy

Manthey
Markley
Marincovich
Matricardi
McGuire
Bloch
Boschert
Boyd
Boxwell
Bratcher
Braun
Brick
Brittain
Bruce
Bulfair
Byrd
Carrigan
Cauthen
Cisiecki
Cortez
Cropsey
De Mille
Di Filippis
Dancha
Laney
Le Long
Letcher
Lincoln
Little
Loberg
Longwell
Maier
Modich
Nowotnik
Oler
Olivas
Pointer
Rathburn
Riepe
Trykowski
Peterson
Pretty Bird
Wingo
Hale
Harp
Harvey
Harwell
Haworth
Hix
Hoffman
Hollis
Howell, A. C.
Howell, J. K.
Jenkins

Johns
Kingston
Klaus
Konkolewski
Krist
Laffin
La Loge
Lamb
Ripple
Rose
Sanfilippe
Savona
Scena
Seckman
Smith
Stasiunas
Stenman
Troped
Vittorio
Waldman
White
Young
Eubanks
Evans
Feeley
Foley
Forney
Friskey
Gandy
Glisson
Grieco
Guerci
Gumina
Hammer
Rispoli
Saulovich
Schaefer
Schlueter
Schmotzer
Sprague
Staszak
Stiliha
Tabijan
Taylor
Tenpenny
Moreland
Niswander
O'Brien
Olender
Overmann
Parris
Partain
Paslak
Paul

Petty
Pierce
Reo
Thomas
Tobach
Todhunter

Trujillo
Ulmer
Ulrich
Walley
Witterschein
Wright

Yerges
Yessen

Privates
Albertson
Andrews

Atkisson
Bailey
Fail
Farley
Fredrickson
Furtado

HEADQUARTERS DETACHMENT

Master Sergeants
Hobson
McClure

Technical Sergeants
Anderson
Richey
Stanton

Staff Sergeants
Conover
Fugate
Katz
Koski
Minton
Munro
Nolan
Prudhon

Sergeants
Carlson
Fredericks
Hayward
Hickling
Jepson
McKinley
Nee
Newkirk
Roemisch
Rosen
Stangel
Stover
Zbojovsky
Roop

Corporals
Arcco
Brown
Bruno
Burger
Cherrito
Crites
DePratt
Dochak
Dutton
Hendrickson

Miligi
Nash
Newenhuis
Norgard
Phillips
Proscia
Savoie
Shubert
Simpson
West
Lichtenberg
Loewen
Wilcox

Technicians 5th Grade
Flattum
Gropp
Parker
Tidwell
Petler

Privates First Class
Andrews
Armour
Cestola
Cleveland
Cook
Engleson
Flatequal
Floerke
Grasser
Hansen
Ikerd
Kennedy
Millisent
Hollenpeck
Laughlin
Luecke
Maletto
Means
Nahaas
Nagel
Porter
Ridenour
Sachs
Schuchard

Sundt
Thiel
Trammel

Privates
Allen
Buelow

Costa
Easley
Fuller
Knuth
Schuler
Turner
Wells

MEDICAL DETACHMENT

Master Sergeants
Molz

Staff Sergeants
Nicholz
Ostler

Sergeants
Musser
Ehreth
Pipkins
Seal

Corporals
Goehring
Bristow
Slifer

Lefferts

Privates First Class
Behr
Marquez
Murray
Rohr
Schmitt
Weiss
Wood

Privates
Brede
Morgan
Hartmann
Welsh

One of the garrison mess halls, Christmas 1944. (Photo, Wayne E. Rosen)

Appendix I
Branch Camps

From *The History of Camp Concordia: from Site Survey to Deactivation,* edited by Captain Karl C. Teufel (Washington, D.C.: National Archives, Record Group 389, unpubl., 1945), chapt. 3, sect. F:

Introduction: Some prisoners-of-war arrived at Camp Concordia in May 1943, and a goodly proportion of the 3,000 enlisted men and 1,000 officers were on hand by September. All the enlisted men were destined for work, but labor requirements at the Camp, and the necessity of arranging a great many details in connection with work-contracts, postponed the external employment of the Germans until approximately the middle of September. At that time, two Camps, one at Hays, Kansas, and one at Peabody, Kansas, made use of a little more than two hundred (200) prisoners, a too-small percentage of those available. On 9 December 1943, another branch at Hebron, Nebraska, was organized, making use of eighty-seven (87) more prisoners. In early 1944, the coincidence of two problems, *i.e.,* what to do with surplus prisoner-of-war labor, and the problem of getting the badly-needed pulp wood of the Minnesota forests cut, resulted in the establishment, in the period from February to April, of four (4) more branch camps. One of these Camps was closed by 15 July 1944, and the others between then and the end of the year. In the meantime, it appeared wise to higher authority to move the majority of the enlisted men to other locations where they could be more fully employed and more closely administered from the Base Camp. In consequence of this new policy, Concordia's experience with Branch Camps was relatively brief, and by the end of 1944, was definitely destined to be an all-officer camp, maintaining only sufficient men to perform garrison service. The details of these enterprises, however, are worthy of consideration.

Key Personnel of the Branch Camps: Most of the American personnel serving in the branch camps held, in addition to their primary duties, all the other duties devolving upon a Post Commander. They led active lives and responsible ones, with more facets to their tasks than can be treated here. Outstanding persons and their assignments are given below:

Capt. Richard Harding, Commanding Officer of the Minnesota Branch Camps
2nd Lt. Roy Fanning, Adjutant of the Minnesota Branch Camp
2nd Lt. Ewald Schoeller, Commanding Officer Branch Camp 401 (Remer).

Also attached in like capacity to the Peabody and Hebron Camps at various times.

2nd Lt. Neal A. Broyles, Commanding Officer Branch Camp 402 (Bena).
Capt. Marty Ball, commanding Officer Branch Camp 404 (Deer River).
1st Lt. Wolf, Post Exchange Officer Minnesota Branch Camps
2nd Lt. Clem J. Denicke, first Commanding Officer Camp 403 (Owatonna).
1/Sgt. Decuir, Sergeant Major Minneosta Branch Camps
S/Sgt. Dyer, Supply Sergeant Minnesota Branch Camps
Sgt. Edward A. Piette, 1/Sgt. Branch Camp 401

Other Officers who were, at one time or another, engaged in this work were: 1st Lt. Jacob Yockey, 2nd Lt. Oke E. Carlson, Capt. Harry G. Bracken, Capt. Richard Biele, 2nd Lt. Jerich, 2nd Lt. Sitzman, 2nd Lt. Joseph McGovern, Capt. Richard Mulder, 2nd Lt. Sigler, 2nd Lt. Norman Grosshardt. Eight (8) of these men, in addition to Lt. Schoeller, commanded the Hebron Branch Camp while assigned to Concordia. Of all the names included above, only Lt. (now Capt.) Schoeller remains here at the date of writing.

Branch Camp 401, Remer, Minnesota:

On 31 January 1944, 2nd Lt. Ewald Schoeller, CMP [Corps of Military Police], accompanied by thirty-seven prisoners-of-war (including three officers) and eighteen (18) enlisted men American Military Police Escort Guards [MPEG], arrived at Remer, Minnesota, to organize the new branch camp there. The next nine days, preceding the arrival of the main body, these men worked long and hard, alternating "two on - four off" four times daily, with work on the installations filling in the intervals, and with very little time for sleep and none for recreation. At the time, temperatures ranged from 0 degrees at noon to 35 degrees during the nights. Water lines were frozen, broken, or in disrepair, and these could be reached only by laborious digging in ground that was frozen to a level of six (6) feet, and which often had to be thawed by fires maintained for forty-eight (48) hours before excavations could be attempted. The men were equipped with warm arctic-type clothing, kept bonfires burning close to their work, and seemed to have their morale enhanced in inverse proportion to the difficulties and hardships confronting them. They made contests of their duties, and let the contest spirit lead them to compete even in the raising of fantastic beards and mustaches.

On 7 February 1944, the main body of 238 prisoners-of-war arrived, and from then until 5 June 1944, when Camp Concordia surrendered jurisdiction of the project, averaged approximately 248. In a few days, the odds and ends of camp-preparation had been accomplished, and contract obligations became the order of the day. These involved one large contract and three small ones, data on which will be found at the end of this section. Approximately a total of 372,800 man-hours were involved, covering 233 working days. In addition to lumbering operation, the work involved clearing operations, cutting cordwood, and similar tasks. Contracts contained wage-equalization clauses, (12.3% of gross charges to the contractor for lumber scaled), due to labor union action, fixed hourly wage rates due the government, and provided credits to contractors for instruction, supervision, tool rental and maintenance, as well as breakage losses, etc. The largest contract involved a round-trip of thirty-four (34) miles on days when customary routes were passable, and during spring thaws and rainy days, a more circuitous route of sixty-two (62) miles. Occasionally all routes were impassible and work had to stop. Supplies of all sorts and personnel had to be hauled from Remer over dirt roads by Army vehicles (usually driven by prisoners-of-war), and two cars were kept busy hauling equipment out of the mud, back onto icy surfaces, or out of snowdrifts. Frequent repairs and exchange of equipment were customary.

Guard procedure called for onerous work. Six-man guard mounts worked two hours on and four off, while two Corporals of the Guard served twelve-hour tours every day. Two permanent guard-posts, on diagonal corners of the stockade, were established, while the outside gate guard was pulled in during the night to patrol the garrison area. Terrain was favorable to guard measures, since the single road leading into the Camp was easily guarded, and since the density of the surrounding forests made them impractical as escape routes. Two formal head-counts were held daily, and all details leaving the Camp were counted in and out. No efforts to escape, however, were contemplated by the prisoners, since they feared becoming lost and falling prey to the savage Indians and timberwolves said to infest the area, a fear which the American personnel did nothing to alleviate. In fact, prisoners were actually grateful for the protection afforded by American guns and personnel from the neatly exaggerated perils of the Minnesota Forest Primeval.

Life in the Camp was rugged at best. A common mess hall served both Germans and Americans, with only a partition separating the two. Food, cooked by German cooks was good, but not always sufficiently varied. The Remer Mess Sergeant not only supervised food-preparation and mess-hall sanitation at the Camp, but also handled food-distribution for Bena and Deer River as well. Prisoners-of-war performed all fatigue details, and we are informed that very little edible garbage required disposition.

For the first two weeks, sanitary arrangements were hardly adequate, since nine (9) washbowls had to serve three hundred (300) men and the facilities for providing water, disposing of sewerage, etc., were sadly in need of repair. In fact, the water supply never was adequate, a proposed new well not having been drilled until after Concordia surrendered jurisdiction. Later on, a small latrine containing four (4) washbowls, showers, and toilets was furnished American personnel.

A fire-fighting truck was assigned the Camp and two teams were trained in its use. In addition to training classes, the guards got actual experience in helping fire rangers to extinguish two threatening forest fires. The Camp was also equipped with a siren, chemical extinguishers, and G.I. buckets filled with sand or water. Along with fire duties, guard duties, camp duties, prisoner-chasing, etc., American personnel also got daily calisthenics and training classes in basic military information four nights per week. Life in the Minnesota Branch Camps was calculated to kill or cure.

Branch Camp 402, Bena, Minnesota:

This Camp, located a quarter-mile from the town of Bena in Cass County, had formerly been a C.C.C. installation. it has a 2000-foot frontage on the white sand beach of Lake Winnibigoshish (fashioned fifty years ago by damming the Mississippi), and was generally in good condition. Necessary renovations were estimated at $2,425.00. Colonel Vocke inspected and approved the Camp in January 1944. No advance detail was sent, personnel from Remer having been temporarily assigned to Bena to put all into a state of readiness. Little routine preparation was required. Water facilities were adequate, and while some plumbing and wiring needed repairing, the Camp as a whole was in good condition due to its fairly recent occupancy. Extra equipment such as flood lights, chlorination equipment, maintenance shops, and supply facilities were all installed within a few days after the arrival of the prisoners. 141 of these (including three officers), accompanied by twenty-seven (27) M.P.E.G.s under the command of 1st Lt. Neal A. Broyles, CMP, arrived on 7 February 1944, and commenced operations. (Lt. Broyles was followed later by Capt. Marty Ball, CMP, 2nd Lt. Joseph McGovern, CMP, and 1st Lt. Vincent B. Huges, AUS [Army of the United States], as Camp Commander).

The Bena Camp followed the pattern of Camp Remer very closely. Guard arrangements were not so onerous as at the Bena Camp, the stockade being patrolled at night by the guard in charge of the camp entrance in the daytime, assisted by the Corporal of the Guard who made frequent inspection rounds, and also had at his disposal methods of quickly disseminating news of an escape or emergency to Remer Headquarters, the Seventh Service Commands's Director of Security, the Federal Bureau of Investigation, as well as state and local police officials. The system proved efficient at the time of the return to Concordia, when one prisoner of war, apparently loath to depart this beautiful country, hid out, but was apprehended within the hour and entrained. Life of the guards was very similar to that at Remer, training classes being held regularly four times weekly. Their efforts aroused the spirit of omulation in their German charges, who occupied themselves with studies in English, History, government, and like subjects. Classes were held for them in the mess hall, where also a daily news bulletin was read to them.

Four contracts (summarized at the end of this section) were carried through. They involved a total of 127,860 man-hours from 7 February to 1 October 1944. Contracts were similar to those at Remer, with wages averaging approximately sixty cents (.60) per hour, although some of the work was paid for on a piece-work basis. Usual credits were allowed contractors. One or two American guards were used with each work detail.

Branch Camp 404, Deer River, Minnesota:

This Camp, formerly the Cut Foot Sioux C.C.C. Camp, is located twenty-three (23) miles north of the town of Deer River, Itasca County, Minnesota, and is approximately fifty-eight (58) highway miles north of Remer. It is in the Cut Foot Sioux Experimental Forest section of the Chippewa National Forests, where towering Norway pines and many nearby lakes afford a magnificently beautiful and majestic natural background. On 5 April 1944, fourteen (14) M.P.E.G.s arrived to activate the Camp. This group began the routine of converting a C.C.C. Camp into a P.W. Camp, and were joined the following day by 2nd Lt. Oke E. Carlson, CMP, with 131 prisoners-of-war (including one officer) and few additional guards. (Capt. Marty Ball relieved Lt. Carlson a week later, and was himself relived by Capt. Harry Bracken, CAC, in May).

Internal security measures were almost identical with those at Bena, and succeeded without incident. Nor was there much variation in other directions.

Five contracts, lasting from 1 April until 31 October 1944, were undertaken. These involved approximately 217,200 man-hours of work. The work was cutting, peeling, and skidding pulpwood on the whole, and was paid for on the piece-work basis. Details are given in the recapitulation ending this section.

Branch Camp 403, Owatonna, Minnesota:

Owatonna Camp, in Steele County, Minnesota, is fifty-one (51) highway miles south of Minneapolis and some 230 highway miles south of the Headquarters Camp at Remer. It has little in common with the three Northern lumbering camps, being situated in a productive agricultural section. The Camp was composed of buildings leased from the Cashman Hereford Farm, situated just one mile north of the city of Owatonna.

2nd Lt. Clem J. Denicke, CMP, arrived here on 23 March 1944 with a detail of thirty-five (35) prisoners-of-war (including two officers) and ten (10) American guards. Considerable renovations were necessary to bring the Camp up to standard. A large, three-story residence building was used to house the prisoners, while a smaller caretaker's house served the guard personnel. A large garage served as a mess hall, while a small shed became a workshop. Later on, four (4) hutments [a collection of huts] were added. The whole camp was small and compact, simplifying guard and work details. On 4 April 1944, eighty-five (85) more prisoners arrived in the company of eighteen (18) more American guards. Details of guard procedure at Owatonna were very like those at Remer, although naturally on a smaller scale, and acted with complete effectiveness.

Labor contracts at Owatonna were entirely different from those engaging the Northern camps, since the work was predominately agricultural. One large contract for 100 prisoners covered two separate harvesting periods was made with an Owatonna cannery, while two 50-man contracts were drawn with a combination nursery-agriculture concern to cover periods when the cannery contract was not active, thus assuring full-time work for 100 prisoners-of-war. 59,000 man-hours, approximately, were paid for at an approximately hourly rate of fifty-five cents (.55) between 1 April and 15 July 1944. Crops harvested were mostly asparagus, peas, corn and pumpkins.

Branch Camp, Peabody, Kansas:

This Camp, lying about one mile outside the town of Peabody, was designed to make prisoner-of-war labor available for general farm labor. Arnold Berns Jr. and Nelson Poe were the partnership contractors. 112 prisoners-of-war and twenty-three (23) guards of the 480th MPEG Company, under the command of 2nd Lt. Ewald Schoeller, constituted the personnel of the Camp. Conditions at this installation were crude. Both prisoners and Americans lived in perambatal tents from 13 September until 28 November 1943. Latrines had to be dug, and quartermaster boxes employed by all concerned. Washing, personal and otherwise, was performed in the open. Weather conditions were bad through October and November, and the tents proved inadequate protection against them. On 28 November the camp was moved into a large brick garage in Peabody, over which were fourteen (14) rooms, formerly serving as a hotel, which provided comfortable and convenient quarters for the American contingent.

The Camp was highly commended by the surrounding farmers for preventing their crops from rotting in the field. On 1 August 1944, the installation was transferred to the jurisdiction of Fort Riley, Kansas. No record of man-hour employment is longer available here, but this camp was more gainfully occupied from the standpoint of net return to the government than any of the other six branch camps established.

Branch Camp, Hebron, Nebraska:

Hebron is located about forty-five (45) miles north of Concordia. The Camp there occupies the site of an old C.C.C. Camp, was established on 9 December 1943, and passed under the control of the Prisoner of War Camp at Atlanta, Nebraska, on 30 September 1944. It had eighty-seven (87) prisoners-of-war, fifteen (15) American MPEG guards and a Commanding Officer. Contractor was the Thayer County Non-Stock Labor Association, and the contract involved general farm labor.

The Hebron enterprise appears to have been a proving ground for American Officers, no less than nine (9) having been assigned there as Commanding Officers in the little over nine months of the Camp's history.

Branch Camp, Hayes [sic], Kansas:

This short-lived Camp opened on 13 September 1943 and closed on 8 October 1943. It employed one hundred (100) prisoners-of-war, twenty-five (25) MPEG enlisted men, and was commanded by 2nd Lt. Neal A. Broyles. Louis C. Aicher of Hayes [sic], Kansas, was contractor, and the work was general farm work. There is nothing of an outstanding or particularly interesting character to report on the activity at this camp.

BRANCH CAMP STATISTICS:

INCLUSIVE DATES	CONTRACTOR	AVER. AMER. PERS.	AVER. GERM. PERS.	NET TO THE GOVERNMENT
	HAYES[sic], KANSAS			
13 Sept. '43- 8 Oct. '43	1. Louis C. Richer, Hayes [sic], Kansas	26	100	$ 9,295.22
	PEABODY, KANSAS			
13 Sept. '43	1. Arnold Berns, Jr., Nelson H. Poe, John J. Heath (Partners).	24	112	29,811.20
	HEBRON, NEBRASKA			
9 Dec. '43- 30 Sept. '44	1. Thayer County Non-Stock Labor Assoc. (J. R. Kenner, Resident-Agent)	16	87	8,653.32
	REMER, MINNESOTA			
1 Feb. '44- 30 Dec. '44	1. Herman Delin, Cass County, Minnesota 2. Andrew T. Giffen, Fedoral Dam, Minn. 3. Walter C. Andrews, Remer, Minnesota 4. Kelment Farms (E. T. Spartz, Mgr.)	45	248	17,767.07
	BENA, MINNESOTA			
7 Feb. '44- 1 Oct. '44	1. D. C. Dunham Labor Co., Bemidji, Minn. 2. Goss & Richmond, Cass Lake, Minn. 3. Melvin Mettler, Cass Lake, Minn.	28	138	12,642.54

DEER RIVER, MINNESOTA

| 1 Apr. '44-
31 Oct. '44 | 1. Toivo Hovi, Squaw Lake, Minnesota
2. Victor Terho, Squaw Lake, Minnesota
3. Jake Reigel, Deer River, Minnesota
4. Max Loggin Co., Max, Minnesota
5. H. E. Vance, Max, Minnesota | 18 | 131 | 5,006.83 |

OWATONNA, MINNESOTA

| 1 Apr. '44-
15 July '44 | 1. Owatonna Canning Co., Owatonna, Minn.
2. Cashman Nurseries, Owatonna, Minn.
3. Owatonna Nursery Co., Owatonna, Minn. | 21 | 120 | 13,020.78 |
| | | | TOTAL | 96,196.96 |

NOTE: This section written from the records of the Labor Relations Officer, Provost Marshal's Office, PWCK, *passim*. Some data is not available, having been apparently passed along to higher headquarters.

Appendix J
Organization Chart, Concordia Interment Camp

(From Completion Report, Job T1, Concordia Internment Camp, Concordia, Kansas. Courtesy, Marguerite Larson)

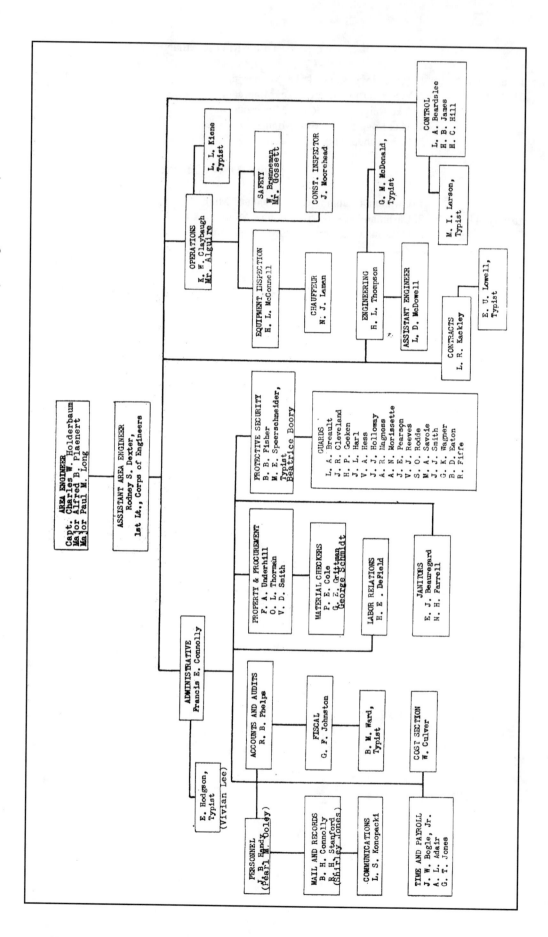

Index

by Lori L. Daniel